Joel Edson Rockwell

The Christian's Work and Rest

Joel Edson Rockwell

The Christian's Work and Rest

ISBN/EAN: 9783337404383

Printed in Europe, USA, Canada, Australia, Japan

Cover: Foto ©Lupo / pixelio.de

More available books at **www.hansebooks.com**

THE CHRISTIAN'S WORK AND REST.

A SERMON

PREACHED IN THE

Central Presbyterian Church of Brooklyn,

MAY 20th, 1866,

ON THE OCCASION OF THE DEATH OF

WARREN ROCKWELL.

By Rev. J. E. ROCKWELL, D. D.

SERMON.

Acts 13 : 36.—For David, after he had served his own generation, by the will of God fell on sleep, and was laid unto his fathers.

These words, uttered by the Apostle in the course of an argument concerning the resurrection of Christ, contain the epitome of a Christian's life, fidelity to God, usefulness to the age in which he lives, and a serene and hopeful death. No higher eulogy could have been pronounced upon David than this,—he served his own generation by the will of God. Here was his crowning excellence and glory; not that he was descended from a long line of illustrious ancestors, or was the possessor of untold wealth, or the occupant of a throne, but that he fulfilled the duties of life cheerfully and faithfully, in obedience to the will of God.

This was the great secret in his life, and in thus obeying the dictates of his better and renewed nature, he as cheerfully did his duty while feeding his father's flocks, as when called to rule over the kingdom of Israel. As the Shepherd boy of Bethlehem he was as faithful and unrepining at his obscure condition, as when he was hearing, after his triumph over the giant leader of the Philistines, the songs of the maidens of Israel.

Nor when he had been annointed by the Prophet as the future king of Israel, and felt kindling within his soul the inspiration of the spirit, and had a dim foreshadowing of what he was to become, did he perform with less fidelity his daily duties, nor allow the hopes of the future to interfere with the work of the hour. Never was there a more pure and disinterested friendship, than that which he cherished for the son and heir-apparent of the throne; never was more loyal conduct than he manifested even to the monarch who was cruelly hunting his life. Nor did this great principle of fidelity to present duty leave him, when seated on the throne. Witness his conduct when, after expressing his desire to build a sanctuary for God, he was assured that he could never attain to that distinguished honor, which must be reserved for his son who should come after him. The check to his generous impulses did not prevent him from doing what he could. But at once setting himself to the work of gathering materials for the temple, he engaged therein as heartily as though he was himself to dedicate the glorious structure that in coming years should rise in its beauty upon the hill of Zion. These elements in the character of David enter to a greater or less extent into the life of every child of God; and are the essential antecedents to such a death as is described in our text.

I. The first thought which presents itself for our consideration is his obedience to the will of God. His morality is all framed after the Divine Statutes, and is developed by a cordial submission and sincere love towards him. He serves his generation, not in accordance with the dictates of a worldly and lifeless philosophy that makes man the centre of all its reasonings and activities, but because he loves God supremely, and has yielded his heart and soul to his service. This was the secret of David's life—to serve God. He drew the grandest motives of all his conduct from Him. He stood in the hey-day of life when the world was pouring its honors at his feet, and said: Whom have I in Heaven but thee, and there is none upon the earth that I desire besides thee. It was because he loved God supremely that he was a faithful subject, an unfaltering friend, a wise and just monarch. His heart was ever turning to God as his Father and Sovereign, and his faith as a lost sinner took firm hold of the hope of a Saviour, which in every age had been the support and comfort of the people of God. Thus he sang amid all the vicissitudes of life 'the Lord is my Shepherd, I shall not want.' And when he had yielded for the time to an overmastering and terrible passion, his sense of obligation to God led his heart to the penitential outbreak, 'against thee, thee only have I sinned,' while his faith took fast hold of the great sacrifice which should be offered on Calvary as he cried,—'purge me with hyssop and I shall be clean, wash me, and I shall be whiter than snow.' Thus is it ever with the Christian. He looks upon all duty as having its origin in our relations to God. It becomes duty because He has commanded it. Nor are we to pause and hesitate at its requirements. If we neglect to improve the one talent we are no less guilty, because he has given to others more and higher duties than he has imposed upon us. And, if we are faithful we shall be no less honored than he who has performed works more conspicuous and arduous. The poor widow who cast in her two mites into the treasury, received even more of the love and approbation of Christ, than the rich men who cast in of their abundance. Her self consecration to God— her performance of duty to the uttermost of her ability, because she loved God and desired to obey him, drew from Christ the blessed assurance, 'she hath done more than they all.

The great measure of all our moral acts, is the extent to which they are performed as a simple obedience to God. The Christian is to do all to His glory. He looks upon himself as not his own. He esteems himself as a poor sinner saved by grace, redeemed to God by the precious blood of Jesus, and as fulfilling a part of the divine plan in his salvation. He seeks to do the will of his heavenly father not *that* he may be saved, but *because* he has been saved, and delivered from death and sin, and made a child of God, and a joint heir with Christ to a glorious inheritance, for the enjoyment of which he is here to be fitted, and to which he will be introduced at his death.

II. And thus obeying the will of God the Christian is faithful to the duties of life, as they daily present themselves before him. This was the secret of the great life of David. It was not one distinguished act that made his name ever after to be remembered, but the faithful discharge of the least and humblest duties of life as well as the more prominent and important. And this is to a greater or less extent the marked and emphatic feature in the life of every Christian. It is the faithful discharge of the duty of the hour that makes up the sum of his moral life. It is thus that he forms habits of fidelity that fit him for the higher spheres of usefulness to which he may be called, and often unconsciously is setting in motion a train of spiritual influences that may be felt long after he has gone from his work to his reward. Drawing his stimulous to duty from the Cross of Christ and the oracles of God, he goes forth to the work of life to serve his generation by the will of God. Wherever work is to be done—there he may be found. He is laboring for a master that he loves, and who has said to him, 'go work to-day in my vineyard'—'what thine hand findeth to do, do it with thy might.' Without a thought or care of what the world may say or think of him, he labors as cheerfully in the shade, as in the more conspicuous walks of usefulness, contented wherever God places him, and grateful that in any way he may serve him.

Yet it is worthy of notice that the acts which a Christian thus performs are by no means limited in their results to what they immediately accomplish. David served his own generation, but the influences he set in motion are felt to-day, and will be felt forever. Robert Raikes, without dreaming of doing more than a simple act of duty toward the poor of his own city, accomplished a work whose blessed power and fruit can never be fully estimated until all its history shall be unfolded amid the record of eternity.

An humble and unpretending Christian engages in some unobtrusive act of piety, never giving a thought as to what the world will say, yet his example may have been a stimulus to some halting heart that has sent it cheerfully forward in a noble christian course. We are not to imagine that our acts are unimportant or profitless because they are unattended by any immediate brilliant results, or because they are unknown to the world. The grandest movements in the natural and moral universe are affected by silent and hidden influences. The vast operations by which the world is made fruitful, and its countless ranges of vegetable and animal life kept in order are carried forward by processes which almost escape our observation. It is not the volcano sweeping along with its flood of fire, nor the deluge wrapping the earth in its funereal shroud—nor the earthquake upheaving the mountains—nor the avalanche falling like a thunderbolt of ice upon Alpine valleys—nor the storm cresting the ocean and scaring the land, that form the forces with which nature accomplishes its most beneficent designs. God binds the universe together by a silent and unseen power that sweeps outward to the verge of creation, and holds the planets in its omnipotent and loving embrace, while it draws a pebble to the earth, and brings the rain-drop from the cloud. He sends the dew, and it moves with a soft and noiseless tread over the springing corn and the opening flowers, and nature is revived as it passes. He gathers the rain within his secret treasure houses, and it wells up in the quiet mountain-spring, where the birds drink and are refreshed, and flows down in silver streams, by whose side the flowers bloom and the grass grows rank and green, and then pours its tribute over the valleys, and mingles its waters with the majestic river and the mighty ocean. Thus is it with the moral influences by which God blesses the world. The acts of quiet, every day duty which the Christian accomplishes are used by him to save and bless.

The stone in the hands of David—and the arrow-shot at a venture was guided by the hand that moves the spheres—the words uttered by Luther and Calvin and Knox and Edwards for their own generation were caught up by the spirit of God, and are echoing still in the hearts of men. The least act done for Christ is never unnoticed by him, nor will it ever fail of accomplishing his own glorious purposes. If he but serve God in his day—and with a faithful and loving heart does the duty of the hour, however humble it may be, the Christian accomplishes the great purposes of his life. For the results he is not responsible. God whom he serves will care for them, and he causes often even that which is sown in weakness to be raised in power.

III. And this leads us to notice the solemn close of the Christian's life as presented to us in the words of the text. He fell on sleep, and was laid to his fathers, and saw corruption. It is worthy of notice, the Apostles seldom speak of the *death* of the Christian. Amid the ancient Catecombs of Rome, where sleep the countless dead of the martyr ages—no allusion to death is seen upon all their monuments. To them the hour of full discharge from work and suffering was invested with no terrors. It was the calm repose of the soul after a life of toil and trial. David did not die. The soul yet lived—his body indeed was laid aside and saw curruption—but he was gathered to his fathers—not alone to the house appointed for all the living, but to that house not made with hands, eternal in the heavens. There he was brought to the general assembly and Church of the first-born—to many over whose graves his tears had fallen—to Jesse whose venerable form had long mouldered in the grave—to the spirit of the gentle Ruth and her noble husband—to Jonathan and Samuel, Moses and Israel and Abraham—to Christ his Shepherd and Saviour, and to God his father and friend. To him dying was but going home—and such is the death of the Christian. It is a sweet rest that follows a life of conflicts and tears and sadness. It is

———A blessed sleep
From which none ever wakes to weep.

It is an entrance to the joy and rest of the better and the higher land.

Such is the work and end of the Christian's life—fidelity to God—and hope in death—followed by eternal happiness and joy. And you will permit me, my dear people, to utter here the feelings not of a pastor, but of a son lately called to watch by the dying bed of a beloved father, and who feels that the theme on which he has dwelt is an appropriate illustration of the life and death of that dear servant of God, who has passed away from his work to his reward.

WARREN ROCKWELL was born in East Windsor, Conn., October 31, 1787. His father, who for nearly 20 years represented his native town in the Legislature of the State, and his grandfather were both successively deacons in the same church at East Windsor, and were descended from a pious ancestry, who as early as 1626 came from Yorkshire to the Colony of Massachusetts for their attachment to the Puritan faith.* His father had an abiding confidence in God's covenant with his people, and I can now recall the fervor and solemnity with which that venerable man, as he lead at times the devotions of our family, prayed that the God of his fathers would be the God of his children and his children's children. In his early manhood my father removed to Leicester, Vt., whither his family had gone while he was absent on business at Charleston, S. C. Here was a feeble congregational church of which his father was made a deacon, and which as its inability to support a stated ministry, appointed him its moderator, who conducted its worship and read a sermon on the sabbath. In the year 1810 a powerful revival commenced in the Church, during which, with an occasional assistance from neighboring pastors a few laymen, led by my grandfather, visited from house to house, and directed inquiring souls to Christ. Among the fruits of this work of grace, were numbered nearly every member of the moderator's family, including my father, and her, who being providentially on a visit there was to be for more than 50 years the partner of his life.

On the 3d of February, 1814, he was married to Miss Sarah R. Wells, with whom he removed to the town of Salisbury, Vt., where he engaged in mechanical pursuits until the Spring of 1817, when he removed with his family to Hudson, N. Y., connecting himself at once with the Presbyterian Church, of which Rev. Mr. Stanton was the pastor. Here, by his diligent attention to business, by his sterling integrity, and by his exalted Christian character, he soon gained the confidence and respect of many of the most influential families of the town, and although an humble mechanic was received and welcomed by them as a friend and a guest. As his worldly cir-

* See Note on last page.

cumstances, improved and he was able to give suitable entertainment to his friends, his house became the transient home of many whose praises was in all the churches.

Among my earliest memories of my home are the faces of many a noble Christian minister and layman, now gone, or still busy in his work. David Abeel, then a pastor at Athens, N. Y., was a frequent guest in his family, and in his quiet parlor conversed and consulted with him concerning his hopes and aims as a Missionary to China. There, too, the beloved Whiting, of Syria, was at home, and many others like him who enjoyed his Christian sympathy and hospitality. In the year 1825, he was ordained a ruling elder by Rev. Dr. Chester, then the pastor of the Church, and who ever cherished for him a warm affection. Soon after his removal to Windsor he became interested in the Sabbath School, with which he was long connected, either as teacher or superintendent, and in the Tract and Bible Societies of the County held active and responsible relations.

When the great movements in behalf of Temperance commenced, he at once took a prompt, bold stand in its behalf. One day a number of gentlemen from the eastern part of Columbia County were his guests, whom, as usual he invited to his sideboard to furnish themselves with the spirituous liquors which were the common beverage of all classes. They declined to take any, adding that they had been thinking it best for the friends of good morals, to abandon the custom. He conversed with them freely on the subject, and in a few days his decanters disappeared forever from his table, and he became thoroughly and warmly identified with the grand reform, by which thousands have been saved from drunkards' graves. He gave of his time, means and influence to the movement. He rode over the country addressing large gatherings of the people upon the subject, and directing and organizing societies for the promotion of the cause. When the Sons of Temperance sprang up as an auxiliary to the work, he soon identified himself with them, and was long an efficient and honored member of their State and National Councils.

Almost the last work he did in his annual visits to the city with whose interests he was so long identified, was to re-organize and revivify the Division which he had himself first assisted in establishing. He also, for four years edited and conducted a paper devoted to the cause of Temperance, bringing to the work the powers of a vigorous and clear mind, and good practical sense and judgment. He was also deeply interested in the cause of popular education, and while holding a seat in the city councils, rendered efficient service in the establishment of a complete system of common schools, and in the erection of suitable buildings for their accommodation.

During all these years of earnest labor in the general cause of public morals, he did not neglect his own family; nor was he without precious evidence of God's blessing upon his labors. While conducting a mechanical business which required the aid of a large number of men and apprentices, he expected all who were bound to him, and who were members of his family, to attend morning and evening worship, supplying each one with a Bible, out of which he read in turn at the daily service of prayer. He watched carefully over their morals and lives, insisted on their regular attendance at the worship of the sanctuary, and conversed with them familiarly and faithfully on the great subject of a personal interest in the great salvation.

During one of the periods of revival experienced in the church at Hudson, and while his family was unusually large, all but one of those who then composed it became hopefully pious. His heart was at that time greatly exercised for those who were then for a time committed to his care. Among them was one young man who had during all the revival manifested no special interest for his soul. One day, while speaking of his case to two of his intimate friends and co-laborers, it was resolved that one of them should endeavor to bring the subject of religion before him, while the other two should continue in prayer for God's blessing upon the interview. My father invited the young man into his office, frankly telling him for what purpose. One of the three friends, a godly and earnest man, met him and opened to him the matter of his soul's salvation. The other two retired to pray. The interview lasted nearly two hours. The young man has been for nearly thirty-five years a consistent and faithful member of the church, and dates his conversion from that office and that interview. He knows of no other time when he became a child of God. Those three friends are now united in a better world, while he still lives to admire the wonders of redeeming love.

Towards the close of the year 1856, Mr. Rockwell was invited to act as a distributing agent for the Brooklyn City Bible Society, for the purpose of having the city fully explored and supplied with copies of the word of God. The work, though arduous, was an inviting one to him, who having declined the business that had thus far employed his time and energies, did not care to spend the remainder of his days unemployed. He removed at once to this city, where he has ever since been actively employed in labors among the poor and needy. His heart soon became deeply interested in the work of exploration and supply as a Bible agent. He was thoroughly systematic in his work, which continued for more than two years, at the end of which time the Society suddenly determined to give up its plan of distributing the Scriptures by means of an agent. During the period of his employment in this work he visited more than 26,000 families, and circulated among the destitute nearly 4000 copies of the Word. The fruits of his labors here were abundant, and his works still follow him. His journal is rich in its relations of interviews with the poor, the afflicted, the ignorent, the bigoted and the vicious. His kind and gentle manner of approach, his venerable appearance, his quiet dignity, his strong common sense, his tact in dealing with every variety of character, and his true Christian courtesy and spirit won for him an entrance, and gained for him a respectful hearing where others might have met with insult and rebuff. It was always a matter of regret that he had not been permitted to finish the exploration and supply of the city, learning as he did by a rich experience the necessity and the benefit of such a work.

In one of his reports he remarks: "Sometimes I meet with bigotry, often with nature in her untutored coarseness, but rarely with designed rudeness and insult. In some sections of the city I have discovered a lower strata of degredation, guilt and poverty, than I had supposed could exist in any Christian or even civilized community, and certainly lower than outcast humanity with all its appalling depravity could ever teach without the aid of *strong drink*. Yet in such dens of infamy I have sometimes seen the eye that was blackened by violence fill with tears, and the bruised and battered face of woman in her degredation show marks of tenderness and contrition, as the Bible, so long neglected has been held up to her view, and her attention called by a few words of kindness to Him who said to one, and who will say to all who come to him '*go, and sin no more.*'"

When his labors for the Bible Society were terminated Mr. Rockwell was appointed a Missionary by the Brooklyn Tract and Mission Society, in which work he continued until his death. Here in this blessed field of labor he has continued year after year, visiting the poor and the ignorant, the afflicted, the sick and the dying, faithfully and lovingly, bearing to them temperal relief and comfort, and the richer blessings of the Gospel of peace.

Year after year he has labored on, with an untiring zeal, and an ever deepening interest in the work. Many a child of poverty and want—many a sufferer upon a bed of pain and anguish—many a family in affliction and sorrow, has looked for his daily visits with a growing interest, and has welcomed him as a minister of mercy and comfort. Many a member of this and of other churches in this city has been brought into the fold by his efforts and prayers, which a faithful God has owned to the conversion of their souls. It has been to me often a source of rich instruction, to sit down with him at evening, and listen to his account of the work of the day. Almost the last work he performed was to assist in the funeral services of a soldier, whom he had found in his visits, dying from exposure in one of the prisons of the South, and who was under God, led by his instructions, to Christ, and died in a blessed hope in him.

When it seemed probable that the remainder of his days would be spent in this city, he renewed his relations to this church; ever retaining, however, a deep and abiding affection for the church in Hudson, which he had for more than thirty years served as an elder and trustee. One of his last requests upon his dying bed was that I should write a letter to his old pastor, Mr. Leavitt, and express his sincere pleasure and joy at hearing of a revival which had lately blessed and strengthened his church.

Although he came to a congregation where he was henceforth to be only a private member, he was by no means disposed to be an inactive or useless one. Many a Christian here will remember long his fervent prayers and his earnest exhortations. Few will forget his earnest exercises on the day of prayer for colleges, at the commencement of the recent work of grace among us. With what seriousness and solemnity he urged us to fidelity ; with what unction and fervid importunity he plead with God, his own precious covenant and promises.

Soon after his coming among us, the young mens' Bible class was organized, of which he became the teacher, and in which, to the last, he retained the deepest interest.

Two of that noble band of beloved youth, Smith and Fox, left the class at the commencement of the late war, and fell, the one at Bull Run, and the other at Charleston. He mourned for them like a father, and their likenesses were cherished ornaments of his room. One of which he bequeathed to his class—his dying legacy—that of the noble and lamented Smith.

Even in his hours of partial delerium that dear class was ever on his heart. One morning while I was sitting by his side he started from an uneasy slumber, saying "what a triumphant conclusion of Paul's argument is the close of the eleventh chapter of Romans"—seeing me by him he said 'I thought I was preparing my lesson for my Bible class.

On the 7th of March last, having assisted his feeble wife to the female prayer meeting he passed on to fulfil an appointment with the Missionaries of the Tract Society. He hesitated somewhat about going on account of his infirm health and the unprepitious weather, but duty and his love of his work decided him to go. He returned home with a severe chill, and with the disease fastened upon him which was in a few weeks to loose the silver cord of life. His sufferings were intense, often rising to an agony that seemed intolerable. Yet all was borne with a wonderful patience and resignation to the divine will that none but the Christian could exhibit.

After a long life of more than 78 years, 56 of which had been spent in the service of Christ and his Church, he came to look upon death as an event near at hand. My interviews with him were daily and most precious, and if I draw aside the curtain that you my hearers may look upon the chamber where a venerated and beloved father met his fate, it is to give you one more evidence of the power and value of the gospel of Christ. Among my earlier conversations with him in view of his possible decease, he spoke of his thankfulness for a Godly ancestry, and a pious education and training in the great doctrines of the gospel as taught in the scriptures, and re-affirmed in the Westminster Catechism. 'I have never,' (said he) had a doubt of the Bible nor of the power and willingness of Christ to save all who come to him. His blood needs to be applied daily. When he sent forth his disciples to preach the gospel he said "Lo! I am with you to the end of the world." In that premise, if I am a child of God I have a personal interest and Christ is with me and will be with me to the end. I know that I am a great sinner, every heart knows best its own bitterness, and hence Paul said "I am the chief of Sinners." But my only hope is in the blood of Jesus. I am in God's hand and am content, whatever may be the issue of this sickness."

He enjoyed greatly a hospital chart on which were printed in large type many precious promises, and which I had hung upon the wall so that he could read it. Even when his eyes were blinding with the mists of death they still wandered towards those words, and when he could no longer read them he asked to hear repeated the promise "Though thou walkest through the fire it shall not kindle upon thee."

He had for a long time read with great comfort out of a volume called "Sacred Lyrics from the German" which I had presented to him on the occasion of his Golden

Wedding. One day as I entered his room I found him with the work in his hand. He turned to the hymn entitled "Submission," as expressive of his feelings in view of being laid aside from the work in which he had so long been engaged.

He felt a sadness in thinking that he could no longer minister to the poor and afflicted among whom he had labored; and that he must be laid aside from active Christian effort. Yet, rallying from his dejection, by the thought that all was the ordering of a loving and sovereign God, he read to me with a touching emphasis I shall never forget, the whole hymn, the first verse of which was peculiarly descriptive of his feelings:

> " Thus saith the Lord, 'Thy days of health are over,'
>   And like the mist my vigor fled away,
>   Till but a feeble shadow was remaining—
>   A fragile frame, fast hastening to decay
> The May of life with all its blooming flowers,
>   The joys of life in colors bright arrayed,
> The hopes of life in all their airy promise;
>   I saw them in the distance slowly fade.
> Then sighs of sorrow in my soul would rise;
> Then silent tears would overflow my eyes!
> But a warm sunbeam from a higher sphere
> Stole through the gloom and dried up every tear.
> In this thy will, good Lord! the strife is o'er,
> Thy servant weeps no more."

During one of the visits from his former pastor, Dr. Waterbury, from which he derived great comfort, he handed him the volume, that he might hear the same from the lips which had often ministered to his soul, the the promises and blessings of the gospel. A few days before his death, we gathered in his chamber for family worship. As he lay propped up in his bed, he called to him each member of the household, and taking them by the hand, gave them his blessing. To one he said, " My child, live near to God and put your whole trust in him; do not allow yourself to be drawn aside by the fashions and pleasures of life; use the world as not abusing it; enjoy the blessings of life, but do not set your highest affections upon them. When you come to lie where I now do, you will see that the world is nothing compared with the soul and its interests. May God bless and lift up the light of his countenance upon you."

Thus, like a dying patriarch, he addressed to each in turn some parting counsel, thanking them for their kindness to him, and speaking with evident satisfaction of the years of happiness we had spent together; and then commending to their affection and sympathy, her who would soon be a lonely widow, dependent on them for the care that she should need for her comfort and happiness.

I asked him what passage from God's Word, I should select, and he said the 14th chapter of John; and there, in the hush of evening, I read the blessed words of Jesus, "Let not your hearts be troubled, ye believe in God, believe also in me;" and then kneeling by his bed, we prayed for the presence of him who said "I will never fail thee nor forsake thee."

One day when he was feeling an unusual degree of pain and weakness, I supported him from his chair to his lounge. He spake greatfully of the comfort he received in my assistance, and then said: "Now for strength to trust wholly in God—then the end. O, Lamb of God, that taketh away the sins of the world, grant me thy help."

The Sabbath but one before he died, after giving me some directions in regard to matters to be attended to after his death, he said as I laid him down upon his bed, and he heard the peal of the church bell, "Now, I feel that I want to hear the songs and worship of heaven.

Speaking of his confidence in God he said: "If he gives me to have joy in Christ I shall be thankful, and if not I shall rest content with the simple knowledge that *Jesus saves me.*" In the afternoon he woke from a short slumber and began to give thanks to God for his mercies toward him for the kindness of his children and friends and then prayed that when he came to pass through the waters of the river they might not overflow him and that he might have an entrance to the rest of God's people. One day as I read to him the hymn from the German called Havenward, he said as I finished "O can such glory be for such a poor sinner as I, blessed Jesus grant me thy grace and mercy!

As we were once lifting him into his bed he said God bless you my dear children. You have now to lift me like an infant. Feeling his great and growing weakness he added after a pause, "I have no wish to live—there are many things I would like to see. But our blessed interterview with the Lord Jesus is worth more than they all." I asked him if Jesus was with him now and he replied—"Oh yes, and he comforts me. But when I have these severe spasms I cannot so fully realize his presence. Yet I have peace." Early on the morning of the 27th of April, the family were summoned to his bedside to witness the departure of his Spirit. There in that chamber where he had in long weeks of patient suffering borne his precious testimony to the power of the gospel, we stood by his bed and wept, as we knew that the hour of parting had come. His mind was still clear and cloudless. He said to me, as I leaned over his bed, "Now one brief prayer that Jesus may be with me." I bent down to his ear, and whispered all of words that I could command amid the pressure of sorrow that was filling my own heart : "Lord Jesus, receive his spirit," and again recalled to him the promise which was written upon the leaf of the Hospital chart, hanging upon the wall : "Fear not, for I am with thee ; when thou walkest through the fire, it shall not kindle upon thee, and through the waters and they shall not overflow thee." He caught them as they fell upon his dying ear and they comforted him. He breathed again the name of Jesus; turned one dying look upon his dear wife and family, then lifted his eyes to heaven and closed them forever upon the scenes of earth.

Was it an unwarranted fancy that thought of him as being joined to his fathers—not alone in the grave where their bodies and his see corruption—but as being welcomed by them to that blessed rest where together they see the King in his beauty, and walk in their blissful re-union the streets of the city whose gates are pearl, and enter the temple whose light is the Lamb? Have not those who for years were fellow servants in the church upon earth, met again in the service of the upper and better sanctuary? Have not children and children's children, over whose graves his tears have fallen, met him on the confines of the better land, and caused him to know that the family is still unbroken, though they have for years been nearer than we to their Father's House, where are many mansions.

In the grave-yard at Hudson, through whose grand old pines the soft airs of Spring were sighing their requium over the dead, and amid the graves of the loved and honored who had passed away before him, we laid him down in his dreamless slumber, and felt that of him it might be said, through the grace given unto him, "He served his generation by the will of God."

If I have seemed in this imperfect sketch of one so dear to me, to have intruded upon you, my beloved people, private grief, it has been that I might, in delineating his character, magnify the grace of Christ, and present to you an example of what a private christian may accom if he be but faithful to God.

He rests from his labors, but his works do follow him.

Almost the last message I bore to him from enquiring friends, was one from a poor widow whom he had found in his mission work, and whom he had assisted in obtaining a position where she was earning a comfortable support. As I repeated to him her expressions of gratitude, he lifted his hand and said, "Thanks be to God, that he has made use of such a poor sinner as I am, to accomplish any good." Not long after he ceased from his work in the Bible cause, a city missionary found a family in which he became interested, and on asking the husband and wife how they became Christians, was told that a venerable man, tall and gray haired, called with Bibles, and finding them neglecters of religion, conversed with them upon their souls' salvation, and pointed them to Christ as their Saviour. That conversation was blessed to their conversion. They knew not the name of the stranger, but their blessings and their prayers followed him.

On one occasion he brought to the sesion of the church five converted catholics, to be examined for admission to church ordinances, whom he had instructed and led to Christ.

Let us seek to imitate his example, so far as he followed his Saviour.

My brethren, God has of late called home to himself many of our most faithful and honored members. Let us seek to stand in their lot, and like them serve our generation by the will of God.

And, O, that you who knew and honored the departed —even while you have not yet trusted in the Saviour, whom he loved, would bear in mind that his character was moulded and developed by the gospel. When speaking to him of his death, and of what I should say to you after his decease, he replied : "Make but little of my poor life. I am only a lost and guilty sinner, saved by the grace of God, and dependent wholly upon the blood and righteousness, of the Lord Jesus Christ."

Bear with you this precious message as his legacy for you all. In our dying hour all our philosophy and theology, if we are God's children, will be narrowed down as was his, to this one point, "This is a faithful saying, and worthy of all acceptation, that Jesus Christ came into the world to save sinners, of whom I am chief."

The family of Rockwell is of Norman origin. The first of the name in England was Sir Ralph de Rocheville, one of the knights who accompanied the Empress Maude into England when she claimed the throne of the realm against Stephen. Sir Ralph ultimately joined the eldest son of the Empress Henry II. Plantagenet, and had a grant of three knights fees of land in the county of York, upon which estate the Rockwells have continued until the present time, James Rockwell Esq., of Rockwell Hall, Boroughbridge Co., York, being the representative of the family in Great Britain.

The last great act of the ancestor of this family recorded in English history—is the rescuing of the Earl of Northumberland and Lord Percy, the celebrated Hotspur from the party of the Earl of Douglass at the battle of Halidon Hill, in the reign of Henry IV, by Sir John Rockwell.

The first of the name who settled in America was Wm. Rockwell who arrived at Plymouth, Mass., by the ship Mary and John, in the year 1626. He came with several Yorkshire gentlemen who had become converts to the Puritan faith—and was admitted a freeman of Dorchester, May 18, 1631. He also was one of the first two deacons of the Dorchester Church.

He afterwards removed to East Windsor, Conn., and died May 16, 1640.

Of his descendants, his 2d son Samuel married Mary Norton, of Saybrook, Conn., April 7, 1660. Of their children, John married Anna Skinner. Her son Daniel was born May 30, 1707; married Margaret Loomis, of Lebanon; died March 1, 1789.

He was a deacon of the church in East Windsor, and on his tombstone is spoken of as "one who honored his Holy profession living and dying." Of his children, Daniel was born Sept. 4, 1746. He was a deacon, also, in the church of his fathers. He married Esther Bingham. His children are Irene, Noah, Daniel, Esther, Mary Ann, Hannah, Eleazer B., Elvira, Warren, Lora, Alfred, Clarissa.

Memorial Address,

DELIVERED AT

STAPLETON, N. Y.,

JULY 16th, 1876,

By REV. J. E. ROCKWELL, D. D.

MRS. SARAH W. ROCKWELL,

Born Sept. 10, 1788.   Died June 27, 1876.

STATEN ISLAND:
JOHN BALE, PRINTER, AT THE STAPLETON POST OFFICE.
1876.

Memorial Address,

By Rev. J. E. Rockwell, D. D.

The following Address, in memory of a beloved Mother, was made in the ordinary pulpit ministrations of the Pastor of the Presbyterian Church of Edgewater on the 16th day of July, from the words—"He that doeth the will of my Father which is in Heaven, the same is my brother, and sister, and mother."

You will not I trust regard it as an inappropriate introduction of personal feelings into my pulpit ministrations that I add a few words in affectionate memory of a beloved and honored mother, whose life just closed on earth was a beautiful exemplification of Christian principle and experience.

Sarah R. Wells was born of respectable Quaker parents at Claverack, N. Y., September 10, 1788. In her childhood she passed a short time in New York, and then removed with her family to East Windsor, Conn. While yet young she was brought, under the ministry of Rev. Mr. Bartlett, to see the need of a Saviour and to consecrate her life to the service of Christ. Several of the years before her marriage were spent in teaching, for which she had an exceeding fondness and adaptation. While thus engaged she was thrown into the family of Mrs Brown, whose writings—especially the Hymn "I love to steal awhile away"—have endeared her memory to all devout Christians. Their friendship lasted through life, and my mother's recollections of this friend of her youth were vivid and pleasant.

In the year 1814 she was married to Warren Rockwell,

then of Salisbury, Vt., where they resided until the Spring of 1817, when they removed to Hudson, N. Y. Here they entered the Presbyterian Church, then under the pastoral care of Rev. B. F. Stanton, and soon became actively engaged in Christian work in that congregation. Among my earliest recollections are the ordination of my father to the Eldership, and the appearance of my mother as she sat under the pulpit of the old sanctuary surrounded by a group of young ladies, who formed the Bible Class of the Sabbath School in which her husband was Superintendent. I recall also their frequent gatherings at her own modest parlour, when she sought to interest them more fully in their study of the Scriptures and their own soul's welfare, occasionally inviting some clergyman to assist her in the work. She was active and interested in all that promoted the growth of the Church and the progress of the Master's cause.

For many years she held the office of President of the Female Bible Society of Hudson, long a most valuable auxiliary to the Parent Institution.

Her house was the home of Ministers and other Christian gentlemen, and she entered heartily into all plans that furthered reform in morals and the promotion of the Master's Kingdom.

In the year 1854 she and my honored father removed to Brooklyn and made their home at my house. There she renewed her Christian labors and co-operated with her husband in works of Christian activity and benevolence. Among her papers I find memoranda of a mothers' meeting in which she was deeply interested, and where she with other Christian ladies of my congregation held weekly interviews with poor and ignorant women whom they thus sought to benefit and save.

She was a woman of warm sympathies, and stopped at no self-denial or labour which they called her to put forth. Some of the histories of her deeds of Christian benevolence would, if fully told, seem almost like the pages of romance. More than one man in the Ministry has been largely indebted to her for the encouragement and sympathy which cheered him in his early struggles to reach that work, and in her parlour such men as Abiel, of China, and Whiting, of Palestine, and Canfield, of Africa, spoke of the Missionary work to which they were looking as their future field of service for their Master, and shared in her intelligent sympathy with their coming labour. Twelve years ago she met with an accident which henceforth made her a cripple. After months of suffering, patiently endured in her own room, she was again permitted to visit the house of God by the aid of crutches and the supporting arm of her husband. Two years after she became a widow, after more than fifty years of wedded happiness, spent with one whose Christian life was in full harmony with her own. Yet, amid all her afflictions, she possessed an unceasing confidence in her covenant God, which wonderfully sustained her, and enabled her to endure trials with calmness and loving resignation to the divine will. Although laid aside very much from active duty she always did what she could, and never lost her interest in the Church, nor her cheerful and hopeful spirit. That remained with her to the very end. Her love for the sanctuary was deathless. When detained by sickness she always read or listened to my sermon which had been preached on that day, and usually read and re-read it during the week.

Though stricken down by paralysis a few months ago she rallied again and manifested her unabated interest in the work of the Church, retaining her wonderful patience and her strong and characteristic hopefulness.

On the morning of June 20th, while going up to her room after breakfast, she fell backward from the upper stair, which she had reached. I was summoned to her aid in a moment and bore her to her bed from which she was never again to rise. Surgical aid was immediately called, and it was found that there was a fracture of the collar bone and a re-fracture of the thigh.

Although the shock to her system was very great she maintained her wonderful calmness and equanimity and her unfaltering trust in God as her Saviour and friend. By a kind Providence she suffered but little. Her invariable answer to my inquiries after her health was "perfectly comfortable." She enjoyed our daily morning and evening worship around her bed. On Tuesday morning I read to her the 23rd Psalm and the 14th Chapter of John, (the last Chapter I had ten years before read to my dying father at his request); I spoke to her of Him who had said "In my Father's house are many mansions," and knelt in prayer by her pillow. She seemed to enjoy that morning service with a peculiar interest. It was the last prayer she ever heard, for at five o'clock that evening she fell peacefully asleep without a struggle or a groan.

And as I look back over that beautiful life, now closed on Earth to open in the life to come, I recall every where illustrations of the Christian character as described in the words, "doing the will of my Father." Among them was her love of the Bible. It was her daily food, and I think of her now as she used to sit in her old arm chair bending over the precious volume, sometimes lifting up her eyes as I entered the room to smile out a welcome and then to draw my attention to some passage which had peculiarly attracted her notice. One of the last sermons I read to her was written upon a text which she had repeated to me, and which had struck me with new force as she had uttered it. I hardly need say that she was full of the spirit of prayer. How often, when going noiselessly into her room, have I found her upon her knees wrestling with God for blessings on her children and children's children. And how memorable now was her repetition of the prayer, which she taught me in my childhood, and every Christian child has learned,—"Now I lay me down to sleep"—on the evening before she died.

Although her faith in Christ as her only Saviour was undoubted, she had frequently great distrust of herself, and the most abasing views of her own unworthiness and sinfulness. And yet I never knew one whose whole life was more completely under the direction of a competent and enlightened conscience. Her character seemed to be thoroughly saintly. But her estimate of herself was so modest and humbling that she was often led to express a wonder how such a sinner could be saved. Yet when Christ was presented to her mind her faith seemed to grasp Him with a deathless power and undying love. She was wonderfully forgetful of self in her desire to promote the good and happiness of others. They who have known her best will most appreciate that intense sympathy which was continually manifesting itself in acts of kindness and attention to the wants of others. She never wearied in seeking to promote the welfare of all who needed help.

With all the great interests of the Church she was in full and intelligent accord. She read with ceaseless interest the daily history of the work of Christian enterprise, and kept herself fully informed of what was done for the advancement of the Redeemer's Kingdom, and of all the great movements of the Spirit in reviving and refreshing the Church. If she ever indicated a thought of regret at her afflictions it was because she was laid aside from the activities of Christian life. Yet it needed but to remind her that God reigned, and that she could reach Him by faith and prayer, to give her comfort and to re-awaken her cheerful resignation to God's will. When she was brought down to her dying bed she retained all the calmness and hopefulness of her life. We did not care to worry her by explaining to her the full extent of her injuries. So long as she did not suffer we had no wish to produce any needless anxiety or distress. She spoke with her usual serious, tender manner of her hope in Christ alone; talked cheerfully and kindly to the dear ones whom she loved, and who tenderly loved her; spoke with gratitude of the pleasant visit she had enjoyed from her grand-daughter and her little one, who had played upon her knee; listened, on the morning of her death, to a letter from an absent grandson then in the far West; recognized those who stood about her bed; smiled a welcome to her oldest grandson and his wife as they came in; responded to my words that brought the name of Jesus to her mind—and so gently fell asleep and went to see the face of her Saviour and to join the dear ones who had long been waiting for her in the better land. Her memory is that of the just, and it is blessed.

Her sun shall no more go down, and the days of her mourning are ended. Her remains sleep among the representatives of five generations in the beautiful Cemetery upon the Hill, at Hudson, N. Y. There we bore her after the solemn services which were held in this Church, conducted by Rev. Dr. Kip and Messrs. Sinclair and Frazer. When we reached her old home we found that the Elders and members of the Presbyterian Church of which she had long been a member had arranged for a service there. It was a touching and spontaneous tribute to the respect and affection with which she had been regarded. In the Sanctuary where she and her family had often sat, her remains were laid. Services were conducted by Rev. Dr. Holmes, of the Reformed Church, and Rev. Mr. Yiesley, the Pastor of the old congregation; and then we bore her to her last resting place, where, in the midst of scenery of almost unequaled beauty, repose the generations who have gone before her, waiting with her the signal that shall call forth the dust to a new life, under the workings of Christ's mighty power, whereby He is able to subdue all things unto bimself.

CENTENNIAL DISCOURSE.

HISTORY OF THE

First Presbyterian Church,

EDGEWATER, STATEN ISLAND,

By REV. J. E. ROCKWELL, D.D.,

JULY 2, 1876.

STATEN ISLAND:
JOHN BALE, PRINTER, AT THE STAPLETON POST OFFICE.
1876.

Centennial Discourse.

Text.—Psalm 44: 1. "We have heard with our ears, our fathers have told us what work Thou didst in their days, in the times of old."

History is best studied in the light of God's word and providence, and with the distinct purpose in view of gaining a clearer insight into the principles of God's government; of strengthening our confidence in His gracious help, and of stimulating our gratitude for His favours and blessings.

National history is mainly important in its bearings upon the Church of God, and the attentive student thereof will find that while nations have risen and flourished and decayed, the Church has never been destroyed—has never lost its power—and still lives as in the strength and vigour of immortal youth.

Principles never die. God's truth is immutable, and although human institutions may perish, the living embodiment of the Oracles of God, and the conservator of His word and promises, has never disappeared since Jehovah first gathered His people together and set them apart as distinct and peculiar from all the families of the earth. And he who studies most attentively the history of the world will observe that those nations have flourished most, and have been most secure from change, who have most faithfully conserved His truth, and guarded and honored His Church. The Lord's portion is His people, and He raises up or destroys nations just as they accept or resist the progress of His kingdom, and the advancement of His Church. Hence, while the merely worldly philosopher recalls and notes the political, financial and social causes which have been concerned in our national history, the christian identifies it with the developments of divine providence on behalf of the Church, and rejoices to recall what wonders God has here wrought for His people, and what work He hath done in the times of old. Hence it is no impertinent introduction of the Church into the history of our nation, which sets apart this day as a time for reviews of the way that God has led us, and a history of the individual churches with which we are severally associated. No one can read the history of America and not see all the way through the hand of God engaged in opening here a way for His people, not only as a refuge from their enemies, but as the theatre for some of the grandest movements of the Church in subduing the world unto Himself. And while in this work all denominations of Christians are having a part, and while in the establishment and maintenance of free and republican institutions all have been concerned, there seems to be a peculiar fitness in the act of the General Assembly of the Presbyterian Church, which requires of all Pastors that they set apart the first Sabbath in July of this centennial year in our national history to the preaching of historical discourses, which shall collect together and embody the facts which more especially concern their own congregation.

The principles of Presbyterianism are republican; its form of government, which we believe to be scriptural and apostolical, and which was simply modelled after the plan of the Synagogue, is a representative government. Where enough of its people are found to support the institutions of religion, they elect elders to have the charge of their spiritual concerns, and a Pastor to break to them the bread of life.

When three or four churches are found adjacent to each other they organize into a Presbytery or Classis, in which there is an equal representative of elders and ministers. And when these Churches and Presbyteries have increased they unite again into Synods and Assemblies, where the Church or people is still represented by elders, who have an equal voice with the ministers in all their deliberations.

This principle will be recognized as lying at the foundation of our republican institutions, and as manifesting itself in our civil and political arrangements. The rights of every individual are recognized not only in his privilege as a citizen, but in his responsibilities to government and law. The town has its representative in the County, the County in the State, and the State in the Union. The humblest individual has the right of appeal from the decisions of an inferior court to the judgment of the higher, and so may secure justice by a resort to judicatures which are exempt from the prejudice or ignorance which may have worked injury to him in the first processes of the law. This is the principle which distinguishes Presbyterianism as a government, and it was this element which was largely concerned in the early settlement of our country, in the strife for liberty in the great struggle of the Revolution, and in the ultimate organization of our national republican institutions. This form of government, with the exception of England, is that which the Church of the Reformation adopted in its more important features. The Church of Holland, which was the first reformed church that began its work on this continent, was Presbyterian as much as we. The Churches of Geneva, of Switzerland, of Germany, of Bohemia, of Scotland, of France and of Italy, were fully Presbyterian. This was the type of government which the vast majority of the reformed churches assumed, except where kingly power interfered to keep back this great principle that would inevitably work out freedom and popular institutions. Long before the war of the Revolution, the Presbyterian church was established in America. Some of the congregations under the charge of the General Assembly have already celebrated or passed their second centennial, while the Dutch type of the Presbyterian family, as represented in New York, numbers already two hundred and fifty years in the enjoyment of church ordinance. It would hardly be doing justice to the history of Presbyterianism upon this Island to commence and end with the brief review of what this single church has done within the simple score of years of its individual existence. Justice to the theme before us requires a brief survey of what we have heard from our fathers of the work which God has done for them in the times of old.

The early settlements of this Island date back to the year 1638, when amid the snows of the winter the first cabins were erected by a small colony which came out from Holland, under the auspices of the Dutch West India Company. The early colonial records of the State present to us only a few outlines of the events which marked those early attempts at settling the Island with colonists. We can but imperfectly picture to ourselves the appearance of this magnificent bay and its surroundings when these familes first landed upon our shores; those beautiful hills covered with primeval forests; bold headlands which have now disappeared before the pick and the spade of modern industry and improvement; the waters filled with the light canoes of the Monaton Indians, the first lord of this Island; the woods alive with deer and with wild fowl, and sheltering the wigwam of the savage, soon to disappear forever before the advancing tide of civilization. It was not till the year 1661 that any real progress was made in the settlement of the Island. There was here, as elsewhere, the struggle for a foothold with the Indians, who several times made murderous assaults upon the infant colony. Among the first who came hither from the old world was a small colony of Waldenses, who after the last and dreadful persecution of the Papal church, in which thousands of their people were butchered by the hirelings of Rome, first found a shelter and protection in Holland, and at length embarked for America and established themselves upon this Island. In the year 1656 three hundred of this interesting and wonderful people, by the approbation and help of the states of the Hague, to whose protection they had fled, were sent to the New Netherlands in company with several families of the Dutch. And these persecuted Christains formed a home at Oude Dorpe, near the central part of our own beautiful Island. Soon after the Huguenots, who long before the terrible massacre of St. Bartholomew had been oppressed and persecuted by the Papal authorities

of France, came hither and received from the West India
Company grants of land also near the central part of the
Island, a few miles south of the Narrows, where a settlement was commenced and a block house built for protection
against the savages. This is a most interesting and important fact, that this Island should have thus early in the settlement have furnished a shelter and a home to the persecuted
Waldenses of Piedmont and the Huguenots of France, and
that thus its earliest church should have been constituted in
accordance with the Presbyterian model, since the Waldensian
church and the Huguenots were both in their doctrine, order
and discipline, Presbyterian. To this little band of christians,
Dominie Drisius, of the Dutch Church of New York, made a
monthly visit, preaching to them in the French language, and
administering to them the sacraments. It would be pleasant
to be able accurately to picture to ourselves these early Presbyterians of the French, Italian and Dutch type, as they appeared in these occasional services; the joy with which they
welcomed the Dominie as he landed from some quaint looking
vessel or boat that had brought him down from the City, and
the serious and attentive congregation which gathered to hear
him, perhaps in some barn or log house, or perhaps beneath
some broad spreading tree. We can at least know that many
of his hearers came together with hearts full of gratitude and
joy, because they had found here freedom to worship God,
and had the assurance of protection from the enemies that
had sought their destruction. By the earnest and scholarly
investigation of Hon. Henry C. Murphy, while holding the
office of United States Minister to Holland, an exceedingly
interesting manuscript was brought to light and published
under the auspices of the Long Island Historical Society,
which enables us to form some clear conception of the social
condition of our Island in those early days of its settlement.
In the year of 1679 and 1680 Jaspar Dankers and Peter Shuyter left Holland for America to find a home for a sect known
as the Labadists, who for a number of years had created an
unusual excitement amid the Reformed churches. On their
way southward through New Jersey they passed over Staten

Island, and have given a full and entertaining description of three days over its hills and through its forests. Their journal reads thus :—

"Oct. 10; Tuesday.—Finding no opportunity of going to Staten Island we asked our old friend Symon, who had come over from Gouanes, what was the best way for us to get there, when he offered us his services to take us over in his skiff, which we accepted.

"11th; Wednesday.—We embarked early this morning in his boat, and he rowed us to Staten Island, where we arrived about eight o'clock. He left us there and we went on our way. This Island is about thirty-two miles long and four broad. Its sides are very irregular, with projecting points and indented bays, and creeks running deep into the country. The eastern part is high and steep, and has few inhabitants. It is the usual place where ships ready for sea stop to take in water, while the captain and the passengers are engaged in making their arrangements and writing letters previous to their departure. As regards the hilly or middle part of the Island, it is uninhabited, although the soil is better than the land around it; but in consequence of its being away from the water, and lying so high, no one will live there; the creeks and rivers being so serviceable to them in enabling them to go to the City, for fishing and catching oysters, and for being near the salt meadows. The woods are used for pasturing horses and cattle, for being an island none of them can get off. Each person has marks upon his own, by which he can find them when he wants them. When the population of the country shall increase, these places will be taken up. Game of all kinds is plenty; twenty or thirty deer are sometimes seen in a herd. A boy, who came in a house where we were, told us he had shot ten the last winter himself, and more than forty in his life; and in the same manner other game. We tasted here the best grapes. There are now about a hundred families on the Island, of which the English constitute the least portion, and the Dutch and French divide between them about equally the greater portion. They have neither church nor minister, and live rather far from each other and inconveniently to meet together. The English are less disposed to religion and inquire little after it, but in case there were a minister they would contribute to his support. The French and Dutch are very desirous and eager for one, for they spoke of it wherever we went, and said in event of not obtaining Dominie Tessemaker they would send or had sent to France for another. The French are good Reformed Churchmen, and some of them are Walloons. The Dutch are also from different quarters. We reached the Island about nine o'clock, directly opposite Gouanes, not far from the watering place. We proceeded southwardly along the shores of the high land on the east end, where it was sometimes stony and rocky and sometimes sandy, supplied with fine constantly flowing springs, from which at times we quenched our thirst. We had now come nearly to the farthest point on the south-east, behind which I had observed several houses when we came in with the ship. We had also made inquiries as to the village through which we would have to pass, and they told us that Oude Dorp would be the first one we would come to; but my comrade finding the point very rocky and difficult, and believing the village was inland, and as we discovered no path to follow we determined to clamber to the top of the steep bluff through the bushes and thickets, which we accomplished at great difficulty and in a perspiration. We found a little of a road above and below, and nothing but woods through which one could not see. Having wandered an hour or more in the woods, now in a hollow and then over a hill, at one time through a swamp and then across a brook, without finding any road or path, we entirely lost our way. We could see nothing except a little of the sky through the thick branches of the trees above our heads, and we thought it best to break out of the woods entirely and regain the shore. We made our way at last out of the woods and struck the shore a quarter of an hour's distance from where we began to climb up. We were rejoiced as there was a house not far from the place where we came out. We went into it to see if we could find any one who would show us the way a little.

There was no master in it, but an English woman with negroes and servants. We first asked her as to the road, and then for something to drink, and also for some one to show us the road; but she refused the last although we were willing to pay for it. She was a cross woman; she said she had never been in the village, and her folks must work, and we would certainly have to go away as wise as we came. She said however we must follow the shore, as we did. We went now over the rocky point, which we were no sooner over than we saw a pretty little sand creek and not far from there cattle and horses. We also saw the point to which the little path led from the hill above where I was when my comrade called me. We went on to the little creek to sit down and rest and cool ourselves, and then proceeded to the houses which constitutes the Oude Dorp. It was now about ten o'clock; there were seven houses, but only three in which anybody lived. The others were abandoned and their owners had gone to live in better places on the Island. We went into the first house, which was inhabited by English, and there rested ourselves, and eat, and enquired after the road. The woman was cross and her husband not much better. We had to pay her for what we eat, which we had not done before; we paid three guilders in zeewan, though we had only drank water. We proceeded by a tolerably good road to the Nieuwe Dorp, but as the road was in the woods, we got astray again in them. It was dark and we were compelled to break our way out through the woods and thickets. We saw a house at a distance to which we directed ourselves across the bushes. It was the first house of Nieuwe Dorp. We found there an Englishman who could speak Dutch, and who received us very cordially into his house, where we had as good as he and his wife had. She was a Dutch woman from the Manhatans, who was glad to have us in the house.

12th; Thursday.—Although we had not slept well we had to resume our journey with the day. The man where we slept set us on the road. We had now no more villages to go to, but went from one plantation to another, for the most part belonging to the French, who showed us every kindness, because we conversed with them in French, and spoke of the ways of the Lord according to their condition."

The journal gives the account of one more day's journey through the western part of the Island to the Elizabeth ferry, making constant and grateful notice of the kindness received by the French and the Dutch. His narrative gives a pleasant picture of our Island two hundred years ago, and confirms the statement that its original settlers were distinctly and clearly of the Reformed Faith as it was held in Holland, Piedmont and France, which was pure and simple Presbyterianism. In the year 1680, two years after this journal was written, a church was built by the Huguenots at Fresh Kill, in which services were conducted in French. Of this early church only a few stones in the little graveyard around it are left. Not long after a church was built by the Waldenses from Oude Dorp, not far from what was known as the Black Horse Tavern. Rev. Dr. Brownlee, to whose scholarly and patient research we are largely indebted for the church history of our Island, states in his Anniversary Address, that the first traces of a Reformed church on the north side lead back to the year 1680, and that these three churches thus built by Waldensian, French and Dutch Presbyterians, having no settled pastor, were supplied by the Dutch Ministers of New York and New Jersey. In 1697 the Huguenot church at Fresh Kill obtained as a pastor the Rev. Dr. Bonrepos. In 1717 the French and Waldensian churches united with the Dutch and organized a church and built a house of worship at Richmond, which I am told was standing at the time of the Revolution, probably in a little grave-yard not far from the Court House. After this union was formed an English Presbyterian Church appeared to have been organized at Stony Brook, the first site of the Waldensian congregation, for in 1769 a deed was given to the session of this church, and, Consistory of the Reformed church at Richmond, for some land in Richmond on which a church was to be built. "The deed" (says Dr. Brownlee) "mentions the names of Jacob Rezeau and Samuel Broome as the present Elders of the English Presbyterian Church according to the Westminster Confession of Faith, Catechism and Directory agreeable to the present established Church of Scotland. The deed conveyed a small lot, 65 feet by 55, to these parties, as far as I can understand it, the ground on which the present Reformed Church in Richmond stands. The church then standing at Stony Brook was to be removed and rebuilt on this lot." From these historic statements it is evident that Presbyterianism is no novelty on this Island, but was the earliest type of Church order and organization.

If we were called upon to show our Genealogical Tables we might write them somewhat in this form : A colony of Waldenses, the known and admitted successors of the Apostolic church in Italy, came to Staten Island and organized a church at Stony Creek between the years 1656 and 1689. In the same age the Huguenots, fresh from persecutions for Christ's sake and the Gospel's, came from Rochelle and established a church of the same order at Fresh Kill. Near the same town the Dutch (who had fought out the great principle of Religious Liberty before England practically knew what the word meant) established in connection with these Christians a church on the North Side of the Island. In 1717, or a little later, an English Prsbyterian church was organized in the place of the Waldensian church at Stony Brook, and in 1769 built a house of worship in Richmond, whose successor still stands on its old site, and is now the Reformed church at that place. From these united Christian families came the Reformed church at Port Richmond, Brighton, Huguenot and Stapleton ; hence sprang our own. Before leaving this early history of Presbyterianism on Staten Island it is but proper to glance at the relations of our own order to other church organizations. In the year 1704 Rev. Mr. McKenzie came hither as a missionary of the Episcopal Church ; though finding but few of his own faith and order he was kindly welcomed by both the Dutch and the French, and was permitted to hold service in the Huguenot church for seven years, until St. Andrew's was built. In order to bring into the pale of the English Church the Dutch inhabitants, prayer books translated into their language were freely distributed, and so they were gradually introduced to this new form of worship and order. In 1712 the Justices of Richmond County, the High Sheriff, and the Commander in-Chief of Her Majesty's Militia in this County, as well for themselves as in the names of the other inhabitants of the County, members of the Church of England, return thanks to the Society in London for the support of their worthy pastor. "Upon his first induction there were not above four or five in the whole County who knew anything of our excellent liturgy and form of worship, and many of them knew little more of any religion than the common notion of a Deity. And as their ignorance was great so was their practice irregular and barbarous. But now by the blessing of God attending his labours our church increases; a considerable reformation is wrought and something of the face of Christianity is seen around us."

Dr. Brownlee, with a mild sarcasm, calls this "delicious," and speaks of this intolerant ignorance as "celestial complacency." I may be permitted to add that it is "magnificent brass," without alloy, and stupendous impudence of which only a miserable bigot could be guilty; which deserves a monument of lead, on which should be engraved "We are the people, wisdom will die with us." With what cool assumption and outrageous bigotry do these men ignore the very existence of the church which for seven years had given them shelter and a home. With what monstrous arrogance do they speak of Christians who for forty years had been enjoying the ordinances of the church of Waldenses, (the true successors of the Apostolic Church in Italy), whose fathers were preaching the Gospel over Europe when England's priests and people were slumbering in the arms of the harlot of Rome; of the Huguenots, who had waded through seas of blood and persecution for the Gospel of Christ; and of the Dutch, among whom were these magnificent symbols, the Catechism of Heidelburg, and the Confession of the Synod of Dort, who had wrought out the idea of true religious freedom when England was sending out its brutal Claverhouse to Scotland to murder her confessors of Christ in cold blood, and was trying the dreadful but hopeless experiment of seeking to dragoon Scotch Presbyterianism into Prelacy and Kingcraft.

It is worthy of notice that the Moravian Church, which was established a hundred years after the Waldenses and Huguenots had come hither, owes its ministry and its origin to the Waldenses, who carried the Gospel into Bohemia long before the days of Huss and Wickliff; and in this respect that venerable and truly missionary church, though now having Bishops, though it largely limits their power, had a truly Presbyterian origin and parentage. Among the archives at Bethlehem is the original letter, dated in 1762, desiring that a church might be established at New Dorp, as you will notice not far from the early home of the Waldensian Colony. Among the signers are the names of Richard Conner, Stephen and Cornelius Martino, Tunis Egbert, Jacob, John and Cornelius Vanderbilt, Mary Stillwell and Peter Perine. The history of this Island then as to its early settlers is a history of Waldensian, French, Dutch and English Presbyterians, who had enjoyed the ordinances of the Gospel here two hundred years ago. Many of the names yet familiar to the inhabitants of this county are the representatives of those continental presbyterianism, who here sought and found *Freedom* to worship God.

The brief history of our own church, occupying as it does but a space of twenty years, lies within the memory of most who hear me to day. In the year 1849 a Sabbath School was commenced at Stapleton, by members of the Reformed Church at Tompkinsville. From that time religious services were held in the school room with an evidently growing interest on the part of the people. June 25, 1851; thirty-two Christian deciples were organized into a church by the South Classis of New York, and in Sept. of the same year Rev. A. R. Thompson became its pastor, under whose ministry this house was erected in 1852, enlarged in 1854, and a large and flourishing congregation built up. In the year 1856 the Gore Street Chapel was built as a Mission School. This year also witnessed the beginning of a new church which, though styled the First Presbyterian Church of Staten Island, was really the successor of three, which had been established in the first fifty years of the settlement of the Island. In the Spring of 1856 a number of members of the Reformed Church of Stapleton, believing that the time had come for the organization of a new church in Clifton, which then gave promise of a rapid increase in population, met for preliminary deliberation and prayer in the house of Mr. J. D. Dix, and after several meetings and earnest and serious consultation agreed to unite in a new church enterprize, the centre of which should be near the dividing line of the towns of Middletown and Southfield. On the 14th of May, 1856, the church was duly organized at the house of George M. Gerard, in Townsend Avenue, by a committee of the Third Presbytery of New York, consisting of Rev. S. D. Burchard, D. D., A. E. Campbell, D.D., Rev. Washington Roosevelt, D. D., and T. McLaughlin, with Elder David Stevens and J. C. Hines. After religious services, conducted by Dr. Burchard and Mr. McLaughlin, twenty-six persons presented letters from other churches, chiefly the Reformed church of Stapleton, and were duly constituted a church of Christ, under the name of the First Presbyterian church of Clifton, S. I. At the same time Messrs. John D. Dix, E. L. Sexton and G. W. Gerard were installed as Elders, and E. A. Ludlow and R. Davidge were made Deacons. In the evening of the same day Mr. Roosevelt preached a stirring sermon from the words—" The people had a mind to the work." On the following Sabbath the first communion was administered by Mr. Roosevelt. Until the Chapel at Clifton was built services were regularly held at the house of Mr. Dix, or some other equally convenient dwelling. On the 3rd of August, 1856, the Chapel in Townsend Avenue was dedicated to the worship of God; the services being conducted by Rev. Wm. Whittaker, of Greenport, L. I.

On the 1st of October, 1856, Rev. Alonzo Brown was duly installed Pastor of the church. But in consequence of ill health his services were interrupted, and his connection with the church was severed on the 30th of November, 1857.

In April, 1858, Rev. Samuel W. Crittenden was installed

Pastor, and continued in this relation until Nov. 29th, 1859, when he was compelled to ask for a dismission in consequence of increasing ill health. January 25th, 1860, a call was presented to Rev. Wm. H. Taylor, for his pastoral services, and he was duly installed on the 22nd of February, 1860, by the Presbytery of New York, to which body the church had now transferred its relations. After a pleasant and successful pastorate, Mr. Taylor resigned his charge April 18, 1864, and was succeeded by Rev. David R. Frazer, who was installed April 1st, 1865, and after a service every way useful and profitable, was at his own request dismissed on the 1st of November, 1867, that he might accept a call tendered him by the church in Hudson, N. Y. Soon after his dismission the Rev. Dr. Skinner, the pastor of the Reformed church in Stapleton, also resigned his charge, and the way seemed to be opening for a reunion of the two churches. After several preliminary meetings held in each separate congregation, it was agreed that the churches unite under the corporate name of the First Presbyterian Church of Edgewater, S. I. That the property at Clifton be sold and the proceeds used for liquidating the debt upon this property; that the officers of each congregation form the session of the united church. In the month of September, 1868, I took the charge of this people; and these eight years of pastoral service have been to me years of happy labour. During the pastorate of Mr Brown, ten were added to the church by letter. Under Mr. Crittenden seven joined by letter, and fourteen by profession of their faith. Under Mr. Taylor twenty-nine were added by letter, and eight by profession. During the pastorate of Mr. Frazer twelve were received, and fourteen by profession.

Up to the time of the reunion, embracing a period of twelve years, there had been a sure and steady growth. The total added to the church being fifty-eight by letter, and thirty-six by profession. At that time there was in actual communion forty-eight only out of the one hundred and twenty-two who had been members of the church. This fact shows the changes and depletion in population, which made necessary the uniting of the two churches. In June, 1868, at the consummation of the union, thirty-six names were added from the Reformed church. Since then there have been added to the church by letter ninety-six, and seventy-four by profession of faith; in all, one hundred and seventy.

At the union of the two congregations the Session was composed of the following members: Mr. John D. Dix and Mr. E. C. Bridgeman, of the Clifton church, and Mr. Wm. Shaw and Dr. Thos. C. Moffatt, of the Reformed church, Elders; and Mr. Francis McDonald and Mr. Howard Parmele, of the Clifton church, and Messrs. Charles H. Morris and William Standerwick, of the Reformed church, Deacons. Since then Mr. Shaw has left us to reside in Ireland, after a useful and honoured service of eighteen years on this Island. And Dr. Moffatt and Mr. Bridgeman have gone to their heavenly rest from lives of loved and honoured work for the Master, leaving behind them a fragrant and precious memory. Mr. Parmele and Mr. Morris have gone West, where they are still labouring to build up the interests of religion in their respective homes. The places of these brothers have been filled by Mr. Wm. Standerwick and H. L. Butler in the Eldership, and Messrs. Alfred Parmele, B. T. Jacobs, H. L. Butler, Jr., and E. C. Bridgeman in the Deaconate. In the beginning of the year 1872 the congregation adopted as its plan of meeting its yearly expenses what is known as the Bellefont or envelope system, which has as its fundamental principle the support of the Gospel by voluntary offerings, and which only needs the hearty co-operation of all to prove an ample success.

In the year 1874, while I was absent in Europe as the representative of our General Assembly to the Church of Scotland, the Chapel in Broad Street, where our Sabbath School had long found a pleasant home, was burned to the ground by the torch of the incendiary. The event appeared to be one that was every way unpropitious; it seemed largely to interrupt our work as a church, especially among the poor and those who were not in the habit of attending upon the ordinary services of the Sabbath. But the devellopements of

God's providence have shown us that He who could bring order out of confusion could make even the wrath of man to praise Him. The large and commodious room which will soon be completed, the expences for the erection of which have been provided, by the munificence of a single Christian, in a manner which God only could have arranged, is to us an earnest of His power to bless and to build up, which should give us a strong and abiding trust in Him. It has been already a stimulus to our efforts in gathering in the poor and the neglecters of religion to our church, which God has manifestly approved, and on which His blessing has rested.

And now as I close this history I have but to call your attention to the need which is already apparent of a new and more commodious and durable house of worship for this congregation, or at least a thorough repair and enlargement of this. What a memorable celebration of this grand centennial year would it be to begin and complete such a work. I know that the times are dark, yet it may be remembered that the Tabernacle was built, with all its costliness, while God's people were escaping from the long servitude in Egypt, and were yet unsettled in the wilderness, and that the second Temple was rebuilt in the troublous times which followed the long captivity in Babylon. We may not renounce God's service and work whatever are our surroundings. The faith which plans and executes work for Him, even in times of trial and darkness, will secure His abundant blessing. At least let us labour and pray with unceasing earnestness for His spirit to be shed upon us, and for His grace that is able to build us up, to give us an inheritance among all them that are sanctified.

An Address

DELIVERED BEFORE THE SYNOD OF NEW YORK,

BY ITS APPOINTMENT,

IN THE SCOTCH CHURCH, NEW YORK, OCTOBER 23d, 1862,

BY THE

REV. J. EDSON ROCKWELL, D.D.,

MINISTER OF THE CENTRAL PRESBYTERIAN CHURCH, BROOKLYN, N Y.

Published by Request.

NEW YORK:
MISSION HOUSE, 23 CENTRE STREET.
1862.

EDWARD O. JENKINS,
Printer and Stereotyper,
No. 20 North William Street.

ADDRESS.

Fathers and Brethren:

Standing as we do in the midst of commotions and agitations that are stirring our souls to the very depths, and surrounded as we are by the great sea of public and political strife whose angry surges follow us even to the closet and the sanctuary, it is a grateful work to turn our hearts and thoughts away from the dreadful picture of carnage and strife to those holier scenes of joy that await the Church of God, and to those wondrous promises, hastening to their fulfilment, which assure us that all these vast up-heavings are but the necessary preliminaries to the coming of the Prince of Peace, and will eventuate in the enlargement and stability and glory of the Church.

The promises of God to his people are designed for them not alone when all is calm and peaceful, when the sea is smooth and the winds are hushed; but they meet them when the tempest rages, when the ocean is convulsed, and the mountains shake with the swelling thereof. They assure us that Christ our King is walking upon the waters, that he rides upon the whirlwind, and that his voice even the winds and the sea obey. And they point us forward to the ultimate triumphs of his Church, against which, no weapon shall prosper, nor even the gates of hell prevail. While then, as watchmen upon the walls, we look out upon a dark night, and through thick mists, and see the play of the lightnings, and hear the mutterings of the tempest and the crash of the thunder, we may here and there through the rifting clouds see the precursors of coming day, and rejoice to know that its dawning is at hand. Hitherto, for wise reasons, God has permitted sin to enter into the grand experiment which has been going on in the great laboratory of the moral world, that its influence and power may be fully tested. But we have the assurance that eventually he will change the ingredients, and show to the universe what Holiness can do, when by his Grace, all shall know the Lord, and his Church shall everywhere triumph, and infidelity, and superstition, and error, and oppression, and darkness shall have fled away before his coming, whose light is the glory of the upper temple, and whose Kingdom shall stretch from sea to sea, and from the river to the end of the earth. To this great event the eyes of God's people have been turned in every age. They have been taught to pray "Thy Kingdom come," and the wondrous prophecies becoming more and more luminous in the lapse of ages, and the developments of Divine Providence have encouraged them to hope for the dawnings of a day of glory upon this long night of sin, when Christ shall reign over all the earth, and this world, long groaning beneath its load of sin and sorrow, shall rejoice in his supremacy. Daniel in his glorious visions beheld that day, and heard the promise that "the kingdom and dominion and greatness of the kingdom under the whole Heaven shall be given to the people of the saints of the Most High, whose kingdom is an everlasting kingdom, and all dominions shall serve and obey him." And when our faith languishes and grows dim as it looks forth upon the elements of evil and anarchy everywhere prevalent, and beholds the nations still hostile to God, and sees the evil apparently triumphing over the good, it is re-assured by God's own promise, "I will overturn, overturn, overturn it, until he shall come whose right it is." Here, on these promises, we may confidently rest and know that the Church is safe, that God is on the throne, and that Christ in all his divine power and wisdom is King as well as Prophet and Priest, and that he is Head over all things to his Church which he has purchased with his blood.

Nor are we left to walk alone by faith, but here and there the glimmerings of a blessed light appear like the precursors of the dawn of day, and wondrous changes seem to re-echo the words of the Apostle, " the night is far spent, and the day is at hand."

Amid much that is dark, and surrounded by scenes of peril and trial, we may yet look out upon the great field of Christian labour, and feel that the signs of the times are giving promise of good. In all the history of the past, the Church has never had so much to encourage her. God's people have never seen so much to strengthen their faith, and to call forth their full and united efforts for the extension of the Kingdom of Christ. The Bible is now translated into every tongue, and is waiting to be sent to every creature with all its precious messages of mercy. More than forty-eight millions of copies of the holy Scriptures have been published during the present century, which are being circulated, not alone by all the varied agencies in Christian lands, but by more than sixteen hundred missionaries, and more than sixteen thousand native preachers and teachers, who have been converted to God and educated for his service from the midst of heathen degradation. Divine Providence has in the most wonderful, and often in the most unlooked-for manner, removed out of the way obstacles which seemed to be insurmountable in the progress of Christian missions, so that there is now free access to every part of the heathen world. The silence of the remotest sea is now broken by the plash of the steamer, the herald of civilization, and the agent of Christian nations in bearing their influence to every land and nation. Commerce and the intrepid zeal of science have broken in upon African wilds and Asiatic solitudes, and opened to the world vast regions, peopled with teeming millions which have been hitherto unvisited and unknown. The walls of China are broken down, Japan is opening to the

Gospel, Africa is already feeling the influence of commerce in elevating her people, and is opening vast mines of wealth hitherto unknown, which will attract to her shores not the ships of the slave-trader, but merchant fleets, engaged in honorable and civilizing traffic, under whose influence that mighty continent may regain her ancient prestige, when Carthage was the empire of commerce, and Egypt the mother of science. Mahomedan prejudices against Christian nations are fast giving way before the influence of national intercommunion and the fierce fanaticism with which the Turkish, and Persian, and Moorish nations have met the advances of Christian kindness and courtesy, is yielding before the advance of light and truth, while amid the millions of the Papal world there is going on a wondrous change which is rapidly opening their minds to the blessings of civil and religious liberty.

And when we turn from these evident indications for good, as found in the wonderful openings which God's providence is making for the advance of Christian missions, we find that while the Church by no means comes up to the full measure of its strength and duty, yet the last fifty years have witnessed a most wonderful and gratifying progress in this direction.

Much as men who are disposed to look at the dark side may declare that the world is only growing worse—who would be willing to blot out what has been done, and return to the position which the Church was in at the commencement of the present century? Who can trace the progress of modern missions from the hour when the little band of youths at Williams' College began to pray for the conversion of the world, and consecrated themselves to the work of preaching the Gospel to the Heathen until the present hour, and not feel that the Lord hath done great things for his Church? Long before that time, indeed, had the seeds been planted, and were already germinating and shooting upward and giving signs of a coming harvest.

We may trace the great work back to the glorious revivals

which crowned the last century, and which marked the beginning of the present. From that time it was evident that the spirit of missions was awakening throughout the Church. Early in the history of our own beloved Zion we find the principle taking deep hold of the minds of her ministers, that the work of preaching the Gospel to the Heathen was the work of the Church, and although in those days of small things it was evident for a time that there must be a union of all evangelical Christians for the furtherance of the cause—yet that great principle was never lost sight of, and is now manifest, as we see every great division of the Church assuming this work for itself and identifying it with its most cherished movements and operations. And as we go back to the early history of the missionary work, and follow down these few and feeble streams as they enlarge and multiply, and widen and deepen, until they have become a mighty flood, bearing on its bosom the blessings of the Gospel to almost every land, who shall either despise the day of small things, or doubt that the Church has made encouraging progress since it first entered in earnest upon the fulfilment of Christ's command, "Go preach my Gospel to every creature!"

It is not alone upon the arrangements which are made to send out Christian ministers and teachers to the heathen that we are to look, when we would make an estimate of what is now doing for the conversion of the world. This is but a part of the vast system of agencies which God is using for the accomplishment of his purposes and the fulfilment of his gracious promises.

His armory is full of weapons for the destruction of his enemies. His providence has most ample resources for the enlargement and upbuilding of his kingdom. We are not to expect that the institutions of religion will be planted in any nation simply by a few isolated missionaries. God did not so build up his Church in Canaan, but sent there a whole colony that had been fitted for their work amid the discipline of

Egypt and the wilderness. He did not so plant his Church here, but brought hither his people from the shores of the old world where he had prepared them for their work by trials and persecutions. And do we not see this same process going on, by which our Pacific coast has been filled with churches and Christian institutions, and Australia is becoming the home of a vast Christian population, and parts of Africa are already rising to the dignity of a free and enlightened country with all the institutions of our holy religion diffusing their influence far and wide. And it may be that the multitudes which God has been bringing to our own shores are, in his time, to be sent forth with all the institutions of the Gospel that they may make some other lands, now sitting in darkness, the home of the Church and the dwelling place of the Most High.

And then again, God is evidently intending to make the great machinery of commercial enterprise tributary to the upbuilding of his kingdom. It cannot have escaped the student of prophecy how, that many of the exceeding great and precious promises which refer to the latter day glory, connect with it the sea and its inhabitants. As the Church is pointed to her future greatness and glory, she sees the wealth of the nations poured at her feet, and lending her their aid.

But with the multitude of the camels of Midian and Ephah, she beholds the abundance of the sea converted unto God, while the ships of Tarshish come first to bring her sons from far, her silver and her gold with them. And as the providences of God are unrolling his plans, it is evident that he intends to use the sailor as one of the foremost agencies in extending his kingdom. More than three millions of men, chiefly the representatives of Christian nations, are doing business upon the great waters. With an increasing interest and zeal the Church has been turning her attention to this once neglected class of men, and the results of her labour are already manifest. The voice of prayer and praise now ascends from many a ship that spreads her sails to the ocean breeze, and thousands of men are going forth to distant lands upon the peaceful errands of commerce, who are carrying with them all the warm and generous impulses of the sailor, and the manly and unselfish devotion of those whose hearts have felt the love of Christ, and the power of his Spirit; and their influence is felt for good wherever they go. Some of the most encouraging and hopeful aspects of the missionary work abroad, are connected with the fact that so many pious sailors are now representing Christian nations upon heathen shores. Those who have studied most the indications of Providence, and who have most thoroughly understood the character of the Christian sailor, have most wondered that the Church has been so slow to enter upon the work of caring for those who go down to the sea in ships; and of using with them the means that under God may be blessed to their conversion to Christ. The amount of good already accomplished by the scattering of Bibles and tracts among catholic and pagan nations through the means of seafaring men, whose hearts are full of love to Christ, can never be estimated until the records of time are reviewed in the light of eternity.

And when looking over all the appliances which the Church possesses for preaching the Gospel, we ask, What are the results already accomplished? We have no reason to faint or be discouraged, or to doubt whether God intends to use his Church as his agent for spreading over the earth the knowledge of the truth as it is in Jesus.

The representatives of the Church, and even of the American church alone, are found in almost every heathen nation,—amid the coral islands of the Pacific—upon the shores of Africa—on the mountains and plains of Asia, and the hills and valleys of Palestine where prophets and apostles lived and preached. In India and China and Turkey and the Isles of Greece, the American missionary stands as the herald of salvation,—preaching by the press or in the school, or by the wayside, or in the chapel, or from house to house—the news of pardon by the Redeemer's blood. Churches have been gathered amid lands long shrouded in heathen darkness, and many precious souls have been converted and saved by means of those whom we have sent forth to preach the Gospel. Even the catholic world is fast opening to the truth and the light. A wonderful change is evidently going on in Italy. From their mountain fastnesses where they have long hid themselves, the Waldenses, (these ancient witnesses for the truth,) are coming forth and planting their churches and their school of the prophets almost under the shadow of Rome,—while in France the truth is gaining ground, and the precious doctrines of the Gospel are opening upon the minds and hearts even of men who have ministered at the altars of the Papal Church. And with these considerations, may we not look forth hopefully, and with a strengthening faith upon the great field in which we are called to labour? Surely never were the appliances for work so great, never had the Church more encouragement to go forth and thrust in the sickle and reap. Let us then seek to awaken our hearts to the duty of a full consecration to the work of missions in all its varied departments, at home and abroad—in the raising up and education of labourers and in sending them forth to the field. Let us stand by the seashore and give the sailor as he leaves his home some token of Christian love and care. Let us meet the mighty tide of population that is pouring in upon us from the old world, and supply the emigrant with the means of religious instruction and education. Let us send forth the colporteur with his messages of love, to visit every neglected hamlet and desolate home, and leave them some leaf from the tree of life. Let us send forth the embassador for Christ to obey the last command of the Master, "go preach my Gospel to every creature." We cannot doubt the result. The enemies of God may make war upon the lamb, but the lamb shall overcome them. The Church will triumph. The ark is safe. The final victory may even now be near at hand.

Everywhere we look we find the precursors of the day,

and seem to hear the echo of God's word, "The night is far spent." Let us then take courage even while surrounded by trials. We are engaged in a work, the success of which there is no possible doubt. We are labouring for a cause dear to the heart of God himself—for the extension of the Church to which he has said "Thy walls are ever before me. I have graven thee upon the palms of my hands. He that toucheth you toucheth the apple of mine eye." Times of trial and darkness have and may come, but they shall only serve in the end, to manifest more fully the great love wherewith Christ has loved his Church. The promises of God cannot fail, and they all point us forward to the year of jubilee, and bid us labour and pray for its coming. It will surely come. The hour is approaching when there shall be heard the shout of the hosts of God's elect rising from the valleys,—ascending the hills—rolling on in streams ever deepening, over mountains and plains, and seas, sweeping round the world in one mighty and majestic anthem, whose echoes shall be caught by angels and borne heavenward,—" We give thee thanks, O Lord God Almighty, who art, and wast, and art to come, because thou hast taken to thee thy great power and hast reigned."

THE CHRISTIAN MINISTRY.

A SERMON,

PREACHED IN THE

Central Presbyterian Church of Brooklyn,

February 12, 1865.

ON THE FOURTEENTH ANNIVERSARY OF HIS INSTALLATION,

By Rev. J. E. ROCKWELL, D. D.

PUBLISHED BY REQUEST.

BROOKLYN:
"THE UNION" STEAM PRESSES, NO. 10 FRONT STREET, BROOKLYN.
1865.

SERMON.

First Corinthians, 4:1—*Let a man so account of us as of the Ministers of Christ, and Stewards of the Mysteries of God.*

The First Epistle to the Church at Corinth is eminently practical in its character and design, having been written in answer to certain questions addressed from the Church to Paul, and being intended to rebuke and check certain disorders which had arisen among them, partly in consequence of a neglect of discipline on the part of the authorities of the Church, which ought to have been applied for the correction of offences and the good of the offender.

Corinth was to the world in the time of Paul what Paris is now, a gay and brilliant city, where existed a strange mixture of refinement and corruption, of wisdom, philosophy, wit, fashion, splendor, and wealth. Out of these elements a Church had been gathered, under the ministry of Paul, into which, since his absence, divisions and corrupt practices had entered, in the process of which his own rights and prerogatives as an Apostle and minister of Christ had been called in question. The earlier part of his Epistle is therefore, to some extent, an apology and a defence of the Christian ministry, with a statement of its prerogatives and its authority. His design, in the opening chapters of his argument, is to set forth the wisdom of God, as shown in the Gospel, in contrast with human wisdom, as it has appeared in every age, often leading to a rejection of the scheme of mercy through

Jesus Christ, and when manifesting itself in the Church, leading to the formation of sects and parties, and creating serious dissensions among the professed followers of the Lord Jesus. That he might plainly rebuke and thoroughly heal such divisions in the Corinthian Church, he sets forth plainly the distinctive features of the Christian religion, recalling to their minds that in all his ministry among them he had known nothing but a crucified Saviour; that avoiding the discussion of any question of merely worldly wisdom and human philosophy, he had set before them Jesus Christ as the only hope of guilty and lost sinners. Remembering the words of the Saviour, "And I, if I be lifted up, will draw all men unto me," he had held up the cross as the grand rallying point for saved sinners, around which the high and the low, the rich and poor, the wise and the unlearned, might gather and feel that they were all one in Christ. In the consciousness that in this respect he had performed his great duty as an Apostle and minister of the Gospel, and that for the fidelity with which he had met his obligations he was responsible to God, and not to man, he plainly declared that with him it was of very little importance what the world, or even the Church, thought of him. Human judgment, whether it came in the form of praise or of censure, of approbation, or scandal and reproach, was nothing to him, who judged not even himself, but left all for the decisions of the Great Day, looking then for acceptance not in his own righteousness, but in the perfect obedience and sacrificial sufferings of the Son of God. It is in this connection that the words of our text occur: "Let a man account of us as of the servants of Christ, and stewards of the mysteries of God."

In the words which follow he notices the fidelity which is required of those who are set apart to dispense to men the messages of the Gospel; and in a few brief and emphatic passages, which seem to be both historical and prophetic, sets forth the toils and trials of the ministry in a manner so graphic and emphatic that it would seem that none but he who was fully persuaded that it was his duty to preach the Gospel would ever seek to enter that sacred office. He seems to have before his mind a picture of a Roman amphitheatre, with its vast crowd of spectators gathered to witness its inhuman sports, where gladiators were brought out to contend with each other, or with wild beasts, when every other means of entertainment had been exhausted. The world had been in every age the theatre in which God's people had been subjected to sore trials. Patriarchs and prophets and priests have been compelled to bear witness for the truth often amid fiery trials. Christ, the great Captain of our salvation, was made perfect through suffering; and now his ministers were to be called to follow him who had sent them forth as sheep in the midst of wolves. Hence, the Apostle declares: "I think that God hath set us the Apostles last, as it were, appointed unto death, for we are made a spectacle unto the world, and to angels, and to men. Even unto this present hour we both hunger and thirst and are naked, and are buffetted, and have no certain dwelling-place, and labor, working with our own hands; being reviled we bless, being persecuted we suffer it, being defamed we entreat; we are made as the filth of the earth, and are the offscouring of all things unto this day." Such was the Apostles' view of the experience of the Christian ministry, and yet he who wrote these words declared that when called to this work he conferred not with flesh and blood. He it was who blessed God that he had counted him worthy, putting him into the ministry; and who, when writing to his youthful friend and companion, said: "He that desireth the office of a bishop desireth a good work." These statements, so strangely discordant, may be all harmonized by the words of our text, which link them in a golden chain of precious ministerial experience: Let a man so account of us as the servants (or the purchased slaves of Christ) and stewards of the mysteries of God.

These words present us for our consideration the divine authority and the special work of the Christian ministry.

1st. Paul everywhere speaks of himself, and through himself, for all who are called to the work of preaching the Gospel as the servants of Christ, using the word "*Doulos*," which was selected to represent a slave or bondman, who either by inheritance or purchase was held to the service of his master. He recognized himself as not his own, but as belonging wholly to Christ. He declared: "Necessity is laid upon me, yea, woe is me if I preach not the Gospel." He felt that he had been called to a work, which, however onerous and painful and self-denying it might be, he could not decline. And although the Holy Ghost witnessed to him that in every city bonds and imprisonments awaited him, yet in his consciousness that he was serving his Master, he declared: "None of these things move me, neither count I my life dear unto myself, so that I might finish my course with joy, and the ministry that I have received of the Lord Jesus to testify the Gospel of the grace of God." He regarded himself as bought with a price. He had been purchased at the amazing expense of the death of the Lord Jesus, from all the claims of divine justice and law, from sin and eternal death. Christ, who had loved him with an everlasting love, had rescued him from the bondage of Satan and sin, and had redeemed him from their hands by his great work of atonement, and through his own perfect obedience and spotless righteousness had brought him into acceptance with God, and made him his own servant. Hence, the Apostle looked upon himself as not his own. All that he had and was belonged to Christ, and he recognized His right to his full and constant service. What he possessed of talent, or virtue, or influence, or thought, or affection had by that great deed of purchase been transferred from himself, or the world, or Satan, or sin, to whom it had once been appropriated, to the Lord Jesus Christ.

And that transfer had received the cordial acquiescence of his own conscience and will and affection. He was not ashamed of these marks of his new Master which he bore about with him. He felt that it was no dishonor to be the willing and faithful servant of such a Master. He saw no evidence of a loss of manhood in freely calling himself, before all men, the servant of the Lord Jesus. He was not ashamed, as an Apostle and minister of the Gospel, to confess that the credentials of his office were only placed in his hands when Christ had made him his bondman. All this had been the result of that grace which is in common imparted to all true believers. It was the out-working of that everlasting love which God had cherished for his people before the foundation of the world. It was part of that everlasting covenant in which God had pledged to his Divine Son, that he should see of the travail of his soul and be satisfied. It was the development of God's glorious purposes of grace and mercy, in which Christ had, on behalf of his people, magnified and honored the law—suffered in their stead—risen for their justification, appeared in Heaven as their Intercessor, and in due time, sent down his Holy Spirit to convince them of sin, to lead them to Christ for mercy, to renew their hearts, and to commence in them the great work of sanctification by which they should be made to perfect holiness in the fear of the Lord. And the Apostle when setting forth the estimation due to the ambassadors of God, wrote therefore, "Let a man account of us as the ministers or servants of Christ." It was in full accordance with the words of the Master himself, "Ye are my servants; ye have not chosen me, but I have chosen you, and ordained you that ye should go and bring forth fruit, and that your fruit should remain. He that receiveth you receiveth me." The servant of *Christ!* Who would not gladly labor and suffer for such a master? *The Servant of Christ!* That name will be a glorious title of honour, when bonds and fetters, and all the badges of human servitude, with all the tears and sufferings of the oppressed, shall have been lost and forgotten in the resistless progress of Truth, Liberty, and Righteousness, and when Christ shall make all men free, by holding them in bondage to Himself alone, and then giving them the privilege of those whom the truth makes free.

II. But there is a special work imposed upon the Christian ministry, distinct from all others, and separating them by a Divine ordinance from all other employments to which the servants and disciples of Christ are called. As among the servants of Abraham, born in his house, or bought with his money, one was appointed his steward, to whom the interests and affairs of his household, and the custody of his large wealth were committed, so Christ has chosen from his people those to whom he has given a special work which calls them away from the ordinary pursuits and business of life, and in the immediate and full discharge of which they have no opportunity for attention to those objects which ordinarily engross the minds and energies of the world. Their office and duties are here alluded to under the peculiar title of Stewards of the Mysteries of God.

The Gospel, with all its great and glorious truths and histories, and the ordinances of the Church, with all their blessed confirmations of the covenants and promises of God to his people, are evidently here alluded to under the name of Mysteries. The term as used in connection with the Gospel does not imply what is unintelligible or incomprehensible, but in every instance in which it occurs in the Old Testament or the New, refers to something revealed or explained, or which may be understood. Thus Christ said to the Apostles, whom he was training for the Ministry, " Unto you it is given to know the Mysteries of the Kingdom of Heaven." So the Spirit explains to John the Mystery of the Seven Stars and the Golden Candlesticks, and the Mystery of the Woman upon the scarlet-colored beast. In the Apostolic writings the term mysteries is usually applied to the doctrines of the Gospel, once imperfectly known or understood, but now fully explained by Christ and his Apostles. Thus Paul says to Timothy, "great is the Mystery of Godliness," which he immediately explains in his concise but wonderfully accurate description of the incarnation and death of Christ; so he calls the Gospel the "Mystery of Faith," the mystery now made known through, or by means of the Church. "The Mystery of God, and of the Father, and of Christ." With these examples we may easily understand what is meant by the term "Stewards of the Mysteries of God." It is evident that the Apostle would have men regard the ministers of Christ as divinely commissioned to preach the Gospel and administer its ordinances. He thus recalls to their minds the truth that in the Christian as well as the Jewish Church there was a class of men selected and set apart for the work of religious instruction, and which Christ gave to his Church as his ascension gift, when he said, "Go preach my Gospel to every creature."

That sacred work was to be perpetual in the Church. The gift was committed from one generation to another. Paul, who had himself trained the youthful Timothy for the office, warned him "not to neglect the gift which was given him with the laying on of the hands of the Presbytery," and counseled him how to perpetuate his office as a Minister of Christ, when he said "the things which thou hast heard of me, the same commit thou unto faithful men, that they may be able to teach others also." This is the work of all who are called to the office of the Christian Ministry. They are the Stewards of the Mysteries of God, to whom God has committed this trust, the treasure of the Gospel. They come, not as priests, to offer sacrifices, for Christ has offered himself a sacrifice once for all. But with a divine commission in their hand, and with authority bestowed upon them by the great Head of the Church. They come with all the glad tidings of salvation, through the Redeemer, to declare to lost and sin-ruined man, the terms on which he may be saved; to urge him to reconciliation with God; to announce to him the news of pardon and peace; and to call him to repentance. All his work is summed up in the great commission which he holds in his hand from the Master, "Go preach my Gospel to every creature." The doctrines, the invitations, the ordinances, the promises, of that Gospel are committed into his hands, together with all needful care and discipline and watch over the Church, essential to its peace, its order, and its purity. As a steward provides the things necessary to the family, so the Minister of Christ, receiving at His hands the Gospel, dispenses such instruction, warning, counsel, comfort, and guidance, as may be needful, to edify the body of Christ, and to build up the Church. His business is to set forth the claims of the law, the guilt of man and his exposedness to Divine wrath, and the means by which he may be rescued from eternal Death; to lead inquiring sinners to Christ, to point men to the Lamb of God that taketh away the sin of the world; to instruct and guide, and comfort God's people, by a full display of their covenant relations to Christ and his Church, and by a repetition of all these exceeding great and precious promises, on which their hopes are built, and to which their faith must be fully given. He is to do this in season and out of season; in the sanctuary, and in the family; wherever God's providence brings him a hearer; whether it be in the great assembly on the Sabbath, or by the way, or in the house, he is to dispense the Mysteries of God; he is to feed the Flock, to care for the Lambs, to bear on his soul an ever abiding, and ever present sense of responsibility to Christ, and to labor as one that must give account. This is his mission, the work for which God has set him apart, and to which his whole life must be given.

And with these plain and obvious facts before us we see,

I. That the Ministry is a work of awful responsibility, and he who is called to it, may well ask "Who is sufficient for these things?" The pastor is not responsible for results, but for the manner in which he discharges his duty. Christ has not sent him to *convert souls*, that is the work of the Holy Spirit, and Paul or Gabriel could no more perform it than the humblest minister of Jesus. Christ has not made him responsible for the enlargement and upbuilding of the Church, that is *His* work. He represents himself as the Builder. And men err often in judging of a Minister by the immediate success which may crown his efforts. Christ has not made him responsible for the estimation in which the world may hold him. All that lies in the providence of God. But He does require him faithfully to dispense His truth and ordinances, faithfully to warn men to be reconciled to God. And this simple work might fill and angel's hands. It is when the pastor thinks of meeting his hearers at the Judgment, where no mistakes or short-comings can be rectified, and wonders if he have done his whole duty to every soul committed to his care, whether in the discharge of his office he has fully dispensed the Mysteries of God, that his heart sinks within him. And when the Apostle was alluding to this great work he desired those who would form a correct estimate of the Christian Ministry, that they should account of them as Stewards; intrusted with these awful responsibilities,

> "O who can e'er suffice,
> What mortal for this more than angel task,
> Winning or losing souls, thy life-blood's price?
> The gift were too divine to ask.
> Dread searcher of the hearts!
> Thou who didst seal by thy descending dove,
> Thy servant's choice, O, help us in our hearts,
> Else helpless found, to learn and teach thy love."

II. It is obvious, again, that the Ministry need and deserve the earnest prayers and the hearty co-operation of God's people. Paul himself, overwhelmed with a weight of care, and a sense of solemn responsibility, cried, "Brethren pray for us." The minister is but a man, poor, fallible, weak, and erring; subject to all the passions and infirmities of his fellow-men; tempted at all points as they are; feeling as much as they, the cares, anxieties and afflictions of life. And yet, with all these pressures and anxieties upon him, which often rob him of rest, he must comfort others, though his own heart is full of sorrow; he must bring forth from the treasure-house things new and old, whatever distraction may be hindering the full and free operation of his own mind; he must prepare for the services of the sanctuary "beaten oil," food for babes, and for strong men, instruction for the ignorant and the wise, and intelligent, warnings for the impenitent and obdurate, and comfort for the penitent and broken-hearted. All this may seem easy to the man who flatters himself that because he can occasionally deliver an exhortation to his brethren, to which they listen with patience if not with profit, he could as readily take the place of the minister of Christ: yet when we remember that this work is to be done Sabbath after Sabbath, and year after year, we may well ask, Who is sufficient for these things? and say, "Brethren, pray for us, that utterance may be given unto us."

Nor is this view of their work as the Stewards of God's Mysteries diminished when we recall the daily and constant pressure of pastoral and ministerial duties which are laid upon them. They are to visit their flock from house to house; all their deepest sympathies are often awakened at the sick and dying bed of those whom they love, and for whom they cherish a deep affection; households in which they have been welcome guests in times of prosperity, are clouded with gloom and affliction and heavy bereavements: and they are called to minister to these comfort, while their own hearts feel the deep pressure of sorrow, and their own eyes are filled with tears. And when we add to all this the watch and care, which they must have over the Church, the anxieties that press upon them, because of all its varied interests, the duties, often many and onerous, which are laid upon them by the Church in its associated capacity, the part they are to perform in caring for the general interests of religion throughout all the Churches with which they are connected, and the labors which they must undertake in their behalf, we have some faint estimate of what is involved in the words "Servants of Christ, and Stewards of the Mysteries of God." Nor should it be matter of wonder if amid these varied duties a pastor should sometimes seem to fail. Nor need the ministers of Christ think that some strange thing happened to them, when they find themselves the objects of censure and the mark of cruel suspicions and slanders. Against the Master even, false witnesses arose, and men called him Beelzebub. The Apostles were persecuted and put in peril from false brethren. Even a minister as meek and pure as John, wrote "Diotrophes, who loveth to have the pre-eminence receiveth us not. Wherefore, if I come, I will remember his deeds which he doeth, prating against us with malicious words." If such ministers were subject to such trials, can he hope to be exempt who finds himself compassed about with many infirmities: and may he not ask for the earnest prayers of his people, and that they, laboring with him, become "fellow helpers for the truth."

III. Again, it is evident, from the considerations before us, to whom the Ministry is responsible for the fidelity with which their work is discharged. As Christ is their Master, they are to render in their account to Him. The principle that a shepherd belongs to the flock, and is immediately amenable to them, is at variance with all the instructions of the Word of God. Under Christ, The Head, he is accountable to the Church as represented in its Courts. The call of the Spirit to the Ministry, is recognized and sealed by the act of the Presbytery, or whatever representative of the Church stands in its stead, to set him apart formally and authoritively to the work of the ministry. There, and there only, under Christ does his official responsibility rest. There every error and wrong, whether in life or doctrine, which he commits may be judicially examined and reproved. There the injury which he may do to others, or they to him, may be fairly criticised and condemned, censured or acquitted.

And this leads us to notice the great criterion by which to judge of the ministers of Christ. Their work is to open to men the Mysteries of the Gospel, to edify the body of Christ, to instruct, rebuke, and exhort, with all long-suffering, to beseech men in Christ's stead to be reconciled to God. And the judgment of them by the Church is not to be on the principle, and too often manifested in congregations, on which a show-man judges of his wild beasts and puppets, as to the attractions they possess in filling his coffers; nor how far they may seem successful, as a speculation, for the business men of a congregation, in disposing of pews at the highest possible valuation; nor how much revenue they may be able to raise by their varied attractions, but how faithfully and how plainly they preach the Word of Life. Any other estimate than this is unjust and unscriptural. And yet, how many a minister of Christ has been hunted down and persecuted because in some way he has not met the demands of men who have been disposed to estimate him by another standard than that of a Steward of "the Mysteries of God." To this one test should the ministry be brought—Does it meet the requirements of the great commission? Men who complain that they are not edified by this and that preaching, should first ask: Is it God's truth? Is it Christ's Gospel? and if that be admitted, should seriously question their own hearts whether they are in a right state to be profitted by the Word of Life. He who cannot profit by a presentation of Christ, however plain it may be, should begin to examine his own heart for the difficulty. He who truly loves Christ, His Gospel, and the doctrines of His word, will find profit in any discourse, however humble or unpretending, that sets forth Christ as the only hope of the sinner, or that displays any one truth, that has the Cross for its aim and illustration. He to whom the simplest preaching of Christ is profitless and uninteresting, should ask himself whether he may not be like the deaf adder that stoppeth her ears to the voice of the charmer, charming never so wisely.

IV. Again, it is abundantly evident that he who desireth the office of a bishop, desireth a good work. With all its toils and trials and annoyances, it is a blessed and glorious office to which he is called who is made a minister of Christ, and a Steward of the Mysteries of God. What is poverty? What are the struggles and anxieties, and afflictions, and persecutions, which attend the work, to the precious truths with which their minds are familiar, with the sweet and holy communion which they have with God in His word and ordinances, and with the confirmation of Christ's own promise, "Lo I am with you alway, even unto the end of the world." That promise never fails. When all is dark and forbidding; when the ministers of Christ have stood amid storms of persecution; when wicked and unreasonable men have risen up against them; when, like Luther, they are called to bear witness to the truth in the very face of malignant enemies; or like Calvin or Edwards have been hunted down and banished from their work for a time, God has vindicated their cause, and Christ has never forsaken them. Nay, he has raised up and surrounded them with kind and faithful friends, who have nobly stood up with, and for them, making their burdens light and their work easy and pleasant.

V. And with the deep and earnest and experimental conviction that the work of the Ministry is a good work, with many a precious and grateful memory of the years that we have labored together, I come here to-day, on the fourteenth anniversary of my settlement among you, as your pastor, to testify to God's faithfulness to his promises. Of the 126 who were members of this Church when I was called from another field of labor to take the charge of this people, but 47 are now even nominally connected with us; and of that number but 24 are now actually members of this congregation, and statedly worshipping with us. During the last 14 years, there have been added to us 673 members, of whom 259 have been received upon a public profession of their faith in Christ. During the last year, which has been to most of the churches a year of dearth and darkness, 29 have been added to our number, of whom (10) ten were on a profession of their faith. With nearly all who during all these years have thus publicly united with Christ's visible people, I have had personal intercourse, becoming as far as possible familliar with their religious experience, and giving them such instruction and counsel as their several cases required. Within the past year I have preached 107 sermons and 30 weekly lectures; attended 65 meetings for prayer; performed 14 marriage ceremonies, and 28 funeral services; administered the ordinance of Baptism to 24, and made 430 pastoral calls visiting as far as possible every family once, and usually twice during the year, and failing in these attentions only where removals of residence or absence at the time of my call have prevented the accomplishment of my purpose. Remembering also that the Master has committed to my care the Lambs of the Flock, I have scarcely ever permitted a Sabbath to pass without visiting the Sabbath-

School, though seldom feeling that it was proper to interrupt the work of the teachers by any remarks. While on every Communion Sabbath I have taken the whole work of instruction upon me, and have given to the School my pastoral counsels and instruction in connection with their recitation of the Assembly's Catechism; I have commenced also the same work with the Border Mission School, and have been gratified with the prompt and general answers made to that admirable compend of truth, which is one of the standards of our Church.

Nor has this congregation failed in its evidences that it accounts of us as the Ministers of Christ and Stewards of the Mysteries of God. Their acts of kindness and the tokens of their affection have fallen upon me like the dew and the blessed sunshine. Month after month some new act of love, and confidence, and sympathy has come to me. Now in the form of private munificence, supplying my wants in the very time of my greatest need; then in the shape of some anonymous gift, handed in at my door by some unknown friend, or coming as a New Year's Gift; or in timely addition to my wardrobe from kind and loving hands; and always in words of cheer and sympathy, amid scenes of trial and sorrow, and in unmistakable demonstrations from the congregation of unwavering attachment to their pastor.

For all these I can only say, May all who have thus given their proofs of their respect for Christ's ministers, find the blessing which is contained in his words, "He that receiveth you receiveth me." God is my witness, that I have prayed that you all may at last hear from His lips the words, "Inasmuch as ye have done it unto one of the least of these, my brethren, ye have done unto me."

And now, brethren, while anticipating another year of

labor, and asking your prayers and your co-operation, permit me to add, that while now, as ever, regarding myself as the Servant of Christ, and ready, whenever his providence shall plainly call me to go where that providence leads, this Church is bound to my heart by a thousand tender cords. Fourteen years of mutual co-operation and sympathy, have bound me to you with bonds which nothing but Christ can sunder. Here among you are buried the children whom God has already called from my arms to Himself. Here our tears have fallen together over afflictions which we have been called to meet.

We have passed through many a scene of trial and joy together. We have met amid tears and sorrows; at the death-bed and the grave. We have rejoiced together over those who have been heard saying, "Come and I will show you how great things God hath done for my soul." We have met in blessed seasons of communion around the table of our Lord. Here let us again rally around that Cross where he purchased for us pardon, and taught us by His own example the great lesson of forgiveness, as He prayed for his murderers. Here let us, to-day, re-consecrate ourselves to the service of Christ, and the upbuilding of His Church.

Let all uncharitableness, and pride, and ambition, and malice, and wrath, and evil speaking, and anger cease as we open the treasures of the Gospel, and the Mysteries of God, and find we have one Saviour, and one hope, one work, one blessed tie, that binds us to each other and to Christ. Let us labor for the building up of the Church, and earnestly pray the Holy Spirit may rest upon us, and make among us rich and wonderful displays of His saving grace and Almighty power, in the conversion of souls to Christ. Remembering that the Church is to be built up, and souls saved, not by might or by power, but by the Holy Spirit, let our united prayers go up that He would revive and bless us, and give His word success, and put honor upon his own appointed ordinance—the Stewardship of the Mysteries of God.

FRUITFULNESS IN OLD AGE.

A SERMON

PREACHED IN THE

Central Presbyterian Church

OF BROOKLYN,

November 12, 1865,

ON THE OCCASION OF THE DEATH OF

JOHN MORRIS.

By Rev. J. E. ROCKWELL, D. D.

PUBLISHED BY REQUEST.

BROOKLYN:
"THE UNION" STEAM PRESSES, 10 FRONT STREET.
1865.

SERMON.

"The righteous shall flourish like the palm-tree: he shall grow like a cedar in Lebanon. Those that be planted in the house of the Lord shall flourish in the courts of our God. They shall still bring forth fruit in old age."—*Psalm* 92 ; 12–14.

These words are a vivid and beautiful description of a righteous man. They are part of a psalm which celebrates the goodness and grace of God, as manifested in his works, and most especially in his works of Providence and Redemption. They appear in contrast with the transient prosperity of wicked men, who spring up as the grass, and are as suddenly destroyed; who appear for a time to flourish and prosper, but who soon pass away to be seen no more. They are a distinct statement of the work of grace as it is developed in the life and character of the christian. They present him to us under the figure of a palm-tree, which continues green and vigorous all the year through, and whose leaves remain amid the frosts of winter, as well as the more genial heat of the summer months, and whose age is counted not by years, but by centuries. They set forth the aged christian as bearing rich and precious fruits of piety and faith, even while drawing near to the grave, and as giving ample testimony to the power and glory of the Gospel amid the infirmities of life's decline, and while his bodily strength is daily weakening under the influence of age and decay. Taking these words as our guide on the present occasion.

I. Let us enquire first into the Scriptural meaning of the word righteous, as it occurs in this and similar passages. There are evidently but two ways in which a man may become righteous: first, by his own perfect and sinless obedience; and, secondly, by the imputation to him of the righteousness of another. In the first form Adam was righteous until he fell by transgression. Since that hour, neither he, nor his posterity who fell with him, have ever been able to present to God a righteousness of their own which he could accept. 'All have sinned, and come short of the glory of God.' 'By the deeds of the Law, there shall no flesh living be justified.'

It is only therefore in the second form that any child of Adam can become a child of God, and an heir of heaven.

To meet this want of our fallen nature, Christ became flesh; and, having magnified and honored the Law, bore in his own body the tremendous penalty due to our transgression, and thus 'became sin for us, who knew no sin, that we might be made the righteousness of God in him.'

In the arrangements of his grace, and the provisions of mercy, he who accepts of Christ by faith secures to himself the benefits of his merits and death. Thus 'Abraham believed God, and it was counted unto him for righteousness.' And all the way through the Scriptures we meet with the statement, that 'the just by faith shall live.' Christ has taken the place of the believing sinner—he has borne the stripes that he must otherwise have suffered. He has obeyed the law in his behalf, and when he is brought to receive Christ by faith, power is given unto him to become a son of God.

There is no longer to him any condemnation. The law ceases to pursue its claims against him. The perfections and government of God are honored even while he accepts and justifies the sinner. The righteous man, then, is one who, though by nature a sinner, and a child of wrath, and exposed to all the terrors of the second death, has been pardoned for the sake of Christ. He stands acquitted of all legal claims against him. He is clothed upon with the righteousness of Christ, and thus has secured to him the favor of God, and the crown and joy of the heavenly inheritance. This was the righteousness of the saints of old. This was the boast and glory of Apostles and martyrs. This alone is the hope of any sinner, that he may be found in Christ, justified in his merits, washed in his blood, and accepted as righteous for his sake. And this leads us to notice,

II. The fact that the life and character of the Christian is the result of a work of grace in and upon him. The words before us, and those which precede and follow, are a celebration of God's power as indicated in the destruction of his enemies, and in the holiness and joy and salvation of his people. His loving kindness and faithfulness are the themes with which the Psalmist would awaken the chords of his harp, and which he would celebrate upon the psaltery and an instrument of ten strings. And when he turns for illustrations of his theme to the righteous, he speaks of them as planted in the house of the Lord. The sovereignty and providence and grace of God are all concerned in the salvation of the sinner. He is taken in the fulfillment of a divine and gracious purpose, which formed a part of God's eternal counsels. He is led to see his lost and guilty estate, and under the eye of an ever-watchful

Providence is brought within the reach of sacred influences, which exert upon his mind and heart a healthful control, until the Holy Spirit renews his heart, brings him into a cordial reception of the Gospel, and fills him with peace and joy in believing. From this hour a work is begun which will be fully completed amid the joys and holiness of heaven. Yet this work is to be accomplished by the use and enjoyment of the means of grace. As the tree cannot grow without a proper soil in which to stand, or without the rain and the sun—so the Christian cannot flourish except in the midst of those divinely appointed ordinances, which are designed to fill his mind with heavenly truths, and to strengthen his faith, and develop all his graces. Hence he is said to be planted in the house of the Lord. He is brought into the visible Church, where he is fed and nourished by the truths and ordinances of the Gospel. He is surrounded by sacred influences which are ever at work upon his heart and life. He enters his closet, and the word of God opens to him its treasures; while in prayer and holy communion with his Maker, he draws into his soul the richest blessings of Heaven. He enters the house of God, and is fed by the sacred truths of the Gospel as they fall from the lips of Christ's embassadors. He sits down at the table of his Lord, where he commemorates his sufferings and death, and his heart is refreshed and strengthened and comforted by the sacred ordinance which sets vividly and sensibly before him the great sacrifice of Calvary. He looks upon the administration of Baptism, and receives new impressions of the grace of God in his covenant with his people, and their seed after them, of which it is the seal. He visits the place of prayer, and his spiritual strength is renewed by the precious communion and fellowship of the saints. While with all these means of grace the Holy Spirit sheds his own blessed influences upon his heart, strengthening his faith, increasing the power of his gracious affections, enlightening his mind, confirming his hope, and giving him the ability to overcome sin, to walk in the fear of God, and to manifest in all his life the beauty and glory of the Gospel.

III. And the results of this work of grace in the soul are set forth in the words before us with great clearness in three important particulars.

1. The first result is Growth. When true grace is given to a soul—more is given. When there is the blade—then follows the ear, and then the ripening corn in the ear. The righteous, says the Psalmist, shall grow like a Cedar in Lebanon. All the imagery of the Scriptures which are used to describe the character and life of the child of God, represents him as increasing in all his spiritual graces. He is first the new born babe, desiring the sincere milk of the word, that he may grow thereby, and then passing upward through the successive stages of the Christian life, becomes the perfect man in Christ Jesus. Nor has any man a right to believe that he has been made an heir of heaven who is not conscious of an increase in faith, and all the graces that are the fruit of the spirit. The law of the Kingdom is 'he that hath clean hands shall grow stronger and stronger.'

2. The second result of grace is Spiritual Prosperity. 'The righteous shall flourish like a palm tree. Those that be planted in the house of the Lord, shall flourish in the Courts of our God.' The natural and normal state of the Christian is one of peace and joy, and spiritual comfort and happiness.

All the provisions of the Gospel look toward this result. Soul prosperity is the proper condition of him who lives near to God. His experiences are not evanescent frames and feelings, now mounting to extacies and intense excitement, and then relapsing into coldness and declension, but they are the steady, calm, and sure effects of faith and love, and clear apprehensions of divine truth, and of all the great and essential doctrines of the Gospel. His spiritual life is hid with Christ in God. The world cannot tell why the lamp always burns brightly. But the word of God shows us the secret pipes from the olive tree, which are ever feeding it with oil. He lives in communion with God in his closet, and the ordinances of the Sanctuary. He builds up his hopes and his character upon Christ alone. His faith takes hold of his truths and promises. His heart clings to him with a growing love. His soul feeds upon his word as heavenly manna, and drinks daily drafts from the overflowing fountain of his grace. Every dispensation of divine Providence, whether it be joyous or sorrowful, brings with it some new experience of the love and grace of Christ. 'All things work together for his good.' Every event of life, ordered as it is by his Heavenly Father, is part of the process by which his graces are strengthened, his passions subdued, and his nature made the more fit for heaven.

3. And with this growth and prosperity there comes also Fertility. Nor is this a temporary result. His fruit drops all the way through life, even down to old age. The means of grace, and the influences of the Spirit are given to man, not that he might simply have joy in his own heart, but that he might thereby be fitted to glorify God here in the upbuilding of his king-

dom and the good of men. Hence our Saviour commands his disciples 'let your light so shine before men, that they, seeing your good works shall glorify your Father which is in heaven.' The true Christian has not alone the leaves of a profession. His spiritual life is not a mere outward show. But all his walk and conversation testifies that he is under the control of true Christian principle, and that his noblest life is drawn from Christ. As he professes to have been born of the Spirit, so he manifests the fruits of the Spirit. His passions and appetites are all controlled and regulated by the law of God. He is kind, and forgiving—unselfish in his motives and acts. He never gives utterance to a slander—nor acts the part of a tale bearer, or a busy body in other men's matters. He has no malice or envy in his treatment of his fellow men. He would rather suffer wrong, than injure either in reputation or person his neighbor. He seeks the peace, harmony and prosperity of the community, and especially of the Church. He does good to all men as he has opportunity. He seeks in every way that the Providence of God points out to him, the upbuilding of the Kingdom—the enlargement and extension of the Church, and the promotion of Truth, Temperance and Righteousness throughout the world. Thus his fruit drops rich and ripe through all the years of his life. Nor when the tree becomes old, and broken by the storms of age, does the leaf yet wither or the fruit disappear. As gray hairs come upon—his ripe christian experience is every way developing itself in judicious counsels, in the administration of comfort to the afflicted, in kindness to the needy, and in the encouragement of the young to an earnest pursuit of knowledge and the attainment of a well-grounded Christian hope;

and in a godly walk and conversation, which becomes more and more spiritual and heavenly as he draws near to eternal realities. Thus, in a calm and serene old age, do the righteous bear the fruits of faith and holiness, until they come down to the grave like a shock of corn fully ripe in its season; and when death comes to take down their earthly tabernacle they fall asleep in Jesus, leaving behind them the savor of a good life, and passing upward to the light and joy and worship of the New Jerusalem.

Such is a brief and imperfect view of the truths set before us in the words of our text. Your own minds will already have recalled, as a vivid illustration of the description here given, the life and character of that venerable servant of God whose grey hairs were a 'crown of glory, because they were found in the ways of righteousness,' and who has but lately passed away from our midst, to join the general assembly and Church of the First-Born, whose names are written in heaven.

JOHN MORRIS was born in the City of Philadelphia, Oct. 13, 1775. His father lost his life with the army at the Battle of Brandywine, leaving him thus at a tender age to the care of a pious mother, to whose instructions he was greatly indebted for many salutary impressions, which never lost their hold upon his mind.

His memory went back with great vividness to the closing scenes of the revolutionary struggle—to the splendid festivities which were held at the declaration of Peace, and to the imposing ceremonies which followed the adoption of the Federal Constitution, and the inauguration of our present form of government. It was pleasant and instructive to hear his reminiscences of those days, and of the great men who were actors in those scenes, and upon whom he had often looked with a boyish delight and wonder. And one almost felt as if he had witnessed the scenes himself when he listened to his minute and graphic description of pageants in which Washington and Franklin and other heroes of the Revolution were the central figures and prominent actors.

In April, 1798, he left his Philadelphia home, and came to the city of New York to enter into business. His journey thither was by stage to the then little hamlet of Paulus Hook, now known as Jersey City, and containing only a population of 10 or 12 persons, where was a single tavern and a ferry, whence sail and row boats took passengers across the river. New York had extended only to the Park, and the City Hall and other public buildings stood in Wall street, around which the wealth and fashion of the metropolis were gathered. The number of inhabitants was less than 60,000. On this side of the river was a small hamlet, at the ferry, built under the hills, then extending to the Wallabout, and reached by sail and row boats, from which a road passing up through farms and orchards to a settlement, the centre of which was the present City Hall, containing, with that at the river, a population of 2,000 or 3,000 souls.

Hills and meadows and forests were seen on every hand, where now a vast city is stretching forth its arms, and covering the land with its beautiful monuments of civilization and art, and taste and wealth. Such was the appearance of these two cities when Mr. Morris came to New York to engage in business; and where for 70 years he was destined to be identified with its interests, and to witness its growth and prosperity. Although not yet a member of the Church, he had enjoyed religious instructions which had left ineffacable influences upon his mind. A single fact will show what was the early training he had received whose fruits were to appear after many days. While yet a child his mother was once reading to him a story from the Bible. As he stood by her knee listening with childish delight and interest to the narrative, he interrupted her with the question 'Is this true.' Yes, my child, was the answer: 'All that you read in the Bible is truth.' Those words he never forgot. Nor did he ever from that hour have one doubt as to the veracity of God's Word. In all his after years he came to its study with entire confidence. His mother's words were ever sounding in his ears, like the echo of Christ's declaration, 'thy word is truth.' Soon after coming to New York he attached himself to the ministrations of the venerable Dr. John Rogers, the pastor of the Wall Street Church. There he was, by the Grace of God, converted, and in June, 1799 was admitted to the fellowship of the Saints. His reminiscences of that eminent servant of God were many and pleasant. Under his instructions he was fed and nourished, and fitted for the long life of usefulness which has just closed its earthly mission. His intercourse with his aged pastor was pleasant and intimate, and when he passed away he assisted the devout men who carried him to his burial. The Churches of New York were at that time blessed with the ministration of men whose names have never ceased to be borne in affectionate and honored remembrance. Our venerable father was permitted to sit at the feet of such men as Drs. Miller and McKnight, and Milledollar and Mason, and from their lips often to hear the precious messages of the Gospel, and he also listened to the first sermon which the venerable Dr. Spring preached, when called to the charge of the Church where he is still a pastor.

With the commencement of his Christian profession began his life of active piety. He found his way to the meetings for prayer, and engaged with his brethren in works for the enlargement and upbuilding of the Church. As early as the year 1809, in connection with the late John Mills, whose name he always mentioned with great affection and respect, he established a meeting for prayer in Spring street, which was then just beginning to be built up in the advance and growth of the city. Beyond it were only scattered houses, standing in the country and surrounded by farms and forests. The whole population of the city at that time was 90,000. A large pond of water, of great depth, then occupied the spot where now the Tombs stand, and its water flowing through Canal street to the North River was crossed by a substantial bridge on Broadway. Hills and valleys and groves everywhere met the eye above this, and meadows stretching down to the river's brink, were sweet with new-mown hay, or alive with flocks and herds which there found pasturage. Making their way over many a vacant square, and along streets not yet thoroughly paved or lighted, Father Morris, and his friend John Mills, looked around for a place in which to establish a meeting for prayer. Their first selection proved an unfavorable one, and but few persons could be gathered there for worship. Another site was tried with little more success. But these pioneers of the Church were not to be easily discouraged. One more place was tried; and here a permanent meeting for prayer was established. The proper centre for a new Church was found. Here month after month, these fast friends made their way at evening, to meet their brethren in social worship. During these labors in the outskirts of the city, the old Wall street Church was demolished to make way for a new and more commodious edifice. At the request of these brethren the pews and pulpit were given to them, and carted up and stored in a shed in Spring street. A few wealthy members of the Church, among whom was the late Col. Rutgers, then bought four lots of ground, on which the first edifice of the Spring Street Church was built. Here a congregation was soon gathered, and a Church organized under the ministrations of Rev. Mr. Perrine, and Mr. Morris was ordained a Ruling Elder therein. Here he labored with earnestness and zeal, and had the privilege of seeing his own daughter Mary, afterwards Mrs. Moon, brought into the Church as one of the precious fruits of a revival with which it pleased God to visit his people.

He used often to refer to these happy days, and to the communion immediately preceding that work of grace, at which but a single person was admitted to the Church. His pastor, Rev. Dr. S. H. Cox, in his prayer, at that time alluding to the fact, prayed that it might be the drop which preceded a plentiful shower. The wish seemed to be prophetic, and the blessing came in answer thereto.

During the administration of President Jefferson, Mr. Morris was appointed to a position in the Custom House, which he retained for thirty years, discharging its duties with singular fidelity, and retaining the good will of all with whom he came into official contact, by the urbanity and kindness with which he tempered the strict and unbending integrity by which he conserved the interests of the government. His religion was illustrated and set forth in his business, as well as in all the walks of life. It made him a thoroughly honest man in his dealings with the world, as well as an active and efficient member of the Church of Christ.

In the year 1824, Mr. Morris removed to the city of Brooklyn, and connected himself with the First Church, then under the pastoral care of Rev. Mr. Sandford. The tree lost neither leaf nor fruit in its transplanting. He at once resumed his earnest labors in the work of his master. Hitherto the efforts in behalf of the religious education of the young, in which he had always been deeply interested, had been confined to a single Union Sabbath School, conducted by members of all the various Churches, and held for convenience in the building used by the Methodists in Sands street. Mr. Morris soon saw that this was not enough to meet the spiritual wants of Brooklyn, even though it was then but a village of only 8,000 or 9,000 inhabitants. He consulted with his pastor as to the propriety of establishing a Sabbath School in their own Church. He was met with doubts and misgivings as to the success of his plan, but determined to try the experiment. Notice of the intention to form such a school was given, and in a few months the lecture room was filled with scholars, and the enterprise was established beyond a question or fear. At the same time, while giving to this work his constant attention, he was busy in establishing and conducting neighborhood prayer-meetings, going with his brethren from house to house, and especially caring for those portions of the village which were most scattered and distant from the Church.

In this work he never wearied. Year after year he

was still busy in this way of doing good. Neither cold nor heat, nor storm nor darkness, kept him from fulfilling the appointments thus made from week to week. He had the names of all the praying members of the Church who attended these services, and saw that they were each called to take their part at proper times. He was careful also to bring forward as leaders in these meetings such men as he thought proper for the work, and would place them in the chair while he sat by to counsel and aid. Many there are who bear with them still the memory of these precious scenes, and who recall those golden days of labor and of success in the master's work.

As the population of Brooklyn began to increase, and it became evident it was soon to become a large and important city, Mr. Morris and some of his brethren saw the importance of erecting another Presbyterian Church, to meet the demand of the times. Consulting with his pastor, Mr. Carroll, and the session of whom he had been made a member, the project was soon matured, and a colony was sent forth in the year 1831 to form the Second Presbyterian Church. Mr. Morris was one of the number, and as usual he gave his whole heart to the work. He was at once selected as one of its Elders, and he brought into his new field of labor also the ripe experience of a life· which now had reached its noon-day.

His advice and counsel were of great value in an enterprise like that, and his labors were of acknowledged value both in the conduct of its spiritual and its temperal concerns. The services of Rev. Dr. Spencer were secured as its first pastor, and between him and our venerated friend a strong and lasting friendship grew up, which was never abated, however much they might differ in judgment as to the propriety of measures proposed.

Although the shadows of age were now beginning to lengthen, and his locks to whiten with the frosts of life's winter, he never lost his vigor or tired of his work. It never seemed to enter his thoughts that he should retire from active service and leave hard work to younger men. His heart and spirits never grew old. He seemed as young and vigorous now as when he first avouched the Lord Jehovah to be his God. His eyes still bright and busy, were looking over all the field to see what there was for him to do. He had no disposition to sit down unemployed or idle. Out in what was then the eastern part of the village, under the shadow of Fort Greene, crowned at that time only with grass-grown fortifications thrown up in the war of the Revolution, were a few clusters of houses, built amid half graded streets, and unsightly hills of stones and sand. Farms and orchards and forests were just beyond, where now stands this Sanctuary, with many others which have since been erected.

Groups of neglected children were wandering here and there upon the Sabbath with none to care for their souls. Poverty or vice were seen on every hand. Here was the very spot in which Mr. Morris felt there should be established a Sabbath School. What he proposed he ever had the energy to carry through. Applying to a few of the men of wealth in his Church for means to erect a suitable house, he soon had an earnest and efficient band of teachers at work; and so the first Mission School of the City was established in Prince Street, on the 19th of July, 1834.

The success of this enterprise soon drew attention to the importance of establishing a new Presbyterian

Church in this part of the City. It was evident that the tide of population must roll on and cover all this territory with houses and families. Mr. Morris often conversed with his pastor on the matter, and the proposition was at length made that he should himself go forth with a colony, and lay the foundation for a new Church. It was asking of him what many a one in his circumstances would have felt at liberty to decline. Twice already he had broken away from pastors and friends whom he loved, to engage in the work of Church extension. He was warmly attached to Dr. Spencer, both as an able preacher and faithful pastor and a personal friend. He was surrounded by men with whom he had long labored, and with whom he had taken sweet counsel, as they went to the house of God in company. He was now 72 years old, and might well have asked to be excused from the arduous labors which this new work would impose upon him. Yet none of these things moved him. The tree that had breasted the storms of three score and ten winters was still green and flourishing, and its rich fruit was hanging ripe and fair upon its branches. He yielded to the request of his pastor, and came forth with a colony to form this Church, to which his last labors were given, and in the bosom of which he breathed his last breath. The new congregation was organized in the month of April, 1847, under the pastoral care of Rev. N. C. Locke. Fifteen years ago, at the close of brother Locke's connection with the Church, I became its pastor, and was at once brought into pleasant relations with our venerable father—as the senior Elder of this Church. He was then 75 years of age, but his step seemed as elastic and his spirits as buoyant, and his heart as warm, as a youth's.

In all these years he had never lost the energy and interest he had before manifested in this work of advancing the interests of Christ's Kingdom. His place in the Sanctuary and in the meetings for prayer has ever been filled when his health permitted. With an unflagging zeal he has gone about doing good, assisting the poor, comforting the afflicted, admonishing the erring, and seeking to reclaim those who were gone out of the way. Often in the Sabbath School has his venerable form been seen, as he has watched with an unabated interest the work which was then going on, and on the occasion of the gathering of the children at the anniversaries of our Sabbath or Mission Schools his face has beamed with pleasure, and his voice has often been heard giving some word of encouragement to the teachers, or recalling to the youth there assembled some scenes of his earlier years, the memory of which had been revived by their presence. Neither personal afflictions nor the growing infirmities of age could dampen the ardor with which he engaged in his work. Five times since I have been his pastor have I been called to minister to his stricken household. Early in my connection with this Church a beloved daughter was called away to her rest, and then a son, and successively three of his children's children. He felt these losses deeply, for he had a warm and loving nature, that clung largely for happiness to his family. Yet he never faultered in his work. The more sorely the tree was pressed and crushed, the sweeter and richer seemed to be the fruit it yielded. Amid all these painful bereavements he found strong consolation in the promises of God, and, like David arose from his sorrow and tears and went into the Sanctuary, and resumed the duties of life, chastened and purified and brought nearer heaven by his affliction. And even when his aged eyes were blinded, and he could no longer distinguish even the features of his dearest friends, he never lost his cheerfulness or activity. Leaning upon his staff he still went forth for his daily walks of usefulness, making his way from the house of one friend to another, and still visiting the Sanctuary and the place of prayer. On the Sabbath before he died he was in his wonted seat in this House of God. As he turned away at the close of the services he walked along with a dear young brother whose wife was, after a long illness, just lingering upon the shores of time, and who has since then been called home. His heart beat in strong sympathy with him, and he sought to comfort him by recalling to his mind the precious promises of the Word of God, which had often given his own heart peace amid its sorrows. On the next day he suffered some little inconveniences from a cold which he had taken on the Sabbath. But no alarming symptoms were developed until Friday. Even then he had dressed himself and was about to go down as usual for his morning meal, but was prevailed upon to keep his room. Toward noon it became evident that the end was approaching. And his family and friends gathered around his bedside to witness his departure. I entered his room when made aware of his sickness, and found the dying patriarch literally falling asleep. He was just passing into a state of apparent unconsciousness. Once or twice in response to a question whether Jesus was with him, his lips parted as if he were making an effort to answer. And so he lay during most of the night, gently breathing his life away. There was no struggle—it did not seem like Death. All was so peaceful and calm. The wheels of nature, worn out by constant action, through 90 years, stopped at length, and he was at rest. He left but few sayings as his dying testimony. Nor were they needed, except as precious mementoes of a dying saint. When, early in the day, a member of the family was speaking to him of his increasing illness, he simply expressed a willingness to leave all to God, repeating the words of scripture, "My times are in thy hand." "All the days of my appointed time will I wait till my change come." To another he said, "I am a great sinner, but the grace and blood of Jesus is sufficient to save me, and my trust is in him alone." To his son who, as he saw he was soon to pass away, asked him to give them his blessing, he simply replied. "The Saviour's blessing is better than mine." Thus gently did the aged patriarch fall asleep in Jesus. And his history as it has thus been briefly given, and his Christian character as we have all seen it, are beautiful and striking illustrations of the words which we have chosen for the theme of our remarks. The foundation of the character of Father Morris was a firm faith in God, and reliance upon Christ as his only Saviour. He depended solely upon the merits of his Divine Redeemer as his ground of justification in the sight of God. The prominent traits of his character are familiar to all.

He was consistent in his life with all the professions he had made. He loved the Sanctuary, and was never absent from it when his health permitted him to attend its services. He was eminently an honest man. There was nothing like deception in either his word or his acts. His Religion was not a mere act of the head, but a work of the heart and life. It diffused itself over his whole character. It made him thoroughly earnest and devoted to his master's business. It controlled and regulated his thoughts and appetites and passions. No one could fail to see that he was truly a godly man. His Religion made itself felt in his family, and in all his social relations. It made him a faithful and affectionate husband and father, a warm friend, a loyal citizen, an active officer and member of the Church. It made him set a constant watch over the door of his lips. He was never known to speak ill of his neighbor, nor to backbite with his tongue, nor to circulate an ill or evil report. He had a warm and generous and sympathizing heart. No one who knew him can ever forget the genuine kindness of his nature, which was ever welling up in some kind and loving action or word, and which made him, even in old age, a pleasant companion even for the child. He did not hesitate to speak plainly and frankly his sentiments even to one with whom he most differed. But when speaking of such an one to others it was always with kindness and approbation.

His cheerfulness often manifested itself in a dry humor and a playful manner, that seemed more like the expressions of youth than the more sober feelings of old age, and that threw a wonderful charm over his whole conversation, and set forth his religion with a peculiar grace and loveliness. This manner often was used to impress some special truth or expression with great power. But a few days before his death some old friend who had not seen him for years said to him: 'Why Father Morris I did not know that you were yet in the land of the living.' No, said he, I am in the land of the dying, and then pointing upward he added with a smile, 'The land of the living is up there, I am expecting soon to go to it.'

He did not care much to speak publicly of his own personal experience. He evidently regarded this habit as one which often tended to spiritual pride. His addresses were earnest appeals to Christians to be faithful, and touching allusions to Christ as our only dependence. But he always kept himself and his works out of sight. He gloried only in the Cross of Christ. For many years he had evidently looked upon his great change as near at hand. It was his habit, until his sight failed him, to take the lead of the last prayer-meeting of the year. And his presence and his words of counsel made these seasons occasions of great and solemn interest to all. Every worshipper felt that possibly he was listening for the last time to the counsels of the aged and venerable patriarch. He always spoke of his coming change with calmness, nay with the pleasure of a pilgrim who felt that he was drawing near to his home. In all the long and frequent interviews I have held with him as his pastor, I have felt that he was a living and beautiful illustration of Bunyan's description of the land of Beulah, to which he brought his pilgrims before they crossed the river, 'whose air was very sweet and pleasant,' and 'where they heard the singing of birds, and saw every day the flowers appear in the earth,' and 'had no want of corn or wine.' There he stood for years, waiting until his change should come. One after another of those he loved passed over the river before him, and then the summons came to him, 'set thine house in order, for thou shalt die.' He heard it without a fear. But a few days before, he had been speaking to some friends of the difference in the deaths of young and aged Christians, and quoted the words of one who accounted for it in this wise: The young Christian is full of strong emotion, and when he nears the heavenly world, is often full of joy and extacy at the sight, but with the aged believer the whole is a matter of life-long experience. Death and Heaven have been themes familiar to his mind for years, and so when his time comes he simply falls asleep, and says nothing about what he feels or sees. It was so with our venerable friend. The scene was not strange or new to him. His thoughts had long dwelt upon it. And when the hour of departure came he yielded up his spirit to God, and gently passed from earth to heaven. What a blessed exchange, from cares and sorrows to eternal joy and peace, from the ordinances of the visible Church to the worship of the Redeemed. And he, being dead, yet speaketh. He has left behind him to his family the precious legacy of a good name and a godly example. He has left to the Session with which he was so long connected, the memory of a life consecrated to Christ, and to the upbuilding of his kingdom, for he was an Elder that ruled well, and who was accounted worthy of double honor, and who by faith obtained a good report. He has left to this Church a long record of prayer and efforts for its prosperity, and of devotion to its interests. And he has taught you who are yet without a hope in Christ, that Religion fits a man to live as well as to die. He left not the work of preparation for death to the closing hours of life. In his youth he consecrated himself to Christ, and was by his grace planted in the house of the Lord, where he long flourished and bore fruit even to old age.

Take, then, the lessons of God's Providence and Grace, as they are here presented to you. Remember, ye children and youth, the words which he often spake while yet was with you; recall his godly walk and life, and seek the Saviour while he is near. And, ye men of maturer years, will you not receive instruction in this record of a good man's life and death, and 'Seek first the Kingdom of God and his righteousness.' Our venerable friend left for you this great lesson of the Gospel as his dying message, which spoke of the blood and grace of Christ as his only hopes. O let it be yours. Turn from the world and its pursuits, and make it your great business to make your calling and election sure.

Would you have a useful life and a serene and happy death, trust in him who hath taken the sting from Death and robbed the grave of its victory. Oh, by faith

> "So live that when thy summons comes to join
> The innumerable caravan, that moves
> To that mysterious realm, where each shall take
> His Chamber in the silent halls of death,
> Thou go not like the quarry slave, at night
> Scourged to his dungeon, but sustained and soothed
> By an unfaultering trust, approach thy grave,
> Like one who wraps the drapery of his couch
> About him, and lies down to pleasant dreams."

THE
ONE HUNDREDTH ANNIVERSARY

OF

Hanover St. Presbyterian Church,

WILMINGTON, DEL.,

CELEBRATED THURSDAY OCTOBER 24, 1872.

SERMONS, ADDRESSES, MEMORIAL SERVICES, ETC.

WILMINGTON:
FROM THE "COMMERCIAL PRESS" OF JENKINS & ATKINSON.
1872.

At a meeting of the members and friends of the Hanover Street Church, held in the lecture room, on the evening of the 24th of October, John C. Patterson, Esq., presiding, the following resolution was unanimously adopted.

Resolved, That the addresses and exercises of this Anniversary occasion be published in permanent form as a valuable contribution to the history of the church, and of the community in which it is located,

The Pastor of the church, in connection with Jno. H. Adams and S. Floyd, were appointed a committee to carry this resolution into effect.

HANOVER STREET CHURCH.

PASTOR.
REV. LAFAYETTE MARKS.

FORMER PASTORS.
REV. JOSEPH SMITH,
" WILLIAM R. SMITH,
" THOMAS READ, D. D.,
" E. W. GILBERT, D. D.,
" ARTHUR GRANGER,
" WILLIAM HOGARTH, D. D.,
" J. E. ROCKWELL, D. D.,
" A. D. POLLOCK,
" WM. C. DICKINSON,
" WILLIAM AIKMAN, D. D.,

ELDERS.
HON. WILLARD HALL,
JAMES T. BIRD,
SAM'L BARR,
JNO. C. PATTERSON,
WM. M. PYLE.

SABBATH SCHOOL SUPERINTENDENT.
SAMUEL FLOYD.

ASSISTANT.
D. W. HARLAN.

CENTENNIAL COMMITTEE.
JNO. H. ADAMS.
S. FLOYD,
R. P. JOHNSON,
WM. M. PYLE,
H. P. RUMFORD,
Dr. J. DERRICKSON,
THOMAS McCOMB.

INTRODUCTORY STATEMENT.

The Centennial Anniversary of Hanover Presbyterian Church was celebrated on Thursday, the 24th of October, 1872. The weather was somewhat unpropitious during the entire day; nevertheless the exercises were largely attended throughout, and the occasion was one of great interest to all present. Services were held in the morning, afternoon, and evening, concluding with a social re-union in the lecture room of the Church.

The audience room was handsomely and appropriately decorated for the occasion. Beautiful bouquets and century plants were arranged in front of and around the pulpit, while a long line of evergreens spanned the whole altar and dropping in graceful folds on either side, was extended entirely around the gallery, hanging in festoons in the arches, in which were painted upon white surface, encircled with evergreens, the names of the former pastors of the Church, in regular order, four on each side. The names of Rev. Messrs. Smith and Marks, the first and present pastors of the Church were also to be seen in wreaths above the pulpit. Large oil paintings of Judge Hall and Dr. Gilbert were placed in windows on either side of the pulpit, representative of the Elders and Clergy of the Church. Upon the rear wall were the dates 1772–1872, the former of autumn leaves, the latter in evergreen. Evergreens were also entwined about the lamps in the pulpit, which were kept dimly burning. Much taste was displayed in the decorations, and nothing was omitted that the proprieties of the occasion seemed to demand.

Many who had been former worshippers in the Church were present to participate in the memorial services of the day. The programme was as follows:—

ORDER OF EXERCISES.

---o---

MORNING.

DOXOLOGY.
PRAYER.
MUSIC.
HISTORICAL ADDRESS, by the Pastor, Rev. Lafayette Marks.
SINGING.
ADDRESS, by Rev. J. P. Conkey, Pastor of the Central Presbyterian Church.
SINGING.
BENEDICTION.

---o---

AFTERNOON.

MUSIC.
PRAYER.
ADDRESS, by Rev. Wm. W. Taylor, of Shippensburg, Pa. Subject, "Recollections."
SINGING.
ADDRESS, by Rev. J. E. Rockwell, D. D., of Stapleton, Staten Island, N. Y. Subject, "Events of the Century."
MUSIC.
BENEDICTION.

---o---

EVENING.

MUSIC.
READING OF THE SCRIPTURES.
SINGING.

ADDRESS, by Rev. C. W. Adams, of Waterville, N. Y. Subject, "Elders of the Church."

SINGING.

Original Ode, written for the occasion by E. T. Taylor.

[S. M.] Hail! bright auspicious day
    Hail! glad memorial hour,
We come, with heart and voice to bless
    God's guarding, guiding power;
With grateful, happy hearts
    Our gladsome song we raise,
Children, and children's children join
    Our fathers' God to praise.

We praise Thee, O, our God,
    For what Thy hand hath done;
For garnered fruit, within these walls,
    The trophies grace hath won.
We bless Thee for the truth,
    Proclaimed these hundred years;
For the rich covenant of Thy love,
    Through sunshine, and through tears.

ANTHEM. "Bless the Lord, O, my soul," &c.—Ps. ciii.

[C. M.] Our honored fathers, where are they?
    And mothers, who of old
First taught our infant lips to pray,
    And led to Jesus' fold.

Hidden from sight, but safe with God;
    We treasure all they taught,
Striving to tread the path they trod,
    Seeking the God they sought.

[L. M.] We saw them droop, and fade away,
But mem'ry pictures them to-day;
Faces and forms, to us so dear,
Claim the sad tribute of a tear.

CHANT. "Thou hast been our dwelling place in all generations," &c.—Ps. xc.

[8s. & 7s.] Sweeping through the silent ages,
    Rolls time's rapid, ceaseless stream;
Human life, in changeful stages,
    Passes like a fitful dream;
But while men and nations perish,
    God, from age to age the same,
Will His church forever cherish,
    And preserve Himself a name.

DISCOURSE, by Rev. James M. Crowell, D. D., of Philadelphia, Pa.
MUSIC.
BENEDICTION.

In the afternoon, at the close of Dr. Rockwell's address, the Rev. Noah Price, who was reared in Hanover Church, but now of Philadelphia, was also introduced, and made a brief and touching address to the congregation. He alluded to his former connection with the Church and Sabbath School, and spoke feelingly of the changes which had occurred since his removal from the Church. Although he had wandered from the fold in which he had been brought up, into another denomination, yet he remembered with pleasure that Calvin and Luther both contended for the same great truths, the same Lord and baptism. He concluded by exhorting all to be faithful unto death to the same principles, that they might at last receive the crown of life.

The closing discourse in the evening was delivered by the Rev Jas. M. Crowell, D. D., of Philadelphia, from the words, "Thy servants take pleasure in her stones, and favor the dust thereof." The address was a beautiful and appropriate close of the services of the day, showing why the christian should love the Church, and what results flow from that love. The Choir then sang very sweetly the hymn,

"When shall we meet again—
Meet ne'er to sever?"

The pleasure of the occasion was much enhanced by the tasteful manner in which the music for the day was rendered by the Choir of the Church. The singing of the original ode written for the occasion by E. T. Taylor, formerly a member of Hanover, but now an Elder in the Central Church, was one of the attractive features of the evening. Dr. Rockwell, in a letter to the *New York Observer*, descriptive of the Centennial, says:—

"At the close of these services the present and former members of the Church adjourned to the lecture room, which was tastefully draped and ornamented with flags and flowers, where a bountiful collation had been provided by the ladies of the congregation. Here, until a late hour, old friends met in pleasant and glad re-union. That scene will not soon be forgotten. But one of the former pastors was present; but he found, after twenty years absence, many an old friend, and received as warm and grateful a welcome as when he first came among that people. They have had a noble record of fidelity to the truth, of earnest labor for Christ, and of respect, affection, and hearty co-operation for those who have ministered to them in the gospel. Although three colonies have gone out from them to form other churches, they are still a strong, active, united people, and under their present pastor are increasing in numbers and ability.

"The memorial services of which this notice is made are to be published in a permanent form, and will make a valuable contribution to the historic treasures of the Church. J. E. R."

Some of the former pastors and ministerial members of the Church, who had been expected to take a part in the memorial services, were unable to be present. Of the pastors, Dr. Rockwell, now of Staten Island, N. Y., was the only one present. Rev. C. W. Adams, of Waterville, N. Y., and Rev. Wm. W. Taylor, of Shippensburg, Pa., were both brought up in Hanover Church and Sabbath School. In addition to these, quite a number have gone out from the Church, who are now engaged in preaching the Gospel in this and in other lands. The following letters deserve a place in this introductory notice:—

LETTER FROM REV. ENOCH THOMAS.

CRAIGSVILLE, AUGUSTA CO., VA., *October 10th, 1872.*

REV. L. MARKS—DEAR BROTHER:—

Your favor of the 8th inst. came duly to hand. I was sick abed, but was much cheered by its reception and its kind and fraternal spirit. I have just risen from my sick bed, to make an effort, the best I can, to answer it.

I have much that I would like to say, especially because I know now that I cannot be present on the interesting occasion of your Centennial Anniversary of our dear old Hanover Street Church.

May the Lord Jesus, her adorable head, continue to smile upon her and make her to prosper for many hundred years to come. How many of the old members whom I once knew are living now, I do not know, but I suppose very few. May they flourish as the palm tree, and grow as a cedar in Lebanon, and still bring forth fruit in old age. I would like much to have their names. If I should not come you will please send me a printed roll of the members. I can know from it.

One item in yours was of special gratification. In giving a list of invited and expected guests, the names of Dr. Ellis Newlin and Rev. William Taylor occur. I had not heard from either of these dear brethren for many years. They and I, though marching under the same banner of Presbyterianism, were nevertheless enrolled on the minutes of different Assemblies. Ecclesiastical divisions, with all their different asperities have given place to re-unions, but these after the long interval of thirty years, have not been of such a nature as to bring us yet into the same ecclesiastical body.

How much, alas! how very much are the pleasures of the past sadly mingled with regrets! Notwithstanding all this, it is, my dear brother, pleasing to know that in the approaching anniversary of old Hanover all hearts can unite, all voices join in chorus, and all hands can clasp in fraternal greetings, freely! freely! freely! as they will on the blissful shores of the better land.

Brother William Taylor started with me and we both went together to pursue our studies in an Eastern State. He was one of Christ's sincere and amiable disciples. Please tender to him my very kind, cordial, and fraternal greetings. Dr. Newlin was a junior brother, I suppose now in his prime. We were in different institutions, and seldom met, except a few times in Wilmington. To him likewise tender my kindest regards.

Yours, in Christian Love,

E. THOMAS.

LETTER FROM REV. WM. C. DICKINSON, A FORMER PASTOR.

LAFAYETTE, IND., *July* 10*th*, 1872.

H. P. RUMFORD, ESQ.—DEAR SIR:—

I take pleasure in acknowledging the receipt, in May last, of the kind invitation of a Committee of Hanover Street Presbyterian Church, to attend the exercises with which its hundredth anniversary is to be commemorated in October next. I should greatly enjoy being present with you on so interesting an occasion, and show my respect and veneration for the dear old Church, and my warm personal regard for its members. My stay among them was a brief one, but it created strong attachments on the part of both Mrs. Dickinson and myself to the place and the people, which it would be a great pleasure to both of us to renew.

But I fear we must deny ourselves that pleasure on the occasion proposed. We are to be at the East a few weeks this Summer, and I shall hardly be able to make another journey there in the Fall. I shall be with you in spirit, however, at the time, joining in the benedictions invoked upon the Church, and rejoicing in the honorable record of its century of usefulness and prosperity which will be presented on the occasion.

With very kind regards to all friends in the congregation, and thanks to the gentlemen of the Committee for the courtesy of their invitation,

I remain, very truly, Yours,
WM. C. DICKINSON.

LETTER FROM REV. WM. AIKMAN, D. D., FORMERLY PASTOR OF THE CHURCH.

DETROIT, *July* 31, 1872.

MESSRS. JOHN H. ADAMS AND DR. R. P. JOHNSON:

GENTLEMEN:—I received your kind invitation to be present at the Centennial Celebration of the Hanover Street Church, next October. I have delayed answering positively, hoping that it would be possible for me to attend, but it now seems highly improbable that I shall be able to do so.

You have done well, it seems to me, to make arrangements for such a Centennial Celebration. The history of the old *Christiana* Church, of which Hanover Church is the legal successor, is full of interest, reaching back as it does beyond Revolutionary times, and connecting itself in a very important way with the history of Presbyterianism in the State of Delaware. The history, too, of late years is full of hallowed memories of revivals of religion, and of the lives of those who have walked with God in her communion.

May the gathering of her sons be most pleasant and memorable.

Very Respectfully, Yours,
WILLIAM AIKMAN,
25 *W. Elizabeth Street, Detroit.*

On the Sabbath following the Centennial of the Church, the Sabbath School held its 58th anniversary. The exercises on this occasion were of a very interesting character. The singing by the children, who had been under the training of Mr. Lichtenstein, was very fine. The reading of the "Changed Cross," by Miss Annie Grier, a Bible exercise on the Life of Christ, conducted by the Pastor, and addresses by Rev. E. L. Boing, of Federalsburg, Md., the Pastor, and Dr. R. R. Porter, were among the items on the programme. The large audience dispersed at the close well pleased with what they had seen and heard. The Sabbath School of the Church was organized in 1814, and has been kept up without any interruption from that time to the present. Its present Superintendent, Mr. S. Floyd, has been filling that position for upwards of twenty years. The record of the School has been a long one. The work which it has done has not been in vain. The fruits may be seen on every hand. If time would permit, there is much interesting history that might be introduced in this connection. We regret that the Rev. Dr. Ellis Newlin, of Newark, N. J., was unable to be present at our Centennial. He was expected to give us an address on the history and work of the Sabbath School, which, as a former pupil of the School, he could have done with much interest.

These anniversary exercises have thus been brought to a close, and according to a resolution passed by the congregation on the evening of the Centennial, we have endeavored to put them in permanent form, as matters of history, and as fraught with interest to those who shall come after us. When another hundred years shall have rolled away, we, of this generation will all be sleeping in the dust.

"As for man, his days are as grass; as a flower of the field so he flourisheth. For the wind passeth over it and it is gone, and the place thereof shall know it no more, but the mercy of the Lord is from everlasting to everlasting upon them that fear Him, and his righteousness unto children's children."

L. MARKS,
S. FLOYD,
J. H. ADAMS,
Committee of Publication.

HISTORICAL ADDRESS.

BY THE PASTOR, REV. L. MARKS.

" And of Zion it shall be said, this and that man was born in her, and the highest himself shall establish her. The Lord shall count when He writeth up the people that this man was born there. As well the singers as the players on instruments shall be there. All my springs are in thee." Ps. lxxxvii., 5–7.

In introducing the services of this Anniversary occasion, we extend to you all, as members and friends of this venerable Church, a cordial greeting. Your presence here sufficiently indicates the interest which you take in the past history of this Church. We welcome you all, and rejoice that you have come to participate in these memorial exercises. May the King and Head of the Church command His blessing, life that shall never end!

The God of our creation has endowed us with memory, but not with foreknowledge; we can recollect the past, we cannot disclose the future. When we plant a seed in the earth we know nothing of its future developments. We can only conjecture and hope for the best. Whether it shall develop into a vigorous, long-lived plant, or be suddenly cut down and destroyed, depends upon a great variety of contingencies. Little could the founders of Presbyterianism upon this Peninsula,—which marks its proper commencement upon this continent, —little could they forsee of its subsequent growth and development. But the work which they began in faith and prayer has been blest and continued unto this day. The little seed that was planted by Rev. Francis Makamie, long ago, has grown to be a great tree, whose branches cover the wide extent of our national domain.

The various forms of Protestantism were planted upon this continent by its choicest representatives from the Old World. The storms of persecution which shook the stately tree of the kingdom on the other side of the Atlantic, caused its best and ripest fruit to fall on these western shores, and left the green and the withered to stick to their native branches.

When we dig down to the oldest roots of Presbyterianism we find them underlacing the soil of Maryland, Delaware, and Virginia. The region of country in which we live is rich in historic interest as connected with the growth of Presbyterianism. When these States were dependent colonies of Great Britain; when these cultivated fields were a wilderness; when these cities and towns had scarcely an existence, Presbyterianism had its home here. It must have landed upon this Peninsula sometime previous to the close of the 17th century, for we find that Rev. Francis Makamie, the pioneer of Presbyterianism in this region, died in the year 1708, and previous to his death he had succeeded in establishing several churches in Maryland and Virginia. And here, if time would permit, we might dwell upon a long list of historic names. We might consume all the time allotted to this occasion in reviewing the holy and consecrated lives of men whose praise is in all the churches. Dr. Samuel Davies,—one of the most illustrious men in the history of our country; author of a standard volume of sermons which bears his name; President of Nassau Hall; the man whose cultivated and earnest preaching won the admiration of King George II.,—was born in the County of New Castle, near where the Church of Drawyers now stands. His academic education was received at Faggs Manor, in Chester County, Pa., and his licensure to preach the gospel was given him by the old historic Presbytery of New Castle. Dr. Waddell, the blind preacher of Virginia, whom Wirt has immortalized, received his early training in the academy at Lower West Nottingham, Cecil County, Maryland. Besides these we might make mention of Witherspoon, and a host of others, whose influence has been largely felt in the religious history of our country.

The history of Presbyterianism in this city and in the surrounding region has not, we regret to say, been carefully preserved. In those early days, especially during the excitement of the Revolutionary War, the records of congregations were not carefully kept, so that to give a connected and detailed history of Presbyterianism from its earliest introduction would be impossible. The chain has been broken; the links lie scattered about upon our sessional records, while some of them have been lost altogether. Presbyterianism, however, was established in Wilmington at a very early period of its history. The antiquated structure at Tenth and Market bears upon its northern wall the date of 1740, from which it is clear that there must have been an organization here previous to that time, or more than 132 years ago. Subsequent to that time there is a gap which is not supplied by any records or data with which I am acquainted. Moreover it is not my purpose to give a detailed history of Presbyterianism in this community, even if such a thing were possible. I shall only have time to touch upon the leading points as connected with our own organization. No feeling or interest should control us in this matter, except the desire to know what are the facts of history.

According to the best information that can be obtained, a new and distinct enterprise was commenced in the Eastern part of our city about the year 1772, popularly known at the time as the Second Presbyterian Church, and this continued to be the name of the Church until the year 1787, when, by virtue of an act passed by the Assembly of the State of Delaware, it received the corporate name of the *Christiana* Church. This is the first fact recorded on the sessional records now in our possession. Subsequent to that time it was generally designated as the "Second Presbyterian Church," but it never received that name by any act of incorporation. This enterprise grew out of the preaching of the Rev. Joseph Smith, a man of great popularity and influence, who is presented to us on the Presbyterial records as the first pastor of the Second Church. This worthy man, whose name is so largely associated with the history of Presbyterianism, both in the East and in the West, was born in 1736, in Nottingham, Maryland, not far from the Susquehanna River. He was educated at Princeton, and was licensed by the Presbytery of New Castle, in 1767. His first charge was the congregation of Lower Brandywine, from which he accepted a call in 1768. It appears that he began occasional preaching in Wilmington in 1772, and on the 12th of August, 1773, a call was put into his hands by the Presbytery, from the Christiana or Second Church of Wilmington; this and the Church of Lower Brandywine being afterwards united in one pastoral charge, Mr. Smith accepted the call, and became their pastor October 27th, 1774. In these churches he labored until April 29th, 1778, when the relation was dissolved at Little Britain. Mr. Smith is represented as a man of great force of mind, and possessed of a peculiarly attractive manner in the pulpit. There is much that might be said of his character and labors, if time and space would permit. The history of the origin and growth of the Second Church under the ministry of Rev. Joseph Smith, covers a good many pages of the records of the New Castle Presbytery. Mr. Smith's record, in the main, lies West of the mountains. He and the apostolic McMillan were among the first to lay the foundations of our Western Zion. In 1779 he accepted a call from the united congregations of Buffalo and Cross Creek, Western Pennsylvania, where he continued to labor the remainder of his life, twelve years. The churches which he established are still among the most flourishing in that region. He died in the faith on the 19th of April, 1792. The stone that covers his mortal remains may be seen in the graveyard of Upper Buffalo, Washington County, Pa. Those who would read the story of his trials and triumphs are referred to an exceedingly interesting article in the volume entitled "Old Redstone," on the "Life and Times of the Rev. Joseph Smith."

Our present sessional records, which carry us as far back as the year 1781, make mention of subscriptions that were given for the support of the church, in the list of which we find the historic name of Gunning Bedford, Esq.

The Rev. Joseph Smith was succeeded by the Rev. Wm. R. Smith, for whom a call was made out October 27th, 1779. This call was accepted, and on January 12th, 1780, he was ordained as stated pastor of the Second Church and Lower Brandywine. The connection between these churches was dissolved October 29th, 1785, after which Mr. Smith became pastor of the Second Church, alone. The pastoral relation continued until April 7th, 1795, when it was dissolved for "weighty reasons," the congregation reluctantly concurring. Of the labors of Mr. William Smith, we have but a meagre record. The results of his ministry, running through a period of fifteen years, are now "hid with Christ in God." Its impress has been left upon hearts that have ceased to beat. There is still living and present here this morning one whose infant brow received the water of baptism from his hands.

Passing on to the year 1797, we meet with the pastorate of Dr. Thomas Read, of blessed memory. This eminent servant of God was chosen pastor of the Church on the 7th of August, 1797. He entered upon his labors in January, 1798. It was the distinction of this excellent man to enjoy a long and fruitful ministry. For thirty years previous to his removal to Wilmington, he ministered to the Presbyterian Church of Drawyer's Creek, and under his ministry it is said to have been the most influential and flourishing church in the State. Before his removal to Wilmington, he had passed through the stirring scenes of the Revolution, and was brought into intimate association with General Washington, having assisted the General in laying his plans for the battle of Brandywine, which his perfect knowledge of the country enabled him to do. His labors while in connection with the Church at Fifth and Walnut, and afterwards in connection with what is known as the First Presbyterian Church, are well known and remembered. There are many yet living who can testify to his worth as a man, and to his fidelity as a minister of the gospel. Fifty-five years of his history were spent in "holding forth the word of life;" twenty-five of these were spent in Wilmington, nineteen in connection with the Church at Fifth and Walnut, the remainder, or part of it, in connection with the First Church, at Tenth and Market. The long and successful pastorate of Dr. Read in connection with the Church terminated, owing to declining health, in the year 1817. Those nineteen years of labor were marked with great spiritual power. There were precious ingatherings from time to time of such as shall be saved. I have in my possession now a printed narrative of a remarkable revival that occurred in this Church in 1814. There are still living those who may be claimed as the fruits of that great revival, in connection with which the names of Patterson, Joyce, and Blackburn have become historic. There are present here this morning some whose memory will carry them back, not only to the stirring scenes of 1814, but beyond that into the earlier labors of Dr. Read. He was released from his work in the Church below on the 14th of June, 1823.

There is a fact worthy of notice connected with the first settlement of Dr. Read; it is the amount of salary voted to him in the call. It was fixed at two hundred pounds. This was in the last decade of the eighteenth century. Looking at the mere statement we might fancy that we had fallen upon a time when ministers were handsomely supported, according to the exigencies of the times, but it appears that those were not genuine old English pounds sterling, but a sort of Pennsylvania and Delaware arrangement, representing two dollars sixty-six cents and a fraction, making the salary a trifle over five hundred dollars, instead of a thousand, as might be supposed. Verily, there is nothing new under the sun! and the fashion plate of one generation is equally suited to the next, and the next. And yet we have not outgrown our forefathers in the grace of giving. Those were times when the gospel was appreciated, and men were willing to deny themselves for the Lord's sake; ten, twenty, thirty, and even a hundred pounds were freely subscribed by persons of moderate means in those early days of Presbyterianism. The Church has grown richer, but it can hardly be said that her members have opened their hearts and hands as the Lord hath prospered them.

Immediately after the retirement of Dr. Read, steps were taken to secure another pastor. Accordingly a call was made out for the Rev. E. W. Gilbert, on the 19th of January, 1818. The call was accepted, and on Sabbath, the 15th of February, he commenced his labors, and on Wednesday, the 20th of May, was ordained and installed by the Presbytery of New Castle. At the first meeting of session after the settlement of Rev. Mr. Gilbert, we find the names of Dr. George Monroe, Mr. John Fleming, Mr. David Harbison, and James Smith, as Elders.

The ministry of Dr. Gilbert marks a new era in the history of our beloved Church. I trust it is doing no injustice to others to say that no one has left such an impression upon the Church, or has been so prominently connected with the history of Presbyterianism in this community, as the Rev. Dr. Gilbert. The reasons for this are apparent. His pastorate was a long one, and so far as I have been able to ascertain, it was successful from the commencement to the close. Through it all his hands were upheld by an active, praying people. It is said that the Dr. frequently made the remark, that he could always tell when the people were praying for him; it gave him a power in the study and in the pulpit, little short of an inspiration. Every minister of the gospel needs the encouragement of a praying people. The consciousness of such support becomes his right arm of power. Gospel hearers are but too ready to complain of a stale, drawled-out sermon, but it might not be difficult to make out the connection between that and a fastidious, fault-finding, prayerless, drowsy congregation. "Pray for me," says Paul, "that utterance may be given unto me, that I may open my mouth boldly to make known the mystery of the gospel."

And here, on the scene of his industrious and beneficent life, among his fellow-citizens and parishioners, who knew his virtues so well, and who honor his memory so faithfully, it is not for me, a comparative stranger, to eulogize the man whose time and powers were so largely given to the spiritual welfare of this Church. The labors of Dr. Gilbert are well known in this community. He has written his record upon human hearts and lives. The words which fell from his lips were spirit and life to many now in Christ, and to many more now in glory.

Dr. Gilbert was a man of the greatest simplicity and transparency of character. He was never regarded as a good judge of human nature, inasmuch as he was too unsuspecting for that, but as for himself he was easily read and understood by all who knew him.

He is represented as a man of small stature, quick, nervous habit, and of bright intellect; a man fond of his study, fond of his books, and thoroughly in love with his profession. As a speaker, he was possessed of a rapid utterance, and a shrill, penetrating voice. His tongue was as the pen of a ready writer. His mind was discursive, gathering information from every source, with a decided leaning towards theological and scientific discussion. He excelled as a debater, and never declined the opportunity to measure his strength with an adversary. The sword of truth in his hands was a trenchant blade, that struck fire in many a conflict. Some of his theological and controversial works have been handed down to us in permanent form. From all that we can learn, Dr. Gilbert never excelled as a pastor. He loved his study better than he loved the street, and that implies no disparagement. He excelled in the use of his pen and his tongue. It was in the pulpit, on the rostrum, and amid the excitement of public discussion, that this worthy man of God found a field for the display of his peculiar tastes and talents. Here was his vantage ground, and he never surrendered it to suit the choice or dictation of his people. And Dr. Gilbert was wise. The pulpit is the preacher's throne. It is there that the sceptre of his power is mainly wielded, and all experience goes to show that it is less injurious in all ways to fail in pastoral work than in pulpit work. It is a notorious fact that the ministry of Dr. Gilbert was such as to command the respect of the entire community in which he lived. He was a workman that needed not to be ashamed. He was in the habit of making thorough and conscientious preparation for the pulpit, hence his ministry was one of power in your midst. "He that hath no sword let him sell his garment and buy one." The garment of ease and indolence must be exchanged for the sword, if we would be thoroughly equipped for the ministry of modern times. He that professes to be a preacher of the word must be something more than a door-bell ringer or a pious perambulator. Pastoral work, important though it be, should never be allowed to trench upon the claims of the pulpit; in case it should, the inevitable result is that the Rev. Dr. Windy hitches into the same old rut from Sabbath to Sabbath, and the Rev. Mr. Slender in a marvellously short space of time preaches himself out, and goes away to fascinate some new people with his soft voice and animated manner.

I cannot dwell further upon the labors of Dr. Gilbert in this community. He was twice installed as pastor of the Church. He resigned his charge the first time about 1832. A second call was made out for him on the 10th of October, 1835. This call was accepted and he was re-installed in November, 1836. This last pastorate continued until the 3d of May, 1841, when he was finally dismissed by the Presbytery to accept the Presidency of Newark College.

It was during his ministry that the building in which we now worship was erected. The old stone Church at the corner of 5th and Walnut, though improved from time to time, was found too small for the comfort of the congregation, hence it was found necessary to build elsewhere. The corner of King and Sixth, then called Hanover Street, was chosen as the site of the new Church.

The present building was dedicated on the 12th of March, 1829, and in 1831 the congregation was chartered under the name of the Hanover Street Church; the name of *Christiana* being changed to that of *Hanover Street*. The erection of so large a building was no small undertaking for those days; the people were comparatively poor, yet they devised liberal things for those who were to come after them. So far as the audience room is concerned, no more capacious or comfortable Church has yet been erected in our city.

About one-third of the members remained in the old stone Church, at Fifth and Walnut, and were for a time under the ministry of Rev. Robert Adair, now of Philadelphia; subsequently under that of Rev. Jas. Pickands. The church was continued till the year 1837, when the church building was disposed of to the Baptists, and the congregation dissolved. There is a good deal of interesting history connected with the old building which sheltered the congregation for so many years, and in which Smith, Read, and Gilbert all ministered.

One of the oldest members of the church has handed me a peculiar memento of the early labors of Dr. Gilbert; it is a small piece of pewter with the letters E. W. G. stamped upon it. Some of our younger Presbyterians may be curious to know what it was for; it was used as a token of admission to the Lord's table. These tokens were distributed to the communicants on Saturday preceding the communion, and were collected by the elders on Sabbath, as the members of the Church were seated at the table. What purpose these pewter tokens answered we have never been able to ascertain, nor can the origin of the custom be definitely determined; it still prevails in some parts of the Presbyterian Church. There are those yet living who believe in the "divine right" of tokens. It would be thought sacrilege, almost, to omit them. We have known churches to be almost rent asunder, and worthy elders to take mortal offence, over the discussion of tokens. They would contend for it as earnestly as though it were the little stone of Revelation, with the new name written upon it.

The next name on the list of pastors is that of Rev. Arthur Granger. When he entered upon his labors the records do not show; it was probably in 1832, or immediately after the first retirement of Dr. Gilbert. The account we have of this brother is very meagre. He filled the pulpit of the Church during the time which elapsed between the first and the second pastorates of Dr. Gilbert. He resigned his charge in September 28th, 1835.

We now come to the pastorate of Rev. William Hogarth. A unanimous call was made out for him on the 20th of September, 1841. At this time he was a licentiate of the Geneva Presbytery, of N. Y. This call was accepted, and his ordination and installation took place on Monday, December 6th, 1841. He entered upon his labors under the most favorable auspices, and with all the ardor of a young man. Mr. Hogarth was a man of no ordinary talent, and threw himself heart and soul into his work. It is only just to say that Mr. Hogarth filled a very important place in the history of this Church. The congregation was strong and united, and during his stay among them, many were brought into the church, who have filled prominent positions in it ever since. Some of them are members of this Church to-day, others have gone out and are engaged in doing the Lord's work elsewhere. He still preaches the gospel of the Son of God in a prominent pulpit of Detroit, Michigan. We regret that he is not present with us to-day to take a part in these memorial services. The relation between him and the congregation was dissolved on the 21st of October, 1846, when he was released to take charge of the Presbyterian Church, in Geneva, N. Y. His farewell sermon was preached on Sabbath, the 8th of November.

Soon after the retirement of Dr. Hogarth, the congregation extended a unanimous call to the Rev. Joel Edson Rockwell, of Valatie, N. Y., on the 15th of February, 1847. His installation by the Presbytery took place on May 4th, of the same year. The congregation was in much the same condition at this period, that it had been during the time of Dr. Hogarth,—strong and harmonious. They rallied around their new pastor and gave him every token of respect and confidence. We need not dwell upon these latter pastorates, because they are yet fresh in your memory. They can scarcely be considered as legitimate matters of history.

The labors of Dr. Rockwell closed on the 23d of January, 1851, when he was dismissed by the Presbytery to take charge of the Central Church, Brooklyn. His ministry was a pleasant and useful one, both to himself and to his people. None of the former pastors have shown a more abiding interest in the congregation than Dr. Rockwell, who has come to rejoice with us on this anniversary occasion.

This is as it should be; there may be good and sufficient reasons why a minister should be separated from his people, even where the relations between them are of the most pleasant character; and how pleasant it is to revisit them, feeling that he still retains their love and confidence.

As soon as practicable the congregation took steps to call another pastor. Accordingly a call was made out for the Rev. A. D. Pollock, of Virginia, on the 22d of April, 1852. Mr. Pollock entered upon his labors soon after. The pastorate of this brother was not a long one; it closed some time in the fall of '55. All who knew him unite in testifying to his talent as a preacher and a writer. For freshness and vigor of thought his superior, perhaps, has never appeared in any of the pulpits in this city. His intellect was of a peculiar order, and at times shone with great brilliancy. He is the author of the recent work "Life in the Exode," and still exercises his ministry, though in declining health, in the town of Warrenton, Virginia.

It was at the close of Mr. Pollock's ministry that the Central Presbyterian Church was organized. A large number of the congregation felt it to be their duty to lay the foundation of a new enterprise. This effort was encouraged by a resolution unanimously passed by the session of Hanover Street Church, approving the separation, and bidding those engaged in it God speed. The history of that enterprise is familiar to you all. The building now known as the Central Church, was dedicated to the worship of Almighty God on the 10th of November, 1857.

On the 31st of December, 1855, Rev. Wm. C. Dickinson was chosen pastor. This young brother, however, was never installed. Unwilling to assume the responsibilities of so large a pastoral charge, he remained less than a year. He remained long enough, however, to win the love and esteem of all who knew him, and to attach himself to the congregation with links of remembrance that shall never be broken. The people parted with him sincerely regretting that he felt it to be his duty to decline their call. The paper which he read from the pulpit, assigning his reasons for this step, has been entered upon the Session Book, as a model of Christian courtesy and candor.

The Rev. William Aikman, of Newark, N. J., was chosen pastor on the 2d of June, 1857, and was installed October 30th of the same year. The ministry of Mr. Aikman is the longest which this congregation has been permitted to enjoy since the days of Dr. Gilbert. It covers a period of eleven years. Of the ministry of Dr. Aikman, it is unnecessary to say much; his virtues as a man, and his labors as a pastor are well known, and need no comment at my hands. It is but just to say, however, that the period during which he filled the pulpit of this Church was the most stormy and trying ever known in the history of the Church. During five years of his ministry, the country was involved in a terrible civil war, when there was much excitement and much diversity of interest and opinion, making it exceedingly difficult for a minister to discharge his duty to the satisfaction of all parties. "We speak that we do know." Yet, during all this time, Dr. Aikman remained in his place and continued to discharge his duties under a sense of his responsibility to the King and Head of the Church. He was released on the 19th of May, 1868. He now ministers to a Church in the city of Detroit, and sends his regrets that he cannot be with us on this occasion.

It was during the ministry of Dr. Aikman that Olivet Chapel was built and dedicated. A Sabbath School was organized in the Western part of the city by some members of the congregation, as early as 1849. The first sermon in connection with that enterprise was preached by Rev. Wm. W. Taylor. This continued to grow in size and interest until it was thought best to plant a church in that locality. Accordingly a neat and commodious chapel was erected at the corner of Chestnut and Adams Streets, and dedicated to the worship of God February 7th, 1864, where the preaching of the gospel has been regularly supplied ever since. At the present time the church and Sabbath School are doing a good work under the faithful pastorate of Rev. Alfred J. Snyder.

Immediately after the retirement of Dr. Aikman, a number of persons who had hitherto been connected with Hanover Church, deemed it their duty to withdraw to engage in a new enterprise, and certificates of dismission were granted them for this purpose. These uniting with a number who had already gone out from the Central Church, and with some from the First Presbyterian Church, formed what is now known as the West Church, whose new and beautiful house of worship was dedicated in December last.

Hume, the historian, says that no one can speak long of himself without being egotistical. My connection with the Church as pastor began in January, 1869. I came among you as a stranger from another branch of the Presbyterian family, and with what measure of success and acceptability my work has been done, it is for you to judge. It is but just to say that I have been most cordially received and treated by the people of my charge. We shall leave it to those who come after to write the history.

The history of every Presbyterian Church is largely the history of its pastors, but we might couple with this statement also, the lives of its elders. It has been the distinction of this Church almost from its beginning to be under the supervision of a faithful corps of elders. In this respect it will not suffer in comparison with any church within our knowledge. The first mention of a meeting of Session occurs about 1796; no names however are given. The first election of which we have any account, took place in 1803, when Alex. Fimester and David Harbison were chosen elders. These, together with the names of Dr. George Monro, Mr. James Smith, Mr. Cooke, Watson, Dickson, John Fleming, Matthew Kean, George Jones, Peter Alrich, Thomas Alrich, Jno. B. Porter, Robert Porter, Jno. Patterson, and Wm. Clark, (all now dead and gone,) are familiar to you all, and their record covers a large part of the Church's history. Justice will be done to their memory by another. Of the old members of Session, but one survives, the Hon. Judge Hall, who has already passed his 90th year.

The Sabbath School of the Church was organized in 1814, and has been aiming to do its proper work from that time to the present. Time would fail me to speak of the results which it has accomplished. So far as we can learn, it has never had more than five superintendents. Quite a number of its former pupils are now engaged in preaching the gospel in this and in other lands.

Such, in brief, is the history of this venerable Church. It would be impossible in the limits of an ordinary discourse to go more fully into detail. The salient points have all been set before you. Your own recollection will supply much that I have been obliged to omit. And what means this long and interesting history? Truly, this is a vine of the Lord's planting. We come to-day to bless His guiding, guarding power. These labors of love which cover the wide expanse of a century will never be forgotten. The results of the past are hid with Christ in God, only to appear when we shall appear with Him in glory. It cannot be that so much earnest work; that so many prayers, so many sermons and appeals; that so much teaching and instruction; that so much outlay of time, energy, and talent; it cannot be that all this should go unblest and unrewarded. No! no! "It shall be said that this and that man was born there, and the Highest himself shall establish her." This Church has been blest of God from its beginning until now. You have seen His presence and His power in the sanctuary from time to time. Very little of turmoil or trouble has marked your past history, as little we believe as can be shown in the history of any like Church in the land. Those who have been called to take charge of the congregation from time to time, have not been many, considering the age of the Church, and none of these, so far as known, have ever stained their record, or been separated from the Church without leaving substantial results for good behind them. For this we praise God.

If time would permit, there is much that might be said of the influence of Presbyterianism in the communities where it has flourished, and of its bearing upon the civil and political affairs of our country. It has been, both in this and in other lands, the main bulwark of civil and religious liberty. It is a notorious fact, that in its form it is closely allied with the structure of our civil government. The Revolution of 1776, so far as it was affected by religion, was largely a Presbyterian measure. It was the natural result of those principles implanted in her sons by the English Puritans, the Scotch Covenanters, the Dutch Calvinists, and the French Huguenots. Our Presbyterian ancestry were among the first to set their seal to that immortal document, the Declaration of Independence. Chief Justice Tilghman has remarked that the framers of the United States Constitution borrowed very much of the form of our Republic from that form of church government developed in the constitution of the Presbyterian Church of Scotland. Moreover, Presbyterianism erects around itsself no barrier of exclusiveism; it unchurches none; its hands have never been stained with the blood of persecution; it inscribes upon its banner of truth, forbearance and love; it welcomes to a fellowship in Christian labor all who "call upon the same Lord, both theirs and ours." We take a just pride therefore in her history, and challenge the respect of all that love our Lord Jesus Christ in sincerity.

In this review of the past we are reminded that our period of opportunity and service for the Master hastens to a close. Very soon we shall be gathered to the sepulchers of our fathers. These walls will contain us no more. Others will fill these pews, and others will come forward to receive baptism at this altar. Where will be the congregation of to-day a hundred years hence? I hold in my hand a printed roll of the members of this Church in 1831, and should I proceed to call it now, two-thirds of the answers would be a voice from the tomb. For the destiny that awaits us all, there is but one preparation; the atoning blood of Christ. Seek this and you are safe. Seek this and come joy or sorrow, life lingering long or suddenly fading away, the Abdiel greeting of a well done thou faithful one, shall be your welcome to the tearless scenes of that city that hath foundations, where the leaf never withers and the light never fades. Fix your eye upon the cross and the crown, and remember that

> "Not enjoyment and not sorrow
> Is our destined or way,
> But to act, that each to-morrow
> Find us farther than to-day."

At the close of the historical address, and after singing "The Lord is King," a brief address was made by Rev. J. P. Conkey, pastor of of the Central Church, in which he said that he was there simply as a representative of Presbyterianism, and to express the sympathy of his Church, in behalf of his congregation, with its progress. He spoke, also, of the sadness connected with the idea of age, but felt assured that Hanover Church had no reason for sadness in the gladness of this anniversary day. Looking forward into the future its record should not be viewed by the century, but on, on and on, down the vista of time.

We regret that we are unable to present a more extended report of this address, inasmuch as the author has found it inconvenient to furnish us with a manuscript for publication.

RECOLLECTIONS OF HANOVER STREET CHURCH.

BY REV. WM. W. TAYLOR.

"*I was glad when they said unto me, let us go into the house of the Lord. Our feet shall stand within thy gates, O Jerusalem. Whither the tribes go up, the tribes of the Lord, to give thanks unto the name of the Lord. Pray for the peace of Jerusalem; they shall prosper that love thee. Peace be within thy walls, and prosperity within thy palaces. For my brethren and companion's sake, I will now say: Peace be within thee! Because of the house of the Lord our God, I will seek thy good.*" Ps. cxxii.

I would have you expect nothing from these "*Recollections*" but just what the word naturally indicates; nor let it be a drawback on your interest, that I come not down to the modern days of this sanctuary, but date back fifty years, and linger around the old, original building, where Hanover Street Church lived when it was called the Second Church.

It is still standing on the old spot, Fifth and Walnut, and you may see its stony material and thick walls, though now enlarged over its original size and shape. At first it was square, and I used to hear people say it had been used as a stable by the British, in the Revolutionary War, when it was probably in an unfinished state; at least it needed some repairs after they were done with it. The pulpit was placed on the west side, fitted only for one Preacher at a time, with a small enclosure at its foot, shut in on the front with a railing; a brick paved aisle running in front, North and South, and another shooting at right angles to this, going Eastward to accommodate a large door, set in the East wall, the only way of incoming and outgoing. This was a large two-leafed circular-topped door, the inside fastening consisting of long iron bolts, shooting into grooves at the top, with shorter ones at the bottom; which I have good reason to be acquainted with, and to remember from a somewhat unpleasant and alarming occurrence. On one lecture or prayer meeting night, Wednesday or Friday, when I was a lad of seven or eight, my youthful piety took me to the service, but did not keep me from going to sleep. In company with a much older person, *Sammy Young*, I had taken my seat in the gallery, whilst everybody else was below, who, at the close of the service, very properly left the house and went home, not seeing, for there was no gas in the Church, nor dreaming that two of the worshippers, probably in that condition, were up stairs. I wakened first, and coming to a sense of my condition, lost no time in rousing my companion, and together we groped our way down to the door and so escaped; and this is about the first time I have ever confessed to the sin of sleeping in Church.

How they heated the house in those days I do not remember, or whether any attempts were made, but I can almost see old John Anderson, the sexton, or his poor idiot son, bringing coals in a foot stove for some of the old ladies, every Sabbath morning.

A gallery was built on three sides of the Church, as high as the pulpit, furnished with one row of large square pews all around, having entrance from a little aisle running around the inside of the wall, and finished in front with an open breastwork, made of little turned rods. Right opposite the pulpit, in the gallery, was the pew of old Capt. Geddes and family; on the right of pulpit was my father's pew, shared by the family of Mr. Johnston; the adjoining pew being occupied by the Kirkpatrick's. The pews below were long, rather than square, with straight high backs.

About 1820, the old building was enlarged by advancing the North wall fifteen or twenty feet, into its present size and shape, when a complete transformation was made in pews, pulpit, galleries, and doors, the old windows probably remaining as they had been, on account of the solidity of the walls.

This was thought to be an important event, and a large work among us young folks, who paid our visits from time to time, to enjoy both the demolition and the reconstruction, and I suppose the same views of the importance of the improvement were entertained by the old people. The usual history of such movements, in the conflict of opinion, whether the *old building* was not sufficient, and the enlargement extravagantly great as to the mode of finishing and furnishing, with the probable expense and the ways and means of raising the funds might doubtless be written, but I recollect nothing, but that everybody that I knew was engaged in it. The elders would go to superintend the work and tell stories, and the older boys were ready at the time of plastering to sit up all night and keep the fires going, to facilitate the drying.

One of these stories which I heard from my brother-in-law, Thomas C. Alrich, long afterwards, had respect to some one, who, in relating any matter, had the habit of closing every period by rubbing his hands and saying, "So far, so good." Well, the sight of scaffolding reminded him of an accident that had happened to some acquaintance, who, in climbing or working, lost his balance and fell to the ground and broke his leg; at which point of the story forward come the hands rubbing with the bland expression, "*So far, so good.*"

About the same time that the Church was enlarged, a new lecture room, then called a conference room, was built on Queen, now Fifth Street, adjoining the Church, but some years ago it was removed, and the the spot is now occupied with dwelling houses.

The conference room was brick, having one entrance, in the middle of the wall on Fifth Street, and another door on the opposite side of the house, opening into the back yard. The room was commodious, plastered, and painted white, and furnished with benches with comfortable backs; having a platform on the West end, with a little square recess in the East end wall, made, we boys understood, for a clock, but I do not remember that the clock ever got there; and a little square opening in the ceiling for a ventilator excited much curiosity. This house was used for religious service through the week, and also for the Sabbath School, and I have no recollection of attending Sabbath School anywhere else.

Mr. James Simpson, a shoemaker, living what was then *out Front Street*, and a most worthy man, was the only teacher I can call to mind, and elder Robt. Porter was the Superintendent, assisted by Mrs. Anna Maria Jones, then Mrs. McMullen, Miss Maria Smith, Miss Catharine Ocheltree, Mrs. Gilbert, and the Misses Munro. To this day I can recall an exhortation made to the School, by Mr. Porter, who urged us to be moral and regular in all our ways, not because good habits of themselves would save us, but would keep us in a position where we would be more likely to receive the converting grace of God's spirit, which I have often thought of as an important consideration.

On another occasion, I remember some stranger, a gentleman, addressing us, by which my feelings were greatly moved, but I am sorry to say such a sense of shame came over me for the tears I shed, that before going into Church I went to a pump standing over on Walnut

Street, and still there, to wash the marks from my eyes and face. Our boyish sense of propriety, at this time, was much shocked by seeing Solis, a Jew, at the corner of Hanover and French streets, clarifying quills and cleaning windows on the Sabbath day.

In those days our Sabbath School labors were rewarded with *tickets*, blue and red, four blue securing one red, and four of these purchasing a religious tract, every twenty-four tracts being bound for us by the Superintendent into a handsome volume, and how many of them I became master of, memory fails to recall.

I fancy I saw old Rev. Dr. Read, the predecessor of Rev. Dr. Gilbert, once at least, as he officiated in the Church, and once at a wedding in my father's house. When he died, I was a boy of twelve, attending school in a large, gray stone academy, then standing back of Market Street, on the East side, between what are now Eighth and Ninth streets, and taught by Mr. Allston. He was buried inside the brick Church, on the grounds of the First Church, still standing on the corner of Tenth and Market, and when the ground was opened before the funeral, I entered the building, leaving our play ground for that purpose, and looked down most seriously into the open grave, and I earnestly wished I was to lie there, provided I could have his place in the better world, which I had no doubt was his glorious dwelling place.

The Rev. Eliphalet W. Gilbert was the pastor of the Church and the minister of the word, about whose ministrations my memory is most completely drawn, from my earliest days, to whom my heart warmly and justly clings, with fond and grateful tribute, for through his preaching I was brought, as I hope, to Christ, then into the Church, and my feet helped into the ministry.

Dr. Gilbert was born in New York State, and educated in theology at Princeton. He was a great reader of books, of which he would master a volume a week. He did not, however, take time to write his sermons, but commenced preparation for Sabbath on Thursday and preached extemporaneously without notes in the pulpit and without writing much, if any, in his study. He lived to regret that he had not preserved his thoughts on paper, as I heard him say, when he was pastor of Western Presbyterian Church, in Philadelphia, where he died in the Summer of '52 or '53. He possessed a fine mind, well cultivated and furnished. He was an excellent sermonizer, a good preacher and scholar, and a man of influence; well established in the love and reverence of his people, leaving his post at Hanover Street Church, at his own prompting, to become President of Delaware College, at Newark; which, however, he left and returned to his pulpit,—which a second time he relinquished to resume the Presidency; this resignation of the College being occasioned by its having accepted a lottery scheme to raise funds. Dr. Gilbert visited his people, but in a formal manner.

I remember him from *very early days*, more vividly by his favorite gesture, than the words he said, as he would throw out his arms, bending them in the shape of a W., and when he wound up with some remarks, he would introduce the conclusion by saying, "If these things be true," so and so follows. This gives a good idea of the logical character of his mind at the same time that it expresses his candor and modesty; for he entertained no doubt of the Scripture doctrines he preached, but only of his own argumentative powers. Our pastor's shutting up the Bible was a signal of bringing his remarks to a close.

Our dear old Church has, ever since my recollection, possessed a stout bench of Elders; of whom, in old times, I can recall Robert Porter, John Fleming, Matthew Kean, Thos. C. Alrich, David Harbeson, and George Jones; Judge Hall and Wm. Clark coming in at a later day; and of later members of Session, I need not remind you.

Mr. Porter died in the year 1839, and a published sermon of Dr. Gilbert's occasioned by the event was forwarded to me, in which he was compared with the old High Priest Jehoiada, in the time of Joash, King of Judah; the verse eulogizing him forming the text: that he had done good in Israel, both toward God and toward his house, for which they buried him in the City of David among the Kings, and this was true of Mr. Porter. 2 Chron. xxiv.

I felt very warmly towards Elder Matthew Kean, and Mr. Alrich I loved like a brother, as indeed he was. I loved, because I knew him, and the longer I knew him, and the more I saw him, the stronger grew my respect and affection. He was a man of prayer and maintained a high example of piety. Years did not harden his character and make his heart sharp and angular, but matured him into a mellow ripeness, that showed a preparation for that glory into which he was suddenly drawn, dying in Philadelphia, under a midnight summons, in the Spring of 1865.

Besides the Elders, the Church was blessed in early times with many earnest, believing, and praying Christians, male and female, that set others in motion and became the channel of divine blessing to many, of whom a few names have been given. At one time it would seem there was no christian physician in the Church, nor perhaps in the community, when this praying band of ladies selected a young man, Dr. Thomas, and made him the subject of their earnest and successful prayers.

The same was true of a young editor, Mr. Wm. Mendenhall, of the Wilmingtonian, who long lived an exemplary Christian.

Many old names could I recall, as David C. Wilson, and Allen Thompson, the Geddeses, Porters, Hamiltons, Sellars, Hendricksons, McClurgs, Joneses, Cochranes, Mahaffys, Pattersons, Bushs, Moodys, Monroes, and Smiths, old Mr. Hogg, Guyers, Hendricks, McClarys, and Browns.

I can just remember the death of old Dr. Smith, which was the occasion of great perplexity to my reasoning powers, how a *doctor* could die; that the physician, who was called in to give me pills and jalap, on which I quickly recovered, did not heal himself.

Old Mr. Hendrickson was a fine looking, large made man, tall and broad, the cast and complexion of his face reminding you of what a real Swede should be, and who was proably a descendant of that race, who are ranked among the original settlers of Delaware.

Since my mind has been called to think back, in preparation for these Recollections, a sentiment lodges and presses upon my reflections, like this: The large beneficence and wise outlay of means, in building a church edifice where it is needed, and organizing a Church of Christ.

A church's life may be like that of one of the old Patriarchs, the first century only bringing it through its infancy, that shall continue through the days of Heaven, flourishing like trees of righteousness; its blessed history symboled by the clambering and flowering plant, that holds on and propagates its life from year to year, in growing strength and spreading verdure. If old Hanover is a true sample of all, how long they last, and what a source of blessing of the richest type and largest measure do they become?

And are not we believers who have come up to this celebration, or dwell here and round about, ready to say of our spiritual mother, "The Lord bless thee out of Zion," being ready to give thanks to God for those who laid these foundations, material and spiritual, and have since sustained them?

The old organization still lives and flourishes, though dwelling under another and more commodious roof. The *First Church* has been resuscitated out of its roots, and its branches have been spread in the shape of the Central, the Olivet, and the West.

For a century the gospel of our Lord Jesus has been preached, and the light thereby maintained against outside error; morality has been cherished with the virtues that make communities quiet, orderly, and prosperous, besides the saving grace, that in every generation, and from year to year, has found its way to dead consciences and worldly hearts, to give hope, sanctity, and joy; to enter the household and take hold even of the children's minds; sanctifying the scenes of care and affliction; making the early death in the family a treasure of good; preparing and lifting over into the kingdom of God, our brother, our sister, our father, our dear departed mother; for this has been a living Church, marked by revivals, with praying hearts and working hands, acting as a fountain that sends forth sweet and life-giving waters.

In my early boyhood days I recall a time of excitement in the Church, that affected young and old. We young persons held prayer meetings among ourselves, and exhorted one another to hold on. We were sent round by the older ones to collect missionary money, furnished with little cards, on which was printed, "God loveth the cheerful giver; "Freely ye have received, freely give," and similar passages of scripture. How many were received into the Church at this revival, I do not know, but some of us younger were taken under the care of the Session. I thought myself a christian at that time, but I am now persuaded otherwise, for I fell away greatly, and had no deep convictions of sin. I still recall to memory a young man, an active member of the Church in those days, by the name of McCall, who tried to help us on. In the work of the revival, our pastor, Mr. Gilbert, had assistance from the Princeton theological students, one of whom, the late Dr. Henry Ludlow, was quite effective. An exhortation from him, which must have been delivered in the old unaltered Church, I have never lost from my recollections, as he spoke of Noah building the ark and warning his fellows of what would come, when the graphic young preacher made the sound of every hammer stroke as it fell upon the nail-head, resound and enforce the Patriarch's cry, *Prepare to meet thy God!*

The revival of the Winter and Spring of 1827, is most memorable to me, when the same faithful Church members were abundant in their labors, and the pastor was again helped by young Princeton men, among whom were a Mr. Eastman and Mr. Hervey, who afterwards went to India as a Missionary, and died there of cholera; Rev. Mr. Danforth, of New Castle, Dr. Skinner, of Philadelphia, old Dr. Dickey, and probably other neighboring ministers also assisted. With the state of the Church immediately before this revival, and the means to bring it forward, I am unacquainted. I probably was not aware of what was going on among the good people, till my attention was arrested by a sermon of the pastor's, and my fears of God's anger for my sins vividly awakened thereby, on Sabbath, February 4, 1827, and I could, perhaps, point out the very seat I occupied in the old edifice, as I could certainly tell the text used on that Sabbath day, so blessed to me. "*I pray thee have me excused.*"

I strangely lost my impressions upon stepping outside the door of the Church after the morning service, but they returned the next Monday evening with great pungency, and I was numbered among the anxious and prayerful, until I found hope in Christ. Christian friends came around me to counsel and urge me. Mr. Alrich encouraged me by the thought that I might be the means of winning many souls. Mr Hervey sought me behind the counter, where I was for the time employed, and Mrs. Anna M. Jones put into my hands Doddridge's Rise and Progress of Religion in the Soul, by the reading of which I seemed to be led, step by step, into the kingdom of God. Upon finding relief, my emotions at first were not very vivid; I hoped that God had heard my incessant prayers, and christians appeared like friends, but the reading of the Scriptures, especially the New Testament, soon led me into the sweetest fields of thought and feeling. Christ was in my heart, and I knew that I had never known happiness before.

During the period of my convictions my whole previous life appeared but one lengthened sin, because I had never acted from a sense of God's glory, but Jesus cleansed my sins away; I needed no arguments to convince me of original sin and total depravity, for I saw it in my own heart, yet Christ, the second Adam, stood in my behalf, against all the evil wrought by the first, unto whose service in the ministry, from the first I devoted myself.

I have allowed my own experience in this revival to be made so prominent in these recollections, because it may give a true recital of what happened to many others at the same time, for on the communion Sabbath, that gathered in the fruits of the work, thirty-seven stood up to together to take the vows of God.

Those who approached me in christian love doubtless labored for others, and the same good work that was wrought of God for me, made many others glad. I now renewed my acquaintance with the Sabbath School and became a teacher of little boys, the Superintendent at this time being, probably, Mr. Belknap, a school teacher.

In connection with the revival, our meetings in the conference room were frequent through the week, at night, and were seasons of great interest and religious ardor. There was much singing and exhortation, and the trouble many a time of our pastor was to get the people to break up and go home. He was much afraid of anything bordering on the irregular, and ten o'clock was an hour beyond which he did not feel easy to stay; but as fast as he dismissed them the fragmentary parts would heal up for further exercises, and this would happen again and again.

Nor shall I ever forget a certain evening when a young convert besought her sister to come to Jesus, throwing her arms about her, hanging on her neck and crying, "do, sister, do;" "do, sister, do come!" with a paroxysm of importunity, love, and gushing tears. For my own part, such was my interest that I was impatient for the meeting time, and literally ran through the streets to the dear conference room, and to show the earnestness of others in the great work, I heard at the time of two young women who were so engaged that they determined not to sleep on a certain night till they had found the Saviour, and before the morning light they rejoiced in the light of His countenance.

The young Princeton brethren were desirous of bringing out the young converts to take a part in the services, and one evening I was invited, and perhaps urged to mount the little platform and say something about my feelings. I felt that I was among friends and had no fear, but by the time I stood up and faced the room full, they proved too many for me, and I could not speak a word; the moisture of my tongue was entirely dried up, and the tongue clave to the roof of my mouth, nor could I even move my jaws, and there remained nothing for me but to leave the platform and sit down; yet I had no sense of shame, I thought I had tried my best; I could not do worse, and hoped I would do better the next time, and indeed I did speak shortly afterward, I hope to edification.

In connection with this revival a young men's prayer meeting was established and held Sabbath evening's before Church, in the conference room, and missionary labors, in the shape of Sabbath Schools, and prayer meetings, and tours of tract distribution on Sabbath afternoons were entered upon, in Brandywine village, and in other directions and up the Brandywine, in which excursions I was permitted to take a part, in company with Judge Hall, Thomas Mahaffy, and others.

At the communion in the Spring of 1827, to which I have referred, many united with the Church whose names I have forgotten, and of whom I have known little or nothing for many years. Judge Hall, I believe united at that time, and Thomas McCorkle, my brother James Alexander Taylor, James Porter, son of Alexander Porter, Archibald Robertson, a Mr. W. Hendrickson, Miss Margaret Bowers, and Miss

Frances Thompson. The pastor's house on French Street above Seventh, seemed then out of town.

I am quite sure Rev. Mr. Danforth was present on this communion Sabbath, but Dr. Skinner, then of Philadelphia, preached the sermon, whose text was the language of the crucified thief: "*Lord, remember me!*" That Sabbath night, after the services, as we lingered in the sanctuary, James A. Taylor, James Porter, long since Capt. Porter of the merchant service, and myself were standing together when Dr. Skinner, after conversing with us, expressed the desire that he might know, *after ten years*, that we held on in the good way.

I hope this is the case with us all, my dear brother having been for many years an Elder in the Presbyterian Church, but Captain Porter, though living, I have seen but once or twice since that day. How many have passed away since my recollections have dated themselves! embracing all of that generation, of whom the Church has been the nurse, through Christ's grace, training up sons and daughters for glory, and introducing them into the kingdom of God; and how few remain, lingering but ready to pass over! Some, who were of my own age are still among you, and of the older, Judge Hall, you still hold, and Mrs. Hall, Miss Martha Kirkpatrick, the Misses Hamilton, Miss Harbeson, and others with whose names I am not so familiar. Mr. Enoch Thomas, a convert, accompanied me to Andover, Massachusetts, to fit for College, both having the ministry in view, whom I had hoped to meet after years of separation, with others who went forth into the ministry, and the dear ex-pastors, only one of whom is present on this animating occasion.

In conclusion, I profess my warmest love for this Church, and give thanks to God continually for throwing me, in my early days, by His wondrous providence, under its sacred influence, and for inspiring the brethren and sisters of the Church in years gone by, with so much love for our souls, and giving them so eminently the spirit of grace and supplications.

And if one, long ago of you, and still so in heart, but of late years not much among you, may give an exhortation to the Church, it is this; the faith of those who have gone before you, *follow;* hold to their love of souls and love of revivals, devise liberal things, expect great things, attempt great things, be forward in every department of Christ's work, nor wait for others, but take the lead, as is your prerogative and privilege, and continue to be the mother examplar to all, the children you have sent forth; by your Godliness to cherish ours; by your light to guide us, in every good word and work.

THE EVENTS OF THE CENTURY.

BY REV. J. E. ROCKWELL, D. D.

No one century, perhaps, since the Christian Church was established has had a record so full of marked and important events as that which has passed since this Church was organized. Changes which have hitherto been the growth of ages, and revolutions which have altered the whole face of society, have been accomplished in a day, and as by the stroke of the enchanter.

One Hundred Years ago! We look back to that period, and think with wonder how events that are now matters of history, were then beyond the wildest visions of philosophers, patriots, and sages.

The awful solitudes of the heathen world were as yet unbroken by the voice of the living teacher. Mighty bulwarks of darkness, ignorance, and superstition stood as apparently insurmountable barriers to the gospel. Italy, Spain, Austria, and the South American States were under the complete dominion of papal superstition, that bade defiance to all efforts to bring their people to a knowledge of the truths as preached by Paul, and re-echoed by Luther, Calvin, and Knox. Turkey, Egypt, Arabia, and the Holy Land were under the dark and cruel power of Mohammedan imposture, that would brook no attempt to offer to its devotees the doctrines of salvation by the cross of Christ. India, China, and Japan, were closed to all efforts to teach their benighted millions a purer religion than that of Buddha, or Confucius, or Brahma. The vast regions of our now teeming West were as yet unvisited by the advancing tread of modern civilization. The wealth of the Pacific was yet unknown. Our mighty rivers and lakes, and the mighty waters of the ocean had not yet quivered under the dash of the swift steamer. The world had not dreamed of our modern appliances of locomotion, that are now carrying population to regions that were but lately the home of the wild beast and the red man of the forest.

This Church began its life just as the stirring scenes of which we are to speak were commencing. America was about to throw off its allegiance to the old world, and begin a new and more brilliant era as a separate and independent nationality. The great mass of the people were undergoing those preliminary agitations, which were to result in the union of the Colonies—the Declaration of Independence, and the war of the Revolution, in which the citizens of this State were to have no unimportant part. Almost within the hearing of the people of Wilmington was fought one of the memorable battles of that eventful struggle. On the night which preceded it, Washington sat in his tent near Stanton, doubtful as to the safest route for his army to take, and unable to obtain from his officers any well defined outline of the roads leading across the State; one of his staff suggested the name of Dr. Read, then at Newark, and afterward the honored pastor of this Church, as one most likely to give him the desired information. The officer was directed to bring him to the camp as speedily as possible. Long before morning the Doctor was with Washington, drawing out a map of the country. Following his directions, the army crossed the State, and the next day met the British troops upon the banks of the Brandywine.

It was in the midst of these exciting scenes, and in such troublous times that the walls of this Zion were built. The very names which we meet with in history, one hundred years ago, will suggest many of the events which mark this century.

Hume, Rousseau, and Voltaire were preparing the way by their infidel literature for the scenes of the French Revolution and its resultant influences. Carnot, St. Just, and Robespierre were busy fomenting those terrible passions that were to make the close of the eighteenth century so fearfully memorable. The first Napoleon was a child of four years, when this Church was beginning its peaceful mission. Blackstone was writing his great commentaries on the laws of England, that are still the instructor and guide of jurists. Hunter was making his memorable discoveries in physiology. Dr. Samuel Johnson was sending forth his magnificent thoughts, that are still an important and brilliant part of English classical literature. Burke, and Pitt, and Fox, and Sheridan, were electrifying the British nation by their fervid eloquence. Howard was doing his noble work as a philanthropist, and awakening the attention of the world to the suffering, and devising plans for their relief. Sir Joshua Reynolds and Benj. West were preparing for themselves an immortality of fame by their works of art. Wesley was working out grand and much needed reforms in the Church. America was everywhere feeling the result of the labors of Whitefield, who had died two years before at Newburyport, but who, though dead, was yet speaking.

As we look over a century filled with the influences of such men, we hardly know where to begin our enumeration of the events which claim our attention. The philosopher would seize upon those facts that illustrate most clearly the progress of science. The politician would look at the mighty changes which have been wrought among the peoples and governments of the world. The economist would present a vast amount of facts that show the mighty progress made in art, science, agriculture, and social and commercial life. But the christian grouping all these together as only means to a more glorious end, would see with wonder and gratitude how God has been using them all in his wondrous providence, for his own glory, for the spread of the everlasting gospel, the upbuilding of his Church, and the growth and enlargement of his kingdom. Look where we may, we see in every revolution and event an illustration of the truth that the only proper light in which to read history, is that which God's word and providence sheds upon it, as connected with the fulfilment of his great purposes of redemption and grace. All the vast changes which have been wrought in the social and political world have been preparatory to some more important advance of the Church toward its final victory over the enemies of God and the Lamb. Inventions and improvements have trod upon the heel, the one of the other, only to prepare the way for some other revolution in the social world, whose resultant influence should be seen in the advance of the Church of God to some new stage in its progress, or some new vantage ground in its conflicts with error and sin, or some fresh victory over its great enemies.

The perfection of the steam engine by Watt, in 1774, was the preparatory step to an entire revolution in the commercial world, that was to link the most distant nations into a common brotherhood, and divest the ocean of half its terrors and perils.

The invention of the spinning jenny, by Arkwright, was the dawn of a new era in manufactures. The discoveries of Galvani were the first important steps in the progress of science and art toward the crowning wonder of the age, the magnetic telegraph. All these changes, begun and completed in a single century, have opened new fields for the Church, and have given it new appliances for carrying on its work, and preaching the gospel to every creature.

Never has any one century seen so many vast changes begun and completed as that whose events we are recalling. There is not a navigable river or lake in the civilized world that has not its system of steamers carrying with them population and wealth, and opening new fields of successful labor to the multitudes that are seeking to subdue the Earth to the behests of our race.

Scarcely a generation has passed since the first railroad was built, and now the whole world seems bound together by these vast links of iron, and the ponderous engine, dragging after it countless treasures of life and commerce, moves without hindrance from the Lakes to the Gulf of Mexico, and from the Atlantic coast to the waters of the Pacific. While to complete the grand ideas of physical life, the electric wires, that are the nerves of the great system, cover this continent with a vast network, and even beneath the ocean are thrilling with thought, and bearing over the world messages of love and peace, and records of mighty revolutions, or ministering to the behests of Commerce, of Science, and of Government. As an essential aid to civilization great improvements have been made in printing, by which the diffusion of knowledge has been immensely increased, and yet all these advances and revolutions have been but the preparatory processes for a still greater work in the extension and enlargement of the Church.

What a succession of wonders has been witnessed during the last century. How marvellously God has been carrying on his work in the world. What stupendous changes, wrought out by the Truth, have been everywhere going on. With what celerity have ideas sprung into life, and become clothed with form, and body, and power.

How emphatic and marked has been the progress of the world in all its highest and noblest interests. Science has sounded the depths of the ocean; brought its solemn mysteries to light; discovered the laws which regulate its currents; analyzed the storms which sweep its surface, and taught the sailor how to evade their influence, or warned him of their approach. Human enterprise has boldly entered the awful solitudes and icy portals of the Polar seas; has explored the interior of Africa, so long an unknown region; disemboweled the earth of its treasures, and revealed to the devout student of nature the wonders of the heavens.

Russia has been shorn of her military glory at Sebastopol, but has yet made wonderful strides in civilization by releasing millions of serfs from bondage, and investing them with the rights of citizens. Austria has shaken off the shackles of a fearful despotism, and awakened to a new life. China and Japan have opened to the world their commerce and their busy ports. Wonderful discoveries have been made in Central Asia, which have thrown fresh light upon Revelation, while busy scholars have been reading the marbles of Egypt, Assyria, and Babylon, and confirming thus the histories and prophecies of the word of God.

It were idle to attempt the enumeration of events so numerous and so important. We can only arrange in three general classes, among which we place,

First. Those changes that have been connected with the removal of obstacles to the spread of the gospel.

For long ages the great adversary to God and his Church has entrenched himself behind fortresses that seemed impregnable. In China, Japan, India, Central Europe, and Southern America, stood up mighty walls of Heathenism, Mohammedanism and corrupt forms of Christianity that appeared to bar all progress of the true gospel. There stood India with her teeming millions, all under the power of grand but false systems of religion, that would admit no light from God's word to shine upon them. But England wanted India for her commerce, and entered and took possession, and the Church followed in her wake upon its peaceful and blessed mission, and sent in its servants to open to the millions of that country the blessings of the gospel. Commerce made its way by war and subsequent treaties to China, without a thought of aiding the Church in her work. But devoted missionaries, headed by Morrison, and Gutylaff, and Abeel, followed with the gospel, and its attendant blessings. And so Japan, long closed against the Church, has thrown down her barriers and sent forth her young men to learn the great lesson of Christian civilization from England and America. A series of wonderful revolutions amid the islands of the Pacific, broke the hold of idolatry upon the minds of of the people even before the living teacher came, and so the missionary found the way prepared for the gospel. Thus, wherever we turn we find that the barriers of Heathen superstition have been broken down, and a great and effectual door is opened through which the Church may enter for its work of preaching the gospel to every creature.

And so too the strength of *Islamism* is weakening and waning. Some of its strong holds have become subject to christian powers. Greece struggled to be free, and in her successful conflict struck a blow at Turkey, that palsied her arm, and now she exists only by the sufferances of Europe. Egypt is a weak and effete nation. Africa is open to the gospel, and the Arab is waiting for the dawning light. Commerce and civilization have in all these nations been breaking down the barriers that have long resisted the progress of the truth.

And so it is with the *Papal Church*. Its political power is waning, and its ability to interrupt or embarrass the work of evangelizing the world is largely destroyed. Its inquisitions are destroyed; its control over monarchs and princes weakened. France desired to be free, and though mistaking the way to true liberty, and wading through troubled seas of blood and revolution, she yet struck a deadly blow at the papacy and gave to her people a taste of religious freedom. By a wonderful train of providences the way has been preparing for the progress of the gospel and protestantism in Mexico and South America. Wars and revolutions and commercial schemes have been the instruments of removing obstacles which seemed almost hopelessly to prevent all efforts at giving to these nations the written word of God, and the instructions of christian pastors and teachers. And more wonderful than all has been the chain of events by which the power of the papacy has been broken in Italy and Austria. Napoleon in his insane attempts to become the arbiter of Europe, if not of the world, is an exile from his country; his army shattered; his bayonets withdrawn from Rome, and Protestant Germany has risen to be the defender of liberty and the oppressed. Victor Emanuel holds his court in Rome under the shadow of the Vatican, where the Pope is his own prisoner, uttering childish anathemas and silly bulls, which even his own priests and bishops no longer fear, and despite which they are seeking to purify the Catholic faith, while the Bible and the protestant Church have every where free course among the people. Even in Spain wonderful revolutions have removed out of the way obstacles to to the truth, and have broken up the influence of the papacy as it has been hitherto felt through the government; so that this ancient home of the fearful and bloody inquisition now welcomes the Bible and the preaching of the gospel, and witnesses the establishment of Churches framed after the apostolic model, with *bishops set over each congregation*, and ordained to their work by the laying on of the hands of the *Presbytery*.

These are some of the wonderful systems of Providence, by which the great obstacles that were opposing the progress of the gospel when this century began, have been removed out of the way. Human agencies have been used, which at the time seemed to have no connection with the work. Nations and Monarchs, and commercial institutions were seeking their own ends and purposes. Wars and revolutions were regarded as merely the human outworkings of some great political principle; but God was overruling all and preparing the way for his Church to enter upon its great work of preaching the gospel to every creature.

Second. And this leads us to notice as a second group of events, those which have been immediately connected with the development of modern missions. In 1789, William Cary proposed in a meeting of ministers to consider the duty of the Church to send the gospel to the heathen, and was for his proposition looked upon as a wild visionary. Yet four years after, the Baptist Missionary Society was organized, and its establishment was followed by the formation of the London and Scotch Societies three years after. From that time the Church began to awake to its great work of sending the gospel to a dying world; and the close of the eighteenth century and the first quarter of this witnessed the uprising of God's people for the conquest of the world to Christ. The organization of mission and kindred societies are the grand events of the century. To the American christian the year 1810 will be memorable as the birth year of the Board of Commissioners for foreign missions. The laborers which they sent forth needed the printed page to aid them in their work, and hence arose Bible societies in Europe and America, which have sent forth one hundred millions of copies of the word of God. They needed a sanctified literature, and then came tract and other religious publication societies. They needed more laborers in the field, and education societies were formed. Africa needed christian men and women, and the Colonization Society arose. They needed religious instructions for the young, and Sabbath Schools sprang into life, when Robert Raikes first obeyed that magic word "*Try,*" which seemed to be angels' whispers answering his questions, what he might do for the neglected children of his native city. Prophecy had declared that the abundance of the sea should be converted to God, and societies were organized to care for the spiritual and temporal wants of the sailor. Finally the Church felt that each division of the army of Christ could best do its work in its own way, and hence arose separate denominational Missionary Boards, and the result has been most marked and beneficent, and the results accomplished have shown the wisdom of Church associations for doing the work of the Church. Thus in a multitude of forms, whose history goes largely to make up the events of the century, has the Church arisen to enter the fields which providence has opened before it, and to do the work of whose results there can be no doubt, and at whose consummation the shout shall go up, The kingdoms of this world have become the kingdoms of our Lord, and of his Christ.

Third. And this brings us to notice the events which have marked the progress of the Church in its work of evangelizing the nations, or which have been for the furtherance of the spread of the gospel.

We go back a hundred years and meet with that grand uprising of America, which was the outworking of the truth, "He hath made of one blood all that dwell upon the face of the earth," and which found its re-affirmation in the declaration that all men are created free and equal. The war of the revolution was largely the result of the principles of freedom which our fathers learned in that blessed Bible which they loved and valued, and which they were not afraid to have taught to their children in the common schools.

Ten years after the world had learned one of its great lessons concerning liberty—as it had seen the results of the conflict in America—it was taught that there could be no true freedom where God was not recognized, and his word and Sabbaths honored. In 1792, France was declared a Republic, and early in the next year her king was put to death, and the *Reign of Terror* commenced. In October the queen was murdered by a brutal mob; a few days later the christian religion was renounced; the Bible buried publicly, and the Sabbath abolished.

Two years were enough to satisfy the people that anarchy was not liberty, and Robespierre and his guilty, infidel associates were brought to the guillotine. Then followed the wonderful career of the first Napoleon, with all his strange alternations of success and defeat, spreading anxiety and alarm through Europe; defeating the Austrians at Lodi; marching into Egypt with thirty thousand men and conquering the Mamelukes in the battle of the Pyramids; invading Syria and being foiled by the gallant defence of Acre; returning to France and suppressing the Directory and taking the Consulate of the Empire; entering Italy and defeating the Austrians at Marengo; forming a treaty at Luneville by which the Rhine was made the border of France; forsaking the cause of liberty and seeking to concentrate all power in himself; made Emperor of France and King of Italy; making Ulm and Austerlitz, and Vienna memorable for his victories; invading Spain and compelling Ferdinand to abdicate; divorcing Josephine and marrying Maria Louisa; annexing Holland to France; entering Russia with four hundred and eighty thousand men, and retiring at length with forty thousand men from burning Moscow; taking the head of a fresh army of three hundred and fifty thousand soldiers; defeated by the allied powers of England, Austria, Spain, and Portugal, and sent to Elba a dethroned Monarch; appearing again in France and taking the field against the Allies;

suffering a final and total rout at Waterloo, and sent to St. Helena; and finally dying on that lone and barren isle, amidst the war of the elements, recalling in his last hours his eventful life, and uttering as his last words the significant *Tete d'Armee*, which showed that the ruling passion was strong in death. The terrible scenes of this grand drama were prolific of good to the world.

The truth began to be seen that God was the arbiter of nations. Evangelical religion began to revive. France felt its influence in the enjoyment of liberty of conscience; the signal rebuke of infidelity; the weakening of the papacy as a political power; the uprising and growth of protestantism, and the diffusion of light and education.

Since that momentous era, with what wonderful and constantly accelerating rapidity have great and important revolutions been affected, which have been either the result of the spread of the truth or providential arrangements for new victories over error and evil.

The islands of the Pacific have cast away their idols, renounced their heathen practices, and become christian nations. Churches, and schools, and printing presses, and happy homes, are the marked and emphatic evidence, in the Sandwich Islands, of the success of the gospel.

Among the Feejees cannibalism has ceased, fearful and desolating wars are ended, and polygamy and infanticide are unknown. Ninety thousand of the inhabitants attend worship, conducted by six hundred and sixty-three preachers. Thirty-six thousand children are gathered in schools, and one-half the population are in possessession of the Holy Scriptures; and all this has been accomplished within the last forty years.

In China missionaries can freely traverse the whole country, and are successfully laboring in many of the great cities along the coast.

In India one thousand stations are opened for Missionary work among the Brahmins, and mighty changes have been wrought in the convictions of that people. At every point Hindooism is giving way before the advancing tide of religious knowledge.

In Madagascar, where the early missionaries were driven away by a pagan and persecuting queen, more than one hundred houses of worship are now filled with attentive hearers. In some of these sanctuaries two thousand persons may be seen gathered on the Sabbath for the worship of the triune God.

In Africa, the colony of Liberia has become an important power on the Western coast, and all along that vast shore are seen the growing lights of the christian Church.

These are but specimens of the wonderful events which have marked the efforts of the people of God to preach the gospel among the heathen. Wherever we turn we see the precursors of the coming day.

Every movement of the political world has eventuated in some new advance of the truth. And it is remarkable how every change has been connected with the removal of some obstacle to the spread of the gospel.

Louis Phillippe, who ascended the throne of France as a liberal Prince, came at length so much under Jesuitical influence as to use his power for the advancement of their purposes. He sent his ships of war to Tahiti, where protestant missionaries were doing a noble work, and opened the way for French brandy and Catholic priests by the mouth of the cannon. He used his power in Greece, and Dr. King was exiled for the time from his home and his labors. He permitted protestant missions to be crippled, and almost destroyed, at the behests of intrigueing and wily Jesuits. Then came the avenging Nemesis in the uprising of his people, and his dethronement and banishment, while the works he assailed were all resumed with fresh power and vitality.

Louis Napoleon tried the same experiment, and filled with the insane hope of revivifying the Roman power was throwing a cordon of French influence and authority around the world.

Taking advantage of our intestine troubles he set his foot upon Mexico and placed his unhappy creature, Maxmillian, upon the imperial throne. Sending his armies to Italy he sought to uphold the tottering power of the Pope, whose predecessor, his uncle had imprisoned. He gained by his efforts the unenviable title of "the youngest son of the Church." He set his foot upon every project that was designed to spread liberty and the truth; and then his fall came, and from being the arbiter and the dread of Europe, he is an exile and a ruined man, while a protestant Emperor takes his place in the grand movements of European politics, and freedom and truth and religion have achieved a noble triumph. Italy, so long crushed under the iron heel of Popery, and whose "beauty was her funeral dower," has been the theatre of mighty revolutions. Again and again her people have risen up to assert her rights and liberties. Amid alternate successes and defeats the truth has been silently making its way, and freedom is dawning upon them. The Pope while pompously declaring his infallibility has only shown his own weakness and folly. His reign as a temporal prince is over, and a wise and temperate monarch sits amid the palaces of the Cæsars, and rules over united Italy. Above all, the Bible, so long a prohibited book to the Italian, is now publicly sold and distributed, and freely read, while the ancient and long persecuted Church of the Waldenses, in its simple and sublime faith, and with a long record of suffering and martyrdom at the hands of papal priests and rulers, is stepping forth from its mountain fastnesses to offer to the nation a pure gospel and an apostolic ministry.

And now, turning from the old world to the new, what a wonderful and eventful era has this century been. In the years 1803 and 1815 the United States paid their tribute to the Corsairs of Algiers (who had hitherto exacted from the commerce of the Mediterranean a tax for its safety) in the form of a naval assault, which compelled the miscreants to renounce their claims, and finally to abandon their depredations.

In the year 1812 began the second war with England, which in a series of brilliant naval victories established our rights upon the ocean, and rebuked the arrogant claims of Britain to her subjects, when protected by the flag of the republic. Then began the growth of our commerce; the rapid enlargement of our territory; the addition of star after star to the banner of our Union; the flow of that vast tide of immigration which has brought to our shores the representatives of every nation to mingle with the original races that formed the old Thirteen States, and which seemed to show the Church that providence, no longer waiting for her to enter on the work of evangelizing the world, was bringing the world to our own door, and re-echoing the words of Christ, Preach my gospel to every creature, beginning at Jerusalem.

To meet the demands of this mighty influx of population; to open rivers in the desert, and highways across our plains and mountains, the land has been crossed and re-crossed with canals, and railroads, and telegraphs. To supply the wants of the people, schools and colleges and seminaries have been established, and Churches built, and supplied with the living teacher. And then to the work, with the divine sanction, glorious revivals of religion have been sent through the power of the Holy Ghost, whereby multitudes have been born to God and made to feel the power of a new life in the soul. To warn the nation not to trust in uncertain riches, fires and floods have at times swept away untold millions of property, and cities and villages have fled before them like a vision. To admonish the nation not to rely upon man, the highest office in the gift of the people has thrice been vacated by the sudden death of the President. To prepare the way for the extinction of great evils a fearful intestine war has gathered its blackness over our land, and in its progress the system of slavery, whose extinction none could have foreseen has disappeared forever.

Out of that great horror what glorious results have issued! what a vast awakening of national love! what a purifying of the political atmosphere! what a union of heart and hand in mitigating the terrors of war by means of the Sanitary and Christian Commissions! what sacrifices and offerings for the country and its defenders! what a consecration of time and influence and property for the spiritual wellbeing of the soldiers who were engaged in the defence of the Union! and when Peace at length waved her olive branch over the nation, what lessons were learned by the world of the self-preserving power of a free people, and of the strength and stability of a Republic with a free church, a free press, free schools, and *free men*! And when this fearful war was over, and the nation was resuming its great work of opening this continent to the world, the Church has been making a wonderful advance towards the fulfilment of the prayer of its great head that they might all be one. During the late civil war, it had been found that when christians of various names were working together for Christ among the soldiers, there was a wonderful drawing together of heart to heart, and a consequent disposition to lay aside those distinctive marks which were unessential to a common christianity. The spirit thus awakened was not lost when these brethren returned to the peaceful pursuits of life, and to their own churches. Then the question arose whether there could not be a closer union of christians, especially of those who in all essential features were alike.

In enumerating these efforts to effect a visible union, it would be a strange omission to leave out of our notice the successive steps by which our own Church has advanced to its present position. This Peninsula witnessed some of the earliest efforts to establish Presbyterianism on this continent. The Dutch type had appeared in New York as early as 1626; the Scotch form was not fully introduced until 1690, when Francis Makemie and John Hampton began to labor on the Eastern Shore of Maryland and planted numerous churches, among which were those of Rehoboth, Snow Hill, and Manokin.

In 1698 the first Presbyterian church of Philadelphia was organized; the date of the venerable structure in which the Presbyterians of Wilmington first worshipped is 1740. In 1741 there was a rupture in the only existing Synod of Philadelphia, arising out of the difference of views in regard to the revival then in progress under the ministrations of Whitefield. This rupture was healed after seventeen years, and the two bodies were united under the name of the Synod of New York and Philadelphia. At the close of the Revolution four

Synods were organized; the General Assembly came into existence in 1789, two months before the adoption of the Federal Constitution. The Assembly was opened with a sermon by Dr. Witherspoon, and Rev. Dr. Rogers, of New York, whose first settlement was in St. Georges in this state, was chosen the first Moderator.

In the year 1802, the plan of union was adopted, by which Congregational and Presbyterian churches were enabled to work together in newly settled districts of the country. Although meant to meet an immediate want, this plan was found to be defective, and too productive of serious evils which at last eventuated in the division of the Church.

In 1812, Princeton Theological Seminary was founded,—the first of those schools of the prophets which have since been increased in numbers and influence as the exigences of the Church have demanded.

In 1816, the Board of Domestic Missions originated,—whose work has so increased that it has been supplemented by the Board of Church Extension and Sustentation.

In the year 1819 the Board of Education was organized. In 1837 the Church assumed the work of foreign missions, by the erection of a Board for this special purpose. The Board of Publication was established in 1838; in 1853 the Church assumed the care of aged and infirm ministers and their families.

Thus it became fully equipped for its work, and though after 1838 divided into two bands, carried on its great plans with increasing zeal and with a growing disposition for a re-union, until in God's good providence the end was happily accomplished. Long before any direct overtures were made for bringing together the two branches of our Church, it was evident the spirit of christian fraternity was gradually increasing. Pulpit exchanges between brethren of the old and new schools,—transfers of ministers from one branch to the other,—co-operation in the work of christian benevolence,—the better understanding of each other's views by frequent interchange of thought and feeling, —and above all the presence of God's spirit among the churches, and united labors among the soldiers of our army in the Christian Commission, were teaching brethren on either side that there were no real barriers to the re-union of the Church. At length overtures were made upon the subject, which, though at first meeting with difficulties and embarrassments, resulted in the formation of a committee of re-union, which proposed terms that, with some few subsequent amendments, were received by the churches as the proper and substantial basis on which all could meet in harmony. Those who took part in, or witnessed these scenes, will never forget them. On the 10th of November, 1869, at Pittsburg, the two streams, so long divided, met together in one broad, deep current, flowing on, we trust, evermore as one of the streams of that river that shall make glad the city of our God,—the holy place of the tabernacles of the Most High.

Such is but a meagre outline of the events which have marked the lifetime of this Church. As we look over all these years, pregnant with changes and revolutions, we exclaim with wonder, What hath God wrought! How plainly do we see every where his hand at work for his Church, his own great namesake! And while we stand and gaze with wonder at the vast movements of divine Providence which have opened the world to the gospel, which have thrown down vast barriers to the truth, which have made the fields ripe for the harvest, caused the sower and the reaper to rejoice together; we are to listen to the summons that calls the Church to earnest and united labor, and says, Thrust in the sickle and reap, for the harvest of the earth is ripe. Wherever we look we see the precursors of the coming day, and seem to hear angel chimes and angel voices joining in the song of joy, and in hallelujahs of praise, while on every side are the clear echoes of God's word, "The night is far spent, the day is at hand."

Solemn and grand events in the past are to be followed by events more momentous and glorious in the future. God is every where at work, fulfilling his wise and wondrous purposes,

> "We are living, we are dwelling
> In a grand and awful time ;
> In an age on ages telling,
> To be living is sublime."

The promises of God cannot fail, and they all point to the year of jubilee, to the conversion of the world to Christ, to the destruction of Satan's kingdom, to the redemption of the world from sin, darkness and sorrow, and bid us labor and pray for the coming of Christ's kingdom.

In the glorious future, the Church is to have a grand and most important part. Then God shall take to himself his great power, and the hallelujahs of his people shall be caught up by angels and borne heavenward, and their burden shall be "THE LORD GOD OMNIPOTENT REIGNETH."

characteristics. Grace was ever manifest in his life. He had a symmetry of character that was beautiful to behold. While not indifferent to the things of this world, no man ever impeached his integrity. His gains were all honest gains. The taint of dishonor did not mar the value of any of his possessions. He was conscientious in the discharge of all his duties; he never permitted his worldly affairs to prevent the discharge of the duties of his eldership. He was chosen a member of Session not long after he became a member of the Church. That he might discharge the public duties of his office to edification, he gave himself to the study of models of prayer. I remember well how fervent his supplications; how well chosen his language, when he led the congregation in social worship. It was both a pleasure and a profit to all who joined with him in this exercise.

His call to leave the earth was unexpected. He had no fears. The words of St. Paul were his words, "For I know whom I have believed, and am persuaded that he is able to keep that which I have committed unto him against that day."

John B. Porter closes the list of these revered men who have departed this life. He was the son of elder Robert Porter He was well named John, for he was a disciple who leaned upon his Master's breast. He was possessed, both by nature and by grace, with a lovely disposition. Calm and discreet in his words, even in disposition, pleasant and kind to all, positive in his opinions, firm in his friendships, wise in counsel. In very early life he mas made an officer in the Sabbath School, and for forty years was never absent from his post of duty, save a single Sabbath, because he was absent from the city.

In a church yard in England there is a monument with this inscription: "Here lies one who never caused but one regret to his friends, and that was that he died." The same words might be inscribed upon the monument of this beloved elder.

I cannot close this brief notice of these good men who have rested from their labors, without speaking of one who was their contemporary, and who with the burden of ninety-two years resting upon him, still abides on the earth.

Williard Hall is a name known and honored of all men. Forty-three years he has been a ruling elder in this Church, and for forty years a successful teacher of young men in the Bible class. When he heard the call of the master he threw himself with all his learning, his legal attainments, his social position, at the foot of the cross, and made a thorough consecration of them to the service of God, to be used for his glory. In every department of christian and benevolent effort he has been a constant worker. Not only the Church, but the State has been the better for his living and his doing. He is not with us this day because bodily infirmity forbids it. He is with us in spirit. He has sent me this note, written this day with his own hand, with the request that I would read it this evening.

"Will the members of the Hanover Presbyterian Church of Wilmington, assembled in Centennial worship, hear a word from one who has partaken oft and much with them in the sweet communion of our adorable and worshipped Redeemer? 'Be ye steadfast and immovable, always abounding in the work of the Lord, forasmuch as you know your labor is not in vain in the Lord.'

Yours in Christ, under the hand of sickness.
WILLIARD HALL."

This afternoon he expressed to a former pastor his satisfaction and happy trust for the future, in that Saviour who has been his chief joy in the past years of his life. With him in the evening time it is light.

The great work of life with these ruling elders was a success. They lived and labored to build up this Church. An hundred years have passed and the Church still continues in vigorous life, with a future rich in its promise of strength and usefulness.

Other prosperous Churches have been reared by those who have gone out from her, and so it will be until the end of the ages. Let us all learn this lesson: Whatever may be our providential position in this life, if we live to bless the world, by working through the Church and for the Church, our labor cannot be in vain.

Then, neither in one century of years, nor in a thousand, will our work or the blessed results of it perish.

ELDERS OF THE CHURCH,

AN ADDRESS BY REV. CARSON W. ADAMS.

A young wife, the mother of two lovely children, once said, "My friends tell me that other parents have as good and as beautiful as my own; I suppose it is so; but I cannot make myself believe it."

I confess to a state of mind very much the same in respect to this city, which is the place of my birth and has been the home of my ancestors for many generations. There are doubtless other cities as beautiful for situation and as tasteful in arrangement as this city; there are other streams as romantic as the Brandywine, and walks as pleasant as those on the margin of its sparkling waters; there are other rivers as lordly as the Delaware, upon whose broad surface I have sailed, and in whose genial waters I have, in youthful days, so often bathed. But there is no city, stream, or river so dear to me, and so comely in my eyes, as these, which were the joy of my early years, and grow in interest and affection as life rolls on.

There are other churches, more grand in proportions, more striking in architecture, more venerable with age, richer in historic interest and importance than this edifice in which we are gathered this evening; but there is no temple of the living God on this earth invested with so much interest to me as this one. It was within these walls that I first began to be interested in the preaching of the gospel. It was within these walls that I found peace in believing in a crucified Saviour. It was at this altar that I made confession of Jesus Christ before men. It was under the influence of the grace of God, given through this Church, that life to me was all changed, and an impulse given that has touched everything with which I have had to do with an eternal interest. Her very stones are precious in my sight.

I am glad to be with you this day and participate with you in this Centennial Anniversary. You have already heard from the eloquent lips of Dr. Rockwell of the many and great changes that have taken place both in church and state during these hundred years. In the few years that my recollection spans, great have been the changes in the appearance of the church edifice, greater still the changes in the congregation which found a spiritual home beneath its roof.

As I look down the broad aisle this evening, I am reminded that with a single exception, every one who sat at the head of these pews has gone to the better country. They were a noble company of men and women, who served well their God and their generation.

You have requested me to speak of that portion of the elect who were called to the honors and responsibilities of the office of ruling elder, and whose labors on the earth have ceased.

Some of these men have rested in the grave more than three-quarters of a century, and there is no record left to tell the story of their lives.

Alexander Femister, Lucas Alrich, William Cook, John Fleming, Eleazer McComb, and James Smith, are names found upon the books of the Church, showing that they were members of Session in the early days. Nothing, is now known of them save a few traditionary anecdotes, which show that they were men well known in their own day as successful in the affairs of this world, and regular and conscientious in the discharge of religious duty.

George Monroe, M. D., was contemporary with some of these men whose names have just been alluded to. He was a well read physician. After having exhausted all the means of medical education in this country, he completed his preparation for the practice of his profession in Edinburgh. He became a devout christian, and served this Church in the eldership with zeal and discretion until the day of his death. He was a man of well cultured mind, open and hearty in his intercourse with his brethren, and known of all men as one who hated all dishonesty and deceit. Death came to him as a thief in the night; he retired in his usual health; when his wife awoke in the morning she found her husband dead by her side. He married the daughter of Col. Hazlett, who was killed at the battle of Princeton. His daughter Lydia married Dr. Gilbert, who was pastor of the Church at that time. Mrs. Gilbert was honored and loved for her zeal and her labors of love among this people.

David Harbison served the Church for some years as an elder. He came to the city from Chester County, Pennsylvania, after he had passed middle life. He did what he could to promote the spiritual good of the people over whom he was called to rule.

John Patterson served the Church with great acceptance for many years. He came to this town from Ireland when a boy. He was through his business life a dry goods merchant. He always valued the privileges of the Church, though he did not connect himself with it till he was past middle life. He opposed the call of Mr. Gilbert, because he let it be known that he would not baptize children neither of whose parents were members of the Church.

Upon this point the new pastor was right, and his faithfulness had its reward. Mr. Patterson was among the first who came forward to confess Christ before men under Dr. Gilbert's ministry. An aged member of the Church told me that she distinctly remembers that Mr. Patterson rose at the communion table and expressed his gratification and thanks to Almighty God that he was permitted to sit with his people and partake with them in the feast of commemoration. He was spared the pains of death. While engaged in his business, in the twinkling of an eye, he was not, for God took him.

His son, John C. Patterson, Esq., now worthily succeeds him as an elder in this Church.

Robert Porter is the next name that appears. He was a man, who in his day, was a power in the Session and in the congregation. He was a printer, a bookseller, and the publisher of "The Delaware Journal," the most influential newspaper in the State at that time.

Like most men of mark, he had strong points of disposition and character. But in him grace abounded. Certain traits of mind and will natural to him would have made him unpopular with men, but under the influence of divine grace, they made him more effective as a christian, and more useful to the Church.

Dr. Gilbert described him as a bold and decided christian; sound in the faith; a man of prayer; a keeper of the Sabbath with Puritan strictness. He loved the sanctuary, and delighted to hear the preaching of the word. Revivals were his greatest pleasure, ever willing to make any personal sacrifice to promote them. He was fully in sympathy with the spirit of the age. He lived at a time when the great Benevolent Societies were founded. He began at once to promote their interests by giving with liberality himself, and urging others to do the same. He was an elder in whom his pastor trusted, and upon whom he leaned. He died at the age of sixty-one. Devout men carried him to his grave, amid the tears of a mourning congregation.

Matthew Kean is a name that brings to the mind many pleasant recollections. He was a man of noble presence, and with him were the instincts of a gentleman and the graces of a christian. He had a well informed mind and a large heart. While he loved his Church and her doctrines, (for he was an intelligent Calvinist,) he was a man of catholic feeling, and loved all who were believers in Jesus. He ever manifested a great interest in young men; he had a love for them; the magnetism of this love was felt in the pressure of his hand, with which he always greeted them. He was a man of prayer, and constant in his study of the word of God. He was a man of sterling honesty. In early life he entered into mercantile business and was unfortunate, but by untiring industry and self-denying economy for many years, he was enabled to discharge all his pecuniary obligations. He fulfilled the injunction of the Scripture, "Owe no man anything, but to love one another." He departed this life at the ripe age of eighty-three. He was gathered to his Father's like as a shock of corn cometh in his season. The memory of this good man is fragrant with the odors of heaven.

The name of William Clark suggests the words of our Lord in respect to Nathanael, "Behold an Israelite indeed, in whom there is no guile." Elder Clark was a man of great amiability of disposition and Christ-like in spirit. He was gifted in prayer, always dwelling much in supplication upon the mercy of God to His children. There was one expression which he used frequently in his supplications at the throne of grace, "Indulgent Parent." The fatherhood of God and his long suffering patience was a constant source of wonder and gratitude to this humble believer.

In my earliest Sabbath School experience he was my Sabbath School teacher. He loved to teach the children the word of God, and continued in this work down to the eighty-third year of his age. His only surviving son, B. S. Clark, serves this Church now as its Treasurer.

George Jones was for most of the years of his life a member of this Church, and also an elder. His life was a quiet one, spent in the diligent pursuit of his business, in which he was very successful. He was an amiable, genial man, a great favorite with his friends. When this Church edifice was erected he had his fortune still to make, but like his contemporaries, he made great sacrifices to secure the completion of the building. He had a love for the walls of this sanctuary; within it many of the happiest hours of his life were spent. He was punctual in the duties of his office as a member of Session. He died in the good hope of a blessed immortality, after he had passed four score years on the earth.

Thomas C. Alrich was an elder, who had a good report of those who were without, and he had also the confidence and the love of all who knew him intimately. He was a man of strong will and other marked

DISCOURSE.

BY REV. JAMES M. CROWELL, D. D.

"*For thy servants take pleasure in her stones, and favor the dust thereof.*" Psalm cii : 14.

It is the doctrine of the word of God that there is a living sympathy among christians as those who make up one body and are animated by one spirit. The ground of this appears in the fact that they are all members of Christ's visible body, which is the Church. And this sympathy not only extends to particular persons; it flows out also, and perhaps especially towards the Church, and all that relates to its good. This has been so in every age. When the king of Israel was bowed in deep contrition before God because of his sins and poured out his supplication for mercy in the fifty-first Psalm, he did not forget the Church, even in the absorption of his own sorrow. "In thy good pleasure, O Lord, do good unto Zion!" And though his heart was broken, yet he cried out as earnestly for the building of the walls of Jerusalem, as he did that his own poor broken heart might be bound up and healed. And when again exalted upon the throne in perfect prosperity, he still prayed for the "peace of Jerusalem." And so in the context here. The allusion to this sentiment is most beautiful and touching. "My days are like a shadow that declineth, and I am withered like grass." But it matters not what becomes of *me*. Let me languish and wither away, provided Zion flourish. Though I myself even pass away, yet thou wilt arise and have mercy upon Zion, and I am content, *that* satisfies me.

It is very likely, brethren of the Hanover Street Church, that during this day of centennial memories and celebration, while your minds have been surveying the past, and you have looked along the way in which God has led you, it is quite probable that some such feeling as this has been in the minds of many among you. Especially have thoughts of tenderest affection to this dear old Church been rekindled upon the altar of *your* hearts, who have the longest been familiar with it and have met with God most often in this hallowed spot. And above all do they who feel like the Psalmist that their "days are like a shadow that declineth" cling with most ardent love to this house of God.

Let me then speak to you a little while.

I. *Of the reasons which should induce us to love the Church.* And
II. *Of the good results which follow from such a love.*

1. As to the reasons for loving the Church. The first is *because of the great elements of power that are lodged in it.*

The Church is one of God's great agencies for bringing men to *Himself.* There are other institutions which tend in this direction, and which are of divine appointment. The agency of home influence is largely instrumental in preparing us for the duty of this life, and for the glory of the life to come. It is to parental training,—to a father's counsel, or a mother's teaching,—that a great many are, under God, indebted for the character they possess, and for their hope of heaven.

By the familiar fireside, beneath the welcome shelter of one's early home, an impression and direction are given to the future destiny. "Although grace does not come *by* succession, it commonly comes *in* succession.

The destiny of children is in a very great measure determined by household influence, and the Bible lays great stress upon this fact and gives most urgent and solemn warnings on the ground of it.

But the matter of which I wish now to speak is the *Church* as a divine institution. The Church in her organized capacity, as an instrument for the establishment and continuance of God's kingdom in the earth. Guarded by God's watchful providence for nearly six thousand years, Zion still has salvation written upon its walls, and praise upon its gates. Look at the many good things that are in it.

1. As the Church of the living God " it is *the pillar and ground of the truth.*"

The sacred oracles belong to Zion and in no place does God's truth carry more authority to the consciences of men than in the sanctuary.

2. As the special guardian *of the Sabbath* too, the Church provides for its proper spiritual improvement. Children trained to come to the sanctuary associate solemnity and reverence with its acts of worship, and often catch impressive glimpses of the meaning of its ordinances; the world on this day suspends the busy operations of its secular industry, and with one accord the people come to hear.

3. Then again God has given to the Church " *apostles, prophets,*

evangelists, pastors, and teachers," and for a purpose nobler and grander than our highest thought, " for the perfecting of the saints ; for the work of the ministry ; for the edifying of the body of Christ."

It is a plan of divine contrivance that has ordained the Gospel to be preached.

There is something in the voice of the living minister that gives the truth itself a deeper and more earnest meaning.

Ministerial influence, great as it is in the sanctuary, pervades also the scenes and relations of domestic life. The faithful pastor mingles with his people as far as his human strength allows, and his other duties permit. He counsels and warns the thoughtless ; he tries to stand between them and the great gulf of a lost eternity ; he directs the thoughtful mind, and the troubled soul, and the weary heart to Him to whom alone they should go, even to Christ; he edifies christians ; he comforts the mourner ; he bears in some measure, as if it were his own, the heavy burden that oppresses the sorrowful ; he prays with his people ; he is alive to every good work ; he visits the sick ; he goes with the dying to the border-land, and he stands among the weepers as they bury their beloved dead out of their sight.

4. But above all the special *promise of the Holy Spirit* is given to the Church. Grace visits the household, but it is chiefly in the Church that God displays His saving power. " He loves the gates of Zion more even than the dwellings of Jacob." The work of grace is carried on and perfected amidst the Sabbath and week-day assemblies of the Church. God in a peculiar manner " dwells in Zion," and is the glory in the midst of her.

II. We have reason to love the Church again, *because it is our spiritual home.*

The right spirit of the christian is that of " *a stranger in the earth.*" He has no real home here but in the Church, and in it he finds a foretaste, and an emblem of the Church above where his rest and his home shall be forever. And this home-love is a most healthy feeling in reference to the Church. It is just the very state of mind in which we should abide. It will induce a quietness, a satisfaction, a repose, which will be found most favorable to real soul prosperity, and the surest token of an approaching blessing.

The text speaks of God's servants taking pleasure " in the *stones* of Zion." Does not that mean that they love it very much as we love the dear spot of our childhood's days, the place of our birth, where we grew up into life? So the Church is the birthplace of souls. " This and that man was born there" should be said of it. Oh, how tenderly, how profoundly do men love the home of their early days. Long years of separation from it in the cold world do not alienate them from the tender memories that gather around it. When far away from it, in the wanderings of this strange life, whithersoever their steps may lead them, their thoughts will turn with living gentleness and tearful remembrance to the place where they were little children, and the dearest place on earth to them will be the home where their parents died. There everything keeps fresh and beautiful, though the old doors creak upon their hinges, and the very porches round the house decay; there the old trees fling out their arms as if in loving welcome, and there the brook leaps gaily along as if it were singing of the happy past.'

> "The sunshine steals through the hanging boughs,
> With a softened holy light, ♦
> And the silent stars gleam purest there,
> In the hush of the Summer night."

Now it seems to me, my brethren, that the true idea of the Church is, that it is our home— our spiritual home—the home of the heart, where we are to live and stay, and grow up, and get ready for our everlasting home. There is the idea of *permanency* about it. It *abides*: we pass away. The Church *stands*. It is a place, not in which we are to tarry for a season only; not in which we are to be transient guests, but in which we are to spend our life as christians; where our names are to be recorded, and our children are to be given to God; where we are to wait and seek for the blessings of the covenant; at whose communion table we are to expect to have our beloved sitting some day, and from whose sweet and solemn and endearing ordinances we are to go up to heaven.

There is nothing to me more beautiful and impressive than this strong devoted attachment which we often see in the case of those who have been worshipping God for many years in the same Church. How delightful to see the tender, clasping affection with which they take pleasure even "*in the stones thereof.*"

II. And now, *as to the happy results of such a love to the Church*, one is

First. An increasing spirit of kindness and conciliation and forbearance towards those who worship with us.

It must needs be in this world of imperfection and varied temperaments and character, that any association of persons continued from year to year will develop some tendencies to alienation from one another. This is so in churches as well as anywhere else. But where the feeling exists among christians, that their Church is their home, where they intend to live and die if possible; there gradually grows up a spirit of tender kindness and mutual conciliation and forbearance, which goes very far to smooth away any unpleasant feeling which may arise, and to remove roots of bitterness and banish unjust suspicions and unkind misunderstandings. The members of the Church are members of the same family, and the Church is *theirs*, their home, their place for labor. The life of the Church is in its members, not in its officers, not in its pastor. *They* may die, or be taken away. the Church in its organic life, remains. And it is a sad fact in the case of any Church, when its life resides in its pastor, or is so connected with him, that no earthly hand but his can hold it together.

The only right theory on this subject is that the vitality of the Church is in the living members of it, and their seed after them. Then, through all changes and through successive generations, it will abide, and grow, and flourish, and bear fruit.

Great changes come to us all in this uncertain world. When any one of mature or advanced life goes back to the scenes of his childhood, he feels that this is so. He knows no one, and no one knows him. Strange little children are playing around him, and new people occupy the houses; many of the names even upon the tombstones are unknown to him. But it is a joy for us to know that *God's covenant stands*, and the *Church abides*, and the promise of God, is unto even "*the generations to come.*"

Second. Another good result of this home-love to the Church, is that it leads parents to cling to the Church where their children were baptized.

The passing years as they roll on exert a great influence in drawing away the children of the Church. Worldliness and fashion, and social connections, and systems of religion more outwardly attractive, throw their snares and temptations around the paths in which our children go. And, therefore, it is of the first importance that they should be trained to love the Church in which they were brought up; to love the *Church* I say, not so much the *Minister*, for if I may use the expression so as to be understood, ministers are emphatically human institutions, *i. e.*, they are only earthen vessels; they are full of weakness and error; are very imperfect and very frail. They change and pass away also. Their strength gives way beneath the pressure of their work; they grow weary and fall by the roadside; but the Church *abides;* its identity holds on; its name and place continue from age to age. "The workmen perish but the work goes on."

And, therefore, it is a good thing to be rooted ourselves, and to have our children rooted in that which will survive; in that which holds on while the years pass away : in the Church of our love and choice through which, amidst all human changes, that river keeps flowing whose streams make glad the city of God. Oh, there is a *power* in this attachment to the Church of our fathers, as a means of leading the soul to God, which we sadly fail to recognize. Sometimes after years have passed away, and the covenant seems almost to have been forgotten by God *Himself*, it turns out at last that He has *not* forgotten the children whose parents were long in heaviness, because they wandered from the instructions of their childhood ; even some whose parents went down to the grave in sadness because of their distance from God,—yea, even some who seem not to have been won back to God by the death of those that nourished and brought them up, even *such* children are reclaimed and brought to Christ through the ordinances of that Church in which their parents worshipped God. They *themselves* go up from the courts of God below, and serve Him in His temple, but God is still in the Church.

He has said it, "This is my rest forever, here will I dwell," and so it often comes to pass that those prayers and tears of christian parents, which seem to be stored away somewhere in the heavens as of no account, if they even entered at all through the veil, turn out by and by to have been laid away only as in the time of drought the summer clouds are laid up, and then like them they pour down a more abundant treasure.

Third. Another good result of this feeling of affection for the Church as our spiritual home is, " *That it leads to a regular and conscientious attendance upon its stated means of grace.*"

And this too, both for ourselves and for those over whom we have authority or influence. The worship of God above everything else, should be attended to as a matter of *principle*, not of impulse, or of fancy, or of fickle taste ; not as that from which we are to gather only entertainment or pleasure, even though it be of a religious kind. God's worship, when correctly considered is the *discipline* of our nature ; it is our soul's *food ;* we are to *grow* by it, to *get strong* upon it, to be *developed into* "men in Christ Jesus." And, therefore, the very best and most healthy feeling that we can have about it is, that it is the regular, stated, constant service of our spiritual home. It is one of the evil tendencies of our day that people crave that form of enjoyment which can be found away from home. The calm and moderate pleasure of the domestic circle is not stimulating enough to them, and so they seek what can be found elsewhere. *And what is worse still,* this same unhappy loss of sympathy,—this same painful separation of parents and children takes place in the matter of religion, and in regard *to the Church.* Children are permitted to go according to the leading of their own foolish fancies, and fall into a state of religious dissipation before their parents are aware of it, while the natural opposition of their hearts to God early makes them crave indulgence in the matter of His worship. When children are left to go to Church *where* they want, and just *when* they want, it seems to me that the likelihood of their conversion is very much diminished. And if they *are* brought to Christ, they will indeed be "*miracles of grace.*"

Oh, how much more beautiful and holy is the sight when parents and children go up for years together to the same sanctuary, as in that most Church going of all lands—Scotland; where the dear kirk is the spiritual home of all the family; where children walk in the same ways of the covenant along which their fathers went, and where the blessings of the covenant seem, so to speak, to come down the generations so naturally and so easily; where, like Abraham, the servants of God "command their children after them to keep the way of the Lord;" where with firm yet gentle hand and with patient untiring prayer, the children are taught to love their spiritual home; and where the beauty of grace in childhood does not fade, and the fragrance does not die.

Oh it is not strange that they who thus love Zion, see their children's children coming into the Church, and that "peace is upon Israel."

And now, as a fitting close to the impressive services of this memorial day, let me appeal to those before me, who are to take the places in which these venerable fathers of this Church have stood.

The passing years have gathered *them* up to the great host of the glorified. Does it not become therefore the great duty of those that survive to take pleasure in the very stones of this beloved Zion, and favor the very dust thereof?

You have, every one of you, some work to do in building up the Church. Its grand mission is to glorify God, and to bless and save the world. There *are* some, alas, that call *themselves* God's *servants,* but they are not *serving.* They profess to be in the vineyard, but they are not *working.* They say they are *soldiers,* but they are not *fighting.* Yet one thing is certain—*The Church will be built.* If you sit still it will be built. But you shall miss the satisfaction of helping in its building. Every stone shall be put into its place, and the pinnacle shall soar aloft towards the sky, but every stone from the foundation to the pinnacle will say to you, "Thou hadst nothing to do with this,—thou hadst no hand in this."

It is said that when Cyrus took one of his guests round his garden, the guest admired it greatly, and said he had much pleasure in it. "Ah!" said Cyrus, "you may enjoy it, but you have not such pleasure in it as I have, for I have planted every tree in it myself."

One reason why the glorious sufferer of Calvary has so much pleasure in His Church, and rejoices over it with joy, is because He *did* so much, and *endured* so much for it.

And so shall it be in some humble measure with all His followers who watch, and toil, and pray, and build for Zion.

May God make you faithful and steadfast.

This is no time for idleness in the Church; there is no room for idlers; it is no time for spasmodic piety; such piety is spurious; it is no time for the mere semblance and form of religion; no time for ritualistic formalism, or sentimental dreaming; it is the time for *work* and for *service*.

Blessed are they who are faithful to duty and steadfast all the time. For the time itself is short. The Master Himself said that "the night cometh when no man can work."

God's workmen are gathering to rest; the curfew-bells are ringing across the weary years; the shadows of the evening time are falling; the blessed ones that do His commandents, that they may have right to the tree of life, are entering in through the gates into the city; and soon for *us*, those gates shall all be *shut!*

THE SAILOR'S MAGAZINE.

Vol. 36.   NOVEMBER, 1863.   No. 3.

Pastors their own Agents.

Much has been written upon the question of Agencies for benevolent Societies—how far they are needful, or may be dispensed with; how far pastors may be relied on to do their work, &a.

Without any desire to agitate this question, we take pleasure in calling the attention of our readers to the following sermon by the Rev. J. E. Rockwell, DD. of Brooklyn. It is the third sermon with which he has favored us, at our request, in the last three years, each having been preached to his own congregation on the occasion of their annual collection for the American Seamens' Friend Society.

Dr. Rockwell's opinions respecting the worthiness of this Society have the more value inasmuch as he is one of its Board of Trustees, and so well acquainted with its operations; while his well established character for honesty and frankness vouches for their fidelity to his convictions.

We commend this sermon, and the fact that a busy city pastor can find time and interest enough to enable him to preach *annually* for our cause, to other pastors; hoping that his example may incite some of them to go and do likewise.

We believe all Agents, who are worthy of their position, would gladly retire from congregations where the cause which they love may have such advocates. One Secretary, who has given the earnest labors of the best sixteen years of his life to the work of sustaining evangelical societies, desires to bargain with any pastor or people who will do this work within their own bounds, that, on this condition, he will cheerfully yield the field to him.

Brethren in the ministry! our appeal is to *you*.

"GO UP NOW; LOOK TOWARDS THE SEA."

A PLEA FOR THE SAILOR.

A Sermon preached in the Central Presbyterian Church of Brooklyn, Sept. 13th, 1863, at the Annual Collection for the A. S. F. Soc. by Rev. J. E. ROCKWELL, D. D.

1st KINGS, 18.—43.—*Go up now, look towards the Sea.*

These words were the command of Elijah to his servant when, at the close of the long drought which had fallen upon the land during the reign of Ahab, he was praying that the windows of Heaven might be opened, and the parched earth revived. Desirous of seeing the first indications of the answer to his prayer, the Prophet, who had retired to the top of Carmel to pray, desired his servant to advance a little nearer to its precipitous sides as it faces the Mediterranean, and look toward the sea, and bring him tidings of the appearance of the sky in the direction whence he knew the rain would approach the land. Six times did the servant bear back to the Prophet the message that "there is nothing;" once more he went, and returned with the news "behold there ariseth a little cloud out of the sea like a man's hand."

Elijah well understood that sign, and saw in it the harbinger of a plentiful shower.

Without pausing to pursue the narrative immediately connected with the words we have chosen for our present contemplation, we propose to make them the guide to our thoughts as we present to you some *considerations upon the Sea*, and those who dwell upon its mighty waters.

To the thoughtful mind the Ocean always has its solemn lessons. Who can even look forth upon that

"Glorious mirror where the Almighty form
"Glasses itself in tempests"

and not think of him who gave the sea its bounds, and who "measureth the waters in the hollow of his hand." What a lesson it reads to us in all its vast upheavings, and the wild roar of its billows, of the power and wisdom and glory of Him who by a word called the waters together and said, "Hitherto shalt thou come but no further, and here shall thy proud waves be stayed."—What an image and emblem is the sea of God's own immensity and eternity. Through how many ages has it rolled on unchanged. The storm sweeps over it but leaves no trace of its fury. Time has been busy; but though the marble monument has crumbled beneath its touch, and the mighty fortress has fallen, and cities and palaces lie in ruins, and the Earth itself shows the marks of its busy fingers,—the sea bears no trace of age or decay.—Generation on generation have risen and stood by its shores, and listened to the music of its ripples and the thunder of its surf—and have passed away.—Yet its dark waters swell and flow, and its wild billows sing their requiem over the dead.

"Time writes no wrinkles on its azure brow,
"Such as Creation's dawn beheld, it rolleth now."

And who can stand and look upon the sea and feel no emotions of wonder and awe and no thoughts of Him who made the Ocean what it is.—What a lesson of our own insignificance and of God's greatness and glory do we learn as we ride upon its heaving billows, or see them breaking at our feet. Its waves instruct us; and its voice joining in the great Anthem of the Universe declares that God only is great.

Its boundless expanse, whose extent no human eye can measure, is a faint image of the infinitude of Him whose power and essence have no limit. And in all its words of peace or wild commotion, of rest or storm, it tells us that He who made it is Almighty and Eternal.

But aside from these general and more obvious lessons of the Sea let us notice

1. The prominence which is given to it in the history of the world. The sea has been and still is the great highway of Nations, while at the same time it has served to divide them one from another. Its waters roll as mighty walls between the Eastern and Western Continents, and they set in between the various portions of the old world and the new, to divide nations that differ from each other in laws, customs and religion. Hence in times of peace, in the ordinary exchange of commerce it is whitened with the outspread wings of ships, bearing the fruits of Art and of Agriculture.—And in times of war it is covered with the fleets of contending nations, and upon its broad bosom often the fate of a belligerent people is decided. When the Persian Monarch who had determined to extend his control over Greece, had marched to Athens flushed with his success at Thermopylæ, he saw his career checked and his power weakened at Salamis, where his fleet of one thousand galleys, carrying each two hundred and thirty men, was defeated and routed by the Greeks with only three hundred and eighty ships. So too the dominion of Rome and the reign of Augustus and his successors was secured at Actium, in the sea-fight between Octavius and Mark Anthony; and the decline of the Ottoman Empire dates from the battle of Lepanto, when the Turkish fleet was destroyed; while Navarino and Trafalgar are recognized in modern history as turning points in the history of Greece and England. These allusions to the past will serve to illustrate the pre-eminence which the Ocean has had

in the history of the world, and in deciding the fate of nations.—And when we "look toward the Sea" we cannot but recall the mighty struggles for Conquest or Liberty, which have there decided the destinies of millions of the human race, and on whose results the interests of the world were suspended.

We look out upon that mighty mass of heaving waters and think that they are mingled with all the mighty struggles of the nations for conquest, or glory, or power, or liberty, and have often seen the oppressor and the tyrant driven back and defeated, when his legions on the land seemed destined to carry woe and misery among the people whom they sought to conquer. The history of all nations has, as one of its most essential and important elements, their work upon the sea either with the peaceful wings of commerce or the mighty struggle for naval supremacy. And when the sea shall give up its dead, a vast multitude, swelling out into untold numbers shall come forth from the silent caverns of the Ocean, who have gone down amid the roar of battle, or the wrath of the tempest—sent forth by the hand of commerce or in the protection of a nation's rights and liberties.

II. Let us notice, again, the frequent mention which is made of the Sea in the Scriptures. Aside from the allusions to the Ocean as an indication of the power and majesty of Jehovah which we every where meet, we find frequent mention made of it as in some way connected with God's gracious purposes towards the Church and the world. It was the sea which he used as his mighty instrument in overthrowing the armies of Pharaoh ;—when its walls stood up like adamant until the people of God had passed through, and re-flowing at his word covered the hosts of Egypt and swallowed them up in one common grave.—The Psalms and the Prophecies are full of allusions to the sea as one of the Divine agents in the accomplishment of his designs for the destruction of his enemies, and the upbuilding and glory of his Church: Isaiah, when beholding the future triumphs of the Messiah's kingdom, sees among the wonders of that day the abundance of the sea converted to him, and her mighty hosts flocking to him as clouds and as doves to their windows ; and Jeremiah beholds the sea used as God's agent in the destruction of his enemies and those of his people, as Babylon is covered with the multitude of her waves! While many of Christ's most mighty works were done by and upon the sea. There he often gathered the people to hear him, and from its hardy sons he selected some of his noblest and most faithful Apostles.

III. With this brief notice of the historical and prophetic interest which is connected with the Ocean, let us turn to some of the lessons of practical importance which we may learn as we look towards the Sea.

1st. Let us think of the multitudes who make it their home in the ordinary avocations of commercial or national life. It is estimated that between two and three millions of men are engaged as sailors, either upon the broad Ocean, or upon the great inland waters of the Eastern and Western Continents. These men go forth as the heralds and messengers of civilization, or the defenders of their nation's honor and liberty, or as the agents of commerce without whom the inhabitants of the great continents and islands of the globe would be as utterly separated and insulated as though occupying different planets. Ever since the Earth was peopled the sea has thus been the pathway of intercommunication. Even when there was no compass to guide the mariner, there were vast fleets which, following the coasts and watching the stars, bore the products of Art and Agriculture, and aided largely in the enriching of the nations by whom they were sent forth;—while as Science in her progress, mapped the trackless Ocean and went before the sailor with her unerring directions, the sea became white with the wings of commerce, until her hardy sons form, now, a nation by themselves.

And this thought reminds us that the dwellers upon the land owe a large debt of gratitude to the sailor for the part he performs in increasing the wealth or in supporting the honor and liberty and adding to the comfort of the nations for which he is engaged. The multitude who have perished on the sea have mainly died in the service of those who live upon the land-Those who are now undergoing the perils of the Ocean, breasting its storms and battling with its billows, or are meeting the enemies of their country in the deadly strife, are serving those who are at home, who are in some way reaping the benefit of their toils and hardships.

If Science and Literature are to be enriched by valuable additions to the stores of knowledge, the sailor must be employed to aid in the work. The gift of the new world to the old, and the peopling of these vast Continents with Colonists from the Eastern Hemisphere, was accomplished by means of the sailor. He it is who enriches the stores of national literature by the volumes which he brings from beyond the sea. He it is who bears to us the fabrics of the looms of other lands in exchange for the products of our farms or the wealth of our mines; or who standing beneath the broad folds of the flag that floats as the symbol of his nation, sustains its honor or dies in its defence.

2nd. Again let us consider the intimate relations that exist between the dwellers upon the sea and the land. Far out upon the deep we behold the lessening sails of a ship, soon to vanish from our sight. Another and another passes away from the land under the pressure of the freshening breeze, and every gallant ship that sweeps away from our sight contains husbands, brothers and sons, the comfort and support of many a household.

How many Wives and Mothers and Sisters will watch each gathering cloud, and as they hear the howling of the tempest, will think of those loved ones far out at sea, and tremble with fear, and watch for the hour that shall restore them to kindred and home. Every noble and manly tar that looks out upon the wild war of the elements, and climbs the tapering mast, or hangs out on the swaying spar over the yawning gulph, and hears the roar of the waters and the sighing of the wind, and knows not how soon the sea may be his grave, has in these long hours of darkness and storm many an anxious thought of mother or wife or children, who keep their vigils for him and daily send up their prayers for his safety.

We can never read of a wreck at sea without knowing that there are those on shore on whom that event will fall a blight to all their hopes.

All around us are those who have special and intimate relations with the sea, and whatever sympathy we manifest for the sailor, whatever we do for his spiritual or temporal welfare, is felt by many a heart that is bound to him by every tie that makes home and friendship dear and sacred.

3d. Again the sea reminds us, as we stand and look forth upon it, of the perils of those who, for our sake, go down upon its waters and make it their home. Yonder lies a wreck, fast bedded in the sand; the waves play madly and freely around it, and on its huge timbers the sea has hung its green mantle of weeds and slime. What a story could that desolate ruin tell, had it but a tongue to speak. How often since it first glided into the treacherous element, which was to be its home, had its broad wings been outstretched to the freshening gale as it sped along its trackless path.

Many an eye, wet with the parting tear, watched the receding vessel until the last sail had sunk below the horizon.—Then came day, and night, and sunshine, and cloud, and the dream of home, until the gale awoke the Ocean from its slumbers and the ship, like a frightened bird, fled before its wrath.

The landsman reposed in peace upon his pillow, and as the voice of the storm howled by his casement, felt only a pleasing sense of his own security. But far out upon the Ocean there was the long struggle with the elements,—the night of watching and fear and despair, the convulsive motions of the staggering vessel as the waves broke over it, the strange and unearthly moaning of its huge timbers as they yielded to the power of the tempest, and the closing scene when, a rugged and shapeless mass, it is swallowed up amid the waters, or is thrown upon the beach to tell, in voiceless eloquence, its sad and impressive story. There it lies amid its solitude and desolation, with the ceaseless roar of the surf and the sighing of the wind for its solemn requiem. The tempest has accomplished its work—the waters are lulled to rest, the moon looks forth in beauty upon the scene; but where are the brave men who made that vessel their home? How many desolate and and widowed hearts will mourn long in bitter grief and agony over the loved and the lost who may never more come back to them.

And yet this is but a faint shadow of the more fearful perils of the soul to which the sailor is exposed. His return in safety to the land may be followed by storms of temptation beneath whose power he falls a hopeless victim. Hardly have his feet touched the shore ere he is beset by crowds of the vile who seize upon him as their prey, and who, if he be not surrounded by Divine influences, will leave him a wreck of health and property and honor and soul.

4. Lastly let us consider the final meeting at the bar of God, when the sea shall at length give up its dead. The Ocean is the grave of untold multitudes. Ever since the first frail vessel trembled upon its faint ripple as it died upon the shore, it has been gathering in its harvest of death,—and its currents have borne them down to unknown depths, and its weeds and shells and caverns have been their windingsheet, their coffin and their grave. Amid the peaceful pursuits of commerce, in exploration of unknown seas, and in the fearful shock of battle, thousands have sunk down to their fathomless graves; and every year is adding to their countless numbers.

But the day is hastening when we shall come forth from the long sleep of death, and the dead of the sea shall meet the dead of the land, all again instinct with life and together meeting around the throne of judgment. What a scene will that be! What memories will then be awakened! What solemn meetings will occur between friends long separated—between the sailor who perished as the victim to the temptations of the land that lured him to his ruin, or from the neglect of those who might have stretched out a hand to save him, and who cruelly turned from him, and permitted him to pass on to ruin unchecked by the Christian influences which, if properly thrown around him, would have saved him.

And now gathering up these threads of thought, let me take them as the basis of a plea for the sailor.

For obvious reasons the work of the Church among seamen must be a special and separate branch of Christian benevolence requiring a special and distinct agency. This agency is the "American Seamens' Friend Society," which carries on its operations

1st. By means of Chaplains for seamen in all the various ports where they most abound.

2nd. By the establishment of Ship Libraries.

3d. By means of Sailors' Homes.— The results of the working of this system form a most unanswerable argument for the Society whose claims I present to-day.

1st. The Sailor evidently needs the sustaining power, the sure guidance, and the blessed comforts of the religion of Jesus Christ. He needs them as we all do in our poor fallen nature—and his peculiar trials and temptations are such as religion can alone meet and overcome.

2d. The Church owes a special debt of gratitude to the sailor, which can best be shown by efforts for his moral and spiritual improvement. As Commerce, Art, Science and Literature are all under obligation to him, so also he aids the Church in her Missionary work—bears abroad her agents and teachers, and printing presses and books, and becomes in many ways the representative of the Church and of Christianity among the Heathen.

3d. The sailor justly claims the sympathies and gratitude of all who dwell upon the land. There is no household however poor which has not some comfort or luxury for the possession of which they are indebted to the sailor. The oil that supplies the lamp is obtained by the sailor. The luxuries of the table, are many of them, brought by him from foreign climes—the raiment that we wear was wrought in the looms of the old world, and never could have reached us but for the sailor. The vast cities rising upon our seaboard, and growing in wealth and power, owe their increasing wealth to the sailor. The flag that we reverence, and that has been honored in every clime, has been borne and protected by the sailor. It was a sailor's heart that prompted the utterance of those memorable words which have become the watch-word of our nation — "Don't give up the Ship."— And shall we refuse to give to him a substantial proof of our sympathy and regard, by providing for him those moral and religious influences that may save his soul, and make him in all his influences a blessing and not a curse?

4th. Lastly, I plead for the sailor, because of the good he is capable of doing when his character is moulded and influenced by the Gospel of Christ. The history of the Church and the Providence of God seem to point to him as one of the most potent agents to be used for the conversion of the world. There was a wonderful significance in the choice which Christ made of his Apostles to whom he was to commit the great work of establishing his Church. When the mind of a sailor receives the truth, he does not hesitate to make known his convictions and experience. He is an earnest man, and when he gives himself to Christ he will make his influence felt, and that for good.

And among the most hopeful signs of the times we now behold, we find coming to us from the sea the voice of prayer and praise as the harbinger of better things, and the foreshadow of the day when the abundance of the sea shall be converted to God and the isles shall wait for his law. On almost every vessel that now leaves our ports may be found some, at least, that are the followers of Christ. On many vessels no spirituous liquors are allowed to be used, and no profane swearing is heard. On others many of the officers are religious men, or the sailors conduct meetings for prayer in the forecastle; and so the voice of prayer and thanksgiving arises from the solitudes of the Ocean, amid the shrill piping of the wind and the deep diapason of the surging sea.

As these men return home, or enter a foreign port, they no longer carry with them those corrupt and demoralizing influences which have too long attended the sailor, but often act as missionaries for Christ, bringing blessing and not a curse.

Who can estimate the value of such a work as may be accomplished by the sailor when his heart is wholly given to Christ. We have seen living illustrations of the power of a Christian sailor which no man could gainsay. The life of Commodore Hudson, who never hesitated to bear his testimony for his Saviour, and who recognized the hand of God in every event of life, was a precious evidence of the power of a sailor when his heart is under the influence of religion.

He was often the Chaplain of his own ship—and never hesitated to throw all his influence, both as a man and an Officer, in favor of morality, benevolence, righteousness, temperance and truth.

And who that ever knew the late gallant and lamented Admiral Foote, will forget what an immense power for good he every where carried with him. What a noble specimen of a man he was! With all the generous impulses of a Sailor subdued and refined and moulded by the grace of God, fearless of dangers, standing unmoved amidst the iron hail that poured upon his ship from the enemies of his Country, trusting wholly in God even with the simplicity of a child, ever thoughtful of the wants and the necessities of others, and especially devoted to the great interests of benevolence and religion, to-day fighting the battles of his Country, and to-morrow entering a house of prayer and acceptably leading the devotion of God's people, wearing himself out in the service of his country and dying the calm and blessed death of the Christian Hero. What an example he was to others!—What an evidence of the power of a holy life, and of the influence of a Sailor when his heart is filled with the love to Christ.

And these illustrations are but two of the many of the hopefulness of the Cause which looks to the Sea as the chief theatre of its operations. When we reach a sailor's heart with Christian influences, we touch an electric chord which may communicate saving truths to men who are now sitting in darkness and the shadow of Death. When you place in his hands the Lamp of God's word, you will soon see that light shining amid other scenes undimmed and unwasted, upheld by a hand that never wavers, and borne onward under the impulses of a heart that never knows fear or shame, and that will not falter even amid persecutions and trials.

Lifes's Answer.
BY THE DEAN OF CANTERBURY.

I know not if the dark or bright
Shall be my lot;
If that wherein my hopes delight
Be boat or not.

It may be mine to drag for years
Toil's heavy chain:
Or day and night my meat be tears
On bed of pain.

Dear faces may surround my hearth
With smiles and glee;
Or I may dwell alone, and mirth
Be strange to me.

My bark is wafted to the strand
By breath divine;
And on the helm there rests a hand
Other than mine.

One who has known in storms to sail,
I have on board;
Above the raving of the gale,
I hear my Lord.

He holds me when the billows smile—
I shall not fall.
If sharp 'tis short; if long 'tis light;
He tempers all.

Safe to the land, safe to the land—
The end is this:
And then with Him go hand in hand,
Far into bliss.
Macmillan's Magazine.

George Whitefield on the Atlantic;
OR THE POWER OF CHRISTIAN KINDNESS AND CONSISTENCY.

A voyage to America, during the last century, was not the comparatively easy thing which, through the onward march of modern science, it has now become. For many long and weary weeks, even months, the sailor to the Western Hemisphere might be kept tossing on the deep by unfavorable winds, or lying in the deep calm, as idle

'As a painted ship
Upon a painted ocean.'

The very length of the voyage, however, which tried their patience, increased the opportunities of usefulness to those who watched for every occasion of doing good to others; and blessed are they that 'sow beside all waters.' The noble evangelist who could say, 'I want more tongues, more bodies, more souls for the Lord Jesus,—had I ten thousand, He should have them all'— and who was going to America to lay out his time and strength in preaching Christ, found in the ship in which he sailed, and which did not reach her haven for four months, a wide door and effectual for the prosecution of the work to which he had devoted himself. A more unpromising outset, and yet a more happy end of labor, perhaps no watchman in the Lord's vineyard ever experienced. To Whitefield the scene was new. He was on board a ship full of soldiers, proverbially a hardened and careless set of men. The naval and the military officers were all determinedly set against religion, and looked on the man of God as a hypocrite and impostor. 'The first Lord's day one of them played on the hautboy, and nothing was to seen but cards, and little heard but cursing and blasphemy.' Mild reproof he made use of, when he heard his Lord's name profaned, yet the effects were at first discouraging. 'I could do no more,' he says, 'for a season, than, while I was writing, now and then turn my head by way of reproof to a lieutenant of the soldiers, who swore as though he was born of a swearing constitution. Now and then he would take the hint, return my nod with a "Doctor, I ask your pardon," and then to his cards and swearing again.'

From the cabin occupants Whitefield turned to the steerage passengers, among whom he moved with so much gentleness and love, that he quite won their hearts, disarmed their prejudices, and was eventually gladdened by obtaining a hearing from the soldiers, whom he styles his 'red-coat parishioners,' and to whom he read and expounded the Bible between decks, twice a day.

No service was as yet allowed to be held in the great cabin; but gradually a way was opened up for this also. The captain of the ship slept in the 'round house.' On Whitfield's solicitation, he gave him permission to retire to it occasionally for devotional purposes, along with a few companions. In the neighborhood of this, the weather-beaten skipper might be seen standing, and overhearing the words of prayer sent up to the throne of God on high.

Who can tell the effect produced on him by listening, it may be, to supplications on his own behalf, poured forth by the very man whose godly ways, on his first embarking, he had so heartily disliked?

Some time afterwards, being invited by the military captain to take a cup of coffee with him, Whitfield embraced the opportunity of telling him 'that he thought it a little odd to pray and preach to the servants, and not to the master.' adding, 'that if he thought proper, he would make use of a short collect now and then, to him and the other gentlemen, in the great cabin.' To this an ominous shake of the head was given, followed up with the remark, 'I think we may, when we have nothing else to do.' It was not, however, till they had experienced a month's detention, from cross winds off Deal that the evangelist's hopes of speaking a word for his Master in the main cabin were gratified. A visible change had come over the ship's captain after his perusing a religious book which Whitfield one day placed on his pillow, in exchange for one on politics which he found lying there, and of which he courteously begged the sailor's acceptance, when next morning, with a smile, he asked if he knew who had made the exchange. About the same time the military captain met him one day, as he came from his wonted work among the common soldiers, and told him that he 'might have public service and expounding twice a day, in the great cabin.'

The scene on board the ship was now greatly changed. The soldiers, who saw from Whitfield's daily efforts for their good, that he was in earnest in seeking their souls' welfare, had been greatly melted under the word faithfully proclaimed in their hearing; and the declaration of the Lord's message of mercy to fallen sinners, was now reverently and attentively listened to on the part of the very officers of the cabin who had at first so hotly opposed the preacher. How true it is that, when a man's ways please the Lord, He maketh even his enemies to be at peace with him; and how often is a consistent and holy walk the instrument of recommending the Gospel to its most inveterate opposers! A patient continuance in well-doing on the part of Christian professors, attests the *reality* of that which is their animating principle, and proves it to be indeed a thing tangible, and not, as many suppose, 'the baseless fabric of a vision.'

The ship touched at Gibraltar to take in more troops, and here Whitfield had an opportunity of preaching on shore, in a place 'in which, being, as it were, a public rendezvous of all nations, he thought he saw the world in epitome.' His preaching here was accompanied with a blessing from above. 'Samson's riddle,' says he, 'was fulfilled here: out of the strong came forth sweetness. Who more unlikely to be wrought on than soldiers! And yet, among any set of people I have not been where God has made His power more known. Many that were blind have received their sight, many that had fallen back have repented and turned to the Lord again: many that were ashamed to own Christ openly, have waxen bold, and many saints had their hearts filled with joy unspeakable and full of glory.'

Once more afloat on the mighty deep, Whitfield realized a blessed answer to his prayers. Instead of having to preach, as formerly, both in the cabin and between decks, the drum was now beat by order of the officers, morning and evening, and all the ship's company assembled on the deck. He now preached, supported by a captain on each side, while the companies of other two ships sailing along with them, being 'now in the trade winds, drew near and joined in the worship of God.' 'The great cabin was now become a Bethel: both captains were daily more and more affected, and a crucified Saviour, and the things pertaining to the kingdom of God, were the usual topics of their conversation.'

How altered the whole aspect of the vessel! 'Cards and profane books were thrown overboard. An oath became a strange thing. The soldiers began to learn to read and write, and the children to repeat their prayers regularly.' The good impressions made were deepened by the breaking out of a fever on board during which Whitfield was unintermitting in his attention to the sick,— crawling on his knees between decks, administering medicines or cordials to them, and such advice as seemed suitable to their circumstances.'

At length they came in sight of thei

desired haven. All on board were naturally joyful at the close of so tedious a voyage; 'but how infinitely more glad,' is the remark of Whitfield on the occasion, 'will the children of God be, when, having passed through the waves of this troublesome world, they arrive at the haven of everlasting rest!'

We cannot close this rapid sketch of the effects produced by the power of kindness, and the force of Christian consistency during a single voyage across the great Atlantic, without reminding our readers that in the circumstances now narrated, GEORGE WHITFIELD displayed a higher amount of moral heroism than perhaps on any other occasion of his eventful life. Those of the Lord's people reading these lines, who may have had long sea voyages, well know the peculiar difficulties which have to be encountered on board ships when the captain and officers are opposed to what is good, and will readily appreciate the tact and courage by which the noble evangelist of last century was distinguished in the first passage to America. Of the months then spent on the broad ocean, Whitfield, writing many years after, takes the following pleasing retrospect: —'Even at this distance of time, the remembrance of the happy hours I enjoyed in religious exercises on deck, is refreshing to my soul: and although nature sometimes relented at being taken from my friends, and I was little accustomed to the inconveniences of a sea-life, yet a consciousness that I had the glory of God and the good of souls in view, afforded me from time to time unspeakable satisfaction.'

The success of those labors, by God's blessing, on which a floating hell was turned into a Bethel, may well stimulate all who are working for the souls of others, to persevere in spite of every discouragement. On the question being put to Judson, when laboring in Burmah, whether he thought the prospects bright for the speedy conversion of the heathen, his answer was, '*As bright as the promises of God.*' Laborers in God's vineyard, in any sphere! it is on the strength of these very promises that you are to cast your line as spiritual fishers for men's souls. Have you labored long without seeing much fruit, and you are sometimes ready to yield to despair? Still let Gideon's characteristic of old be yours.—Though 'faint,' be 'yet pursuing. And among the many means you may employ, forget not to make trial of the law of Christian kindness, and your experience may be that of Henry Martyn, on India's shores, 'The power of gentleness is irresistible.'

"Thou must be true thyself,
If thou the truth would'st teach.

The Russian Navy.

THE appearance in our bay of a small fleet of Russian men-of-war, and the presence in our streets of a number of the sailors of the Czar, naturally excite a desire for some knowledge of the naval strength which the Emperor of all the Russias has at his command.

The war in the Crimea acted as a boundary line between the Russian navy of the past and that of the present, and the fleet as it is found to-day knows but little history beyond the date on which was concluded the treaty of Paris. The last aggressive act of the old navy was the destruction of the Turkish fleet in the Asiatic harbor of Sinope—an undertaking which did not add much glory to the prowess of the Russian Empire. After this display of maritime strength the Russian ships in the Black Sea were sunk in the harbor of Sevastopol; while those of the Baltic sought shelter under the fortifications of Cronstadt; and a few in the north lay rotting under cover of the guns of Archangel.

THE RUSSIAN FLEET BEFORE THE CRIMEAN WAR.

Before this war, Russia possessed two squadrons of about equal power; one stationed in the Black Sea, the other in the Baltic. Each carried about 20.000 seamen, and about half the number of marines and marine artillery men, and the aggregate number of guns was betwen 8.000 and 9.000. These two fleets comprised respectively about 25 ships of the line, 18 frigates, 40 corvettes, and about 20 to 23 steamers. At the Northern ports, in addition to the above preparation of ships, there were about 250 gun-boats. Of this large army of ships in the Baltic, not more than 16 or 18 ships of the line, 10 frigates, and as many corvettes, beside half the number of steamers enumerated, were in a fit condition to put to sea. An official list, indeed, dated 1853, shows the available strength of the Black Sea fleet at that time, to have been composed as follows:

5 Line-of-Battle ships, each carrying...120 guns.
13 Line-of-battle ships, each carrying... 80 guns.
7 Line-of-battle ships, each carrying... 54 guns.
3 Line-of-Battle ships, each carrying from 40 to...... 80 guns.
25 Brigs, corvettes, &c., amounting together to......170 guns.
2 Steam corvettes, each carrying...... 6 guns.

But of these, probably the majority would, by an experienced Naval Surveyor, have been condemned as nearly worthless for war purposes. Russian ships were, for the most part, built of pine, the worst material that could be selected, both as regards durability and its liability to splinter in action; the workmanship was usually very bad. A remarkable example of this was afforded some time ago by a new first-rate line-of-battle ship, the Casarewitch on her way from the Dnieper to the North, putting into Malta for repairs, almost in a sinking condition, propped round and round her hull with cables and hawsers, and yet breaking so fast that her crew were well nigh exhausted with their exertions in keeping her afloat.

THE RUSSIAN FLEET AT THE PRESENT TIME.

Great activity has for some time been prevalent in all the Russian dockyard, and the most strenous efforts continue to be made to repair the loss of their fleet sunk in the harbor of Sevastopol. In 1854, Russia could only number in her navy two or three propellers. Since 1857, several have been constructed. The Baltic fleet has rapidly received re-enforcements, and the squadron in the Amoor on the eastern coast of Asia has been considerably augmented. According to the latest official statement which we have at command (June, 1862), the Russian fleet then stood as follows:

STEAMSHIPS.

Ships of the line...... 9
Frigates—propellers......12
Frigates—paddle...... 8
Corvettes......22
Clippers......12
Floating batteries—armor-clad...... 1
Sloops—armor-clad...... 1
Sloops, gun-boats, &c......79
Yachts...... 2
Schooners......25
Transport ships...... 9
Small paddle wheel steamers...... 6

Total......248

The above are propelled by a force of 37,007 horse power, and carry 2,387 guns.

SAILING VESSELS.

Ships of the Line...... 9
Frigates...... 5
Corvettes...... 3
Brigs...... 3
Schooners......13
Gunboats with rams...... 2
Tenders...... 2
Transport ships......13
Yachts......12

Total......62

These sailing vessels carry 1,304 guns.

The above give a total naval strength of 310 vessels, armed with 3,691 guns. In addition to these, there are three floating docks, and about 300 vessels for harbor service, &c.

THE PERSONNEL OF THE NAVY.

Stood as follows at the beginning of the year 1861.

Admirals and Generals...... 65
Officers of the staff and subalterns.. 3,245
Civil functionaries...... 966
Soldiers and Sailors...... 55,216
Marine Guards and Conductors... 189

Total...... 59,691

The Grand Duke Constantine is the Admiral-General of the fleet. Under him are a commandant of the fleet in the Baltic, five commandants of squadrons, one commandant of the squadron in the Black Sea, and one commandant of the squadron in the Caspian Sea. These offices are filled by Vice or Rear-Admirals.

The Ministry of Marine, which is presided over by the Minister, is divided into eight departments, under the surveillance of Directors and Vice-Directors. These are: 1. The Chancellary. 2. The Department of the Personnel. 3. Hydrographical Department. 4. Commissariat Department. 5. Department of Naval Construction. 6. Audit Department. 7. Medical Directory. 8. Directory of Artillery. In addition to these there are several minor departments, which are charged with the equipment of the Navy, the training of sailors, the superintendence of naval fortresses, &c.

The expense of the Russian Navy for 1862, according to the official budget of that year, was 20,589,831 roubles, or $15,442,373.—*Tribune.*

Slavers in the South Sea.

RECENT English papers furnish particulars of the kidnapping of South Sea Islanders by Peruvian slavedealers, which has excited so much horror and indignation in the Australian colonies. At a recent meeting in Sydney, a clergyman who was for many years a missionary in Western Polynesia, said that early this year as many as from one thousand five hundred to two thousand hapless beings, collected from the different islands, had been conveyed to South America, and at this date the traffic is being carried on with unabated vigor.

It is known that twenty-five vessels have been fitted out in Callao, under pretext that they were going to the South Sea Islands to hire laborers, but in every case they have been used to carry off the natives who fell into their clutches. The dealers have a depot at an island called Easter Island. This island is about thirty-six miles in circuit. It lies in longitude 109 W. and latitude 27 S. It is said that they have completely swept the island of its inhabitants. Seven vessels assembled on the island, sent on shore most of their crews, no doubt thoroughly armed, surrounded the natives, and carried them off. Having carried off the people, they took hogs, poultry, and whatever else they desired, and burned the houses, reserving, no doubt, as many as they wanted for their own purposes. To this island the slavers carry the wretched beings whom they manage to seize, and a schooner plies between the island and the coast, carrying cargo after cargo to slavery and death. These vessels are said to be in whole or in part owned by a mercantile house in Callao, and this house is further said to be connected with a firm of Liverpool.

On board one vessel that called off Samoa there were three hundred natives of different islands, and the captain wished to obtain four hundred more to complete his cargo. It is said that the dealers express a determination to increase the number of their victims to ten thousand. The following incident of the kidnapping operations is given:

A vessel loaded with captives, on the second day after they had been got on board, stood in toward the shore. Some natives, ignorant of the character os the ship, and of what had transpired, went on board. Those in confinement recognized the well-known sounds of their native tongue. They shouted for help, but of course in vain. By desperate efforts they succeeded in breaking a hole in the door large enough to let one through at a time. A number succeeded in reaching the deck, and rushed over the ship's side into the sea, but there were only two or three small canoes, land was a long way off, and some were not able to swim well. The wretches on board fired from the deck upon the helpless natives in the canoes and the water. A boat was lowered, and many were recaptured. Seven only escaped. Among those carried off were thirteen Church members and many candidates. Eighteen wives are left without husbands, and sixty-three children are deprived of their fathers.—*N. Y. Evening Post.*

Quarantine.

If a hundred persons were asked the meaning of the word quarantine, it is highly probable that ninety-nine would answer, "Oh! it is something connected with shipping—the plague and yellow fever." Few are aware that it simply signifies a period of forty days; the word, though common enough at one time, being only known to us through the acts for preventing the introduction of foreign diseases, directing that persons coming from infected places must remain forty days on shipboard before they can be permitted to land. The old military and monastic writers frequently used the word to denote this space of time. In a truce between Henry I. of England, and Robert, Earl of Flanders, one of the articles is to the following effect: "If Robert should depart from the treaty, and the parties could not be reconciled to the king in three quarantines, each of the hostages should pay the sum of 100 marks."

From a very early period, the founders of our legal polity in England, when they had occasion to limit a short period of time for any particular purpose, evinced a marked predilection for the quarantine. Thus, by the laws of Ethelbert, who died in 616, the limitation for the payment of the fine for slaying a man at an open grave was fixed at forty nights, the Saxon reckoning by nights instead of days. The privilege of sanctuary was also confined within the same number of days. The eighth chapter of Magna Charta declares that a "widow shall remain in her husband's capital messuage for forty days after his death, within which time her dower shall be assigned." The tenant of a Knight's fee, by military service, was bound to attend the king for forty days, properly equipped for war.

According to Blackstone, no man was in the olden time allowed to abide in England more than forty days, unless he were enrolled in some tithing or decennary. And the same authority asserts that, by privilege of Parliament, members of the House of Commons are protected from arrest for forty days before the next appointed meeting. By the ancient *Costumale* of Preston, about the reign of Henry II, a condition was imposed on every newmade burgess, that if he neglected to build a house within forty days, he should forfeit forty pence.

In ancients prognostications of weather, the period of forty days plays a considerable part. An old Scotch proverb states:

"Saint Swithin's day, gin ye do rain,
For forty days it will remain;
Saint Swithin's day, and be ye fair,
For forty days 'twill rain nae mair."

There can be no reasonable doubt that this precise time is deduced from the period of Lent, which is in itself a commemoration of the forty days fast of Christ in the wilderness. The period of forty days is, we need scarcely say, of frequent occurrence in the Scripture. Moses was forty days on the mount; the diluvial rain fell upon the earth for forty days; and the same period elapsed from the time the tops of the mountains were seen till Noah opened the window of the ark.

Even the Pagans observed the same space of time in the mysteries of Ceres and Proserpine, in which the wooden image of a Virgin was lamented over during forty days; and Tertullian relates as a fact, well known to the Heathen, that for forty days an entire city remained suspended in the air over Jerusalem as a certain presage of the Millennium. The process of embalming used by the ancient Egyptians lasted forty days; the ancient physicians ascribed many strange changes to the same period; so, also, did the vain seekers after the philosopher's stone and the elixir of life.

Book of Days.

National Thanksgiving.

The following eminently fit and beautiful Proclamation has just been issued by our beloved President, whom may God continue to bless!

By the President of the United States of America.

A PROCLAMATION.

The year that is drawing toward its close has been filled with the blessings of fruitful fields and healthful skies. To these bounties, which are so constantly enjoyed that we are prone to forget the source from which they come, others have been added, which are of such an extraordinary nature that they cannot fail to penetrate and soften the heart which is habitually insensible to the ever-watchful providence of Almighty God.

In the midst of a civil war of unequalled magnitude and severity, which has sometimes seemed to provoke the aggression of foreign States, peace has been preserved with all nations, order has been maintained, the laws have been respected and obeyed, and harmony has prevailed every where except in the theatre of military conflict; while that theatre has been greatly contracted by the advancing armies and navies of the Union.

Needful diversions of wealth and of strength from the fields of peaceful labor to the National defence have not arrested the plow, the shuttle, or the ship. The axe has enlarged the borders of our settlements, and the mines as well of iron and coal as of the precious metals, have yielded even more abundantly than heretofore.

Population has steadily increased, notwithstanding the waste that has been made in the camp, the siege, and the battle-field; and the country, rejoicing in the consciousness of augmented strength and vigor, is permitted to expect a continuance of years with a large increase of freedom.

No human council hath devised, nor hath any mortal hand worked out these great things. They are the gracious gifts of the Most High God, who, while dealing with us in anger for our sins, has, nevertheless, remembered mercy. It has seemed to me fit and proper that they should be solemnly, reverently, and gratefully acknowledged as with one heart and voice by the whole American people.

I do therefore, invite my fellow-citizens in every part of the United States, *and also those who are at sea,* and those who are sojourning in foreign countries, to set apart and observe the last Thursday of November next, as a day of thanksgiving and prayer and praise to our beneficent Father, who dwelleth in the heavens; and I recommend that while offering up the ascriptions justly due to him for such singular deliverances and blessings, they do also, with humble penitence for our national perverseness and disobedience, commend to his tender care all those who have become widows, orphans, mourners, or sufferers in the lamentable civil strife in which we are unavoidably engaged, and fervently implore the interposition of the Almighty hand to heal the wounds of the nation, and to restore it, as soon as may be consistent with the divine purposes, to the full enjoyment of peace, harmony, tranquility, and union.

[L. S.] In testimony whereof, I have hereunto set my hand and caused the seal of the United States to be affixed.

Done at the city of Washington, this third day of October, in the year of our Lord, one thousand eight hundred and sixty-three, and of the independence of the United Statess the eighty-eighth.

ABRAHAM LINCOLN.

By the the President,

WM. H. SEWARD, Secretary of State.

FOREIGN CORRESPONDENCE.

Norway.

F. L. RYMKER, *Chaplain.*

Our Chaplain reports his return from a visit to Denmark, where he remained for some time laboring in the work of the Gospel, with great joy to himself and the friends who gladly welcomed him back to his former field.

As Paul wrought for his own support in his former occupation of tent-making, so does our chaplain, occasionally, in the making of artificial legs, by which means, like the good physician, caring for the bodies of men, he sometimes finds access to their souls.

He mentions G. Huberth, a sailor, who was converted in this country, but returned to Norway to tell his kins folk how great things the Lord had done for him, having mercy upon him, as having commenced his labors in his native place.

For the last quarter's labor, he reports 408 miles travelled, 53 sermons preached, 4 prayer-meetings attended, 6 books, and 2,000 pages of tracts distributed, 3 believers baptized, 91 visits made, of which 5 were to ships or seamen; 6 Bibles and 15 Testaments sold, &c.

Denmark.

REV. P. E. RYDING, *Chaplain.*

This servant of God has furnished us full accounts of his labors in Copenhagen and elsewhere in Denmark. He says of the last quarter:—

"I have visited a great number of vessels, and have had the opportunity to speak to many seamen. Eternity will manifest the fruits of these labors. There is a great desire among seamen to hear the word of God, and a great number of books have been sold to them. It appears that the Spirit of God breathes on these sons of the sea."

He has visited *Sweden* also. Speaking of Nelmo, he says:—

"It is a considerable seaport, and consequently a number of seamen are there. I held several meetings in the houses, but they were not well attended. Among the seamen, however, on board vessels and in the harbor, I had better success. I visited many vessels, and there was a great desire to get books and tracts."

Here he had access to a number of Poles, who had taken shelter here, on account of Russian cruisers. They were Greek catholics, caring little about religion.

Copenhagen.

REV. P. E. RYDING, *Chaplain.*

Speaking of Ronne in Bornholm, he says:—

"At this place there continues to be a good field for labor, and it appears that the Lord has a great people there to be saved, for which reason the enemy shews great opposition. In the northern part of the island, where some time ago great darkness prevailed, several individuals have been awakened. Among these is a man who used to be a most ungodly person; drinking, playing at cards and swearing, were his principal employments, and he was a terror to many. This man attended a meeting, and the word reached his conscience, and his soul was much troubled. He nevertheless pursued his former course, but at the same time he attended the meetings. He began to pray, and at length he found favor in the sight of God, and he is now an humble follower of Christ. The conversion of this man has produced a great sensation in a wide circle—people wonder that so ungodly a person could be converted. May the Spirit of God use him as a means to the conversion of many poor sinners.

In the worst quarters of Ronne, where the seamen live, a little spiritual life appears to have commenced. A daughter of one of the seamen, who was out at service, came home to visit her parents; she attended the meeting, and it pleased God to apply his word to her heart. At length she found peace through the blood of Christ. Having found peace herself, her chief concern was about her mother. God has graciously listened to her prayers. Her mother was induced to attend the meeting; and although she hardened her heart for some time, yet the word of God found entrance into her heart, and she is now sitting like Mary at the feet of Jesus. Mother and daughter are now much concerned about the father. He is out at sea, but they frequently write to him. When he left home they supplied him with tracts and a New Testament. He is a hard-hearted ungodly man, and has lived in sin a great number of years—but they are now sending up their prayers on his behalf to the Throne of Grace, and they entertain the hope that God will graciously listen to, and answer their prayers. There is a considerable religious movement in this quarter—many pray, the one for the other. There is much inquiry after the Word of God, and the desire for reading is very great. My labors in Bornholm are very extensive. Many visit me in my lodgings, both from the town and the country, who inquire after the way to heaven; and there are many places I have to go and teach poor sinners the way of salvation. Lord, may thy Spirit be poured out on this people, and save them from destruction who are strangers to everlasting life.

At Nexo, I visited several families, whom I encouraged to steadfastness. I labored in the neighborhood—spoke to several persons about the one thing needful, and was glad to find several individuals whose joy it was to walk in the ways of the Lord. I then left for Svanike, where I made several house visits, and preached to a few persons, who seemed to hunger after righteousness. From thence I went to Bolshaon, where I visited and preached. A woman who attended the meeting, was seized by the Spirit of God, and convinced of the truth of the word of God. She attended several meetings I held in various places, and I believe she has found favor in the sight of God.

I went to Ankjier, made visits and preached to a good assembly, and there were many who received the word with joy. I conducted a prayer-meeting, and great grace was upon us. I visited the neighboring parts, encouraged the people of God, and conducted a prayer-meeting.

In the parish of Aakirke, I spoke with a female, who is now a sincere believer. She told me that about nine years ago, she had been with some relations where I had come, and has given her two tracts. She took them, and put them in her pocket—but when she went home she read them, and they made a deep impression on her heart which was never eradicated. Nevertheless, it was not strong enough to draw her mind entirely from the world. The seed was however sown; and some years after that, when she heard the word of God being preached faithfully, she was powerfully reminded of what she had read, and the Spirit of God carried on his work in her heart, and she has now for several years found her only comfort in the blood of Jesus, and walks as an humble believer.

God has looked in mercy upon me, poor sinful creature, and permitted me to be an instrument in his hand to promote his kingdom and glory.

I have preached 37 sermons, conducted 12 prayer-meetings; visited about 422 vessels; disposed of 170 Bibles and New Testaments, and 197 religious pamphlets, and distributed about 2,135 tracts."

The Sailor's Magazine.

The American Seamen's Friend Society publish an exceedingly interesting Magazine with the above title, which we commend to the perusal of landsmen as well as seamen. It ought to be widely circulated and extensively read. Men of means could do much good by sending money to the Society for its gratuitous circulation on the land and on the sea. It would be casting bread upon the waters.

N. Y. Observer, Nov. 15.

Marine Disasters in September.

The total losses to American sea going craft reported during September are comparatively light, notwithstanding the severe gales that prevailed in the month. The raids by the Confederate privateers, which have formed such an impressive feature in our monthly reports for a long time, were confined during September to the destruction of but one vessel—the ship Anglo Saxon.

The total losses in the month were 15, namely, 4 ships, 2 brigs and 9 schooners. Of these 7 were wrecked, 3 abandoned, 2 burn, 1 foundered, 1 capsized, and 1 is missing.

The following are their names, &c., including nearly an equal number of foreigners, bound to or from an American port.

[The nature of the disaster is indicated as follows. *w* for wrecked; *a.*, abandoned; *b.*, burnt; *f.*, foundered; *c.*, capsized; *m.*, missing.]

SHIPS.
B. R. Millan, *a*, from New York for Cadiz.
Anglo Saxon *b*, [*] from Liverpool for New York.
Santa Claus *a*, from Callao for Hamburg.
Anderson (Ital.) *w*, from Lisbon for New York.
Tropic, *m*, from Philadelphia for San Francisco.
Loussiana, (Nor.) *a.*, from New York for Antwerp.

BARKS.
Gaspar, (Chil.) *f*, from Pisagua for New York.
Geo. Sands, (Ham.) *w*, from San Francisco for Hong Kong.

BRIGS.
Gitana, (Br.) *w*, from New York for Kingston, Ja.
Trade Wind, *w*, from Matamoras for New York.
Helen Jane (Br.) *w*, from New York for Oporto.
Clarence (Br.) *w*, from New York for Barbadoes.
Emily *f*, from New York for Boston.
Eliza Ann McAdams, (Br.) *w*, from Sagua for New York.

SCHOONERS.
Martha, *w*, from Musquash, N. B. for Boston.
A. O. Small, *w*, (Fishing vessel of Provincetown.)
Susan, *w*, from Elizabethport for New Haven.
Golden Rod, *b*, [†]
Spray (Br.) *w*, from Boston for Cornwallis.
Leader, *c*, from Fall River for New York.
Winona, *w*, from Elizabethport, for New Haven.
Jessie (Br.) *w*, from Rio Grande for New York.
Roderic Random, (Br.) *w*, from Inagua for Boston.
Wave, *w*, from Bangor or Hartford.
R. E. Cock, *w*, (Fishing vessel of Provincetown.)
Rush, *a*, from Boston for Beaufort, N. C.
Clifton (Br.) *w*, from New York for St. Johns, N. F.

Partial losses are not included in the list. The total value of the above domestic craft is estimated at $210,000.

[*] Burnt by Confederate steamer Florida.
[†] Destroyed rebels in Chesapeake Bay.

—Journal of Commerce.

	Vessels.	Value.
Total losses for January	44	$1,885,300
Total losses for February	50	1,396,500
Total losses for March	41	1,534,000
Total losses for April	44	2,151,500
Total losses for May	26	2,501,000
Total losses for June	49	2,636,500
Total losses for July	30	2,031,000
Total losses for August	28	1,500,300
Total for seven months	352	$15,536,550

Notice.

Subscribers to the Sailors' Magazine, who are not in the habit of binding them, will confer a favor by returning the following numbers by mail, viz:— January, April, June, July, September and October, all of 1863. Address *Sailors' Magazine*, New York.

Receipts for September, 1863.

NEW HAMPSHIRE.

Boscawen, Estate of George Coffing for Peter Coffing,	10 00
Harrisville, Children,	5 50

VERMONT.

Fairfax, Cong. Ch., (in part.)	4 55
Fayetteville, Cong. Ch ,	4 00
Georgia, Cong. Ch., Ships Library,	12 65
" Bapt. " " "	13 15
Montpelier, Congregational Church,	19 88
Pittsford, " "	12 00
St. Albans, " "	30 25
Wells River, " "	11 00
Westford, Congregational Church const Rev. C. C. Torrey, L. M.,	20 85

MASSACHUSETTS.

Andover, Late B. F. Punchard's Estate closed,	62 20
Attleboro, Ladies Seamen Friend Soc'y,	15 00
Dudley, Congregational Church,	10 00
Fall River, Rev. Mr Thurstons Church,	97 80
Georgetown, Ladies Benev. Soc'y,	6 00
Hamilton, Congregational Church,	6 75
Mattapoisett, " "	4 11
Medfield, Mrs. Sarah A. Goodale,	2 00
North Bridgewater, First Cong. Ch.,	10 60
North Chelmsford S. Sch Ships Library	27 62
" " Mrs. T. F. Wood, self, L. M.	20 00
Orange S. School,	5 18
South Hadley, Dea. Geo F Camp, First Cong. Ch., per Rev R. Knight,	22 00
Tewsbury, Cong. Ch., $20 from Geo. Lee, Ship Library,	40 00
Woburn, Rebecca Rogers, Ships Library,	10 00

CONNECTICUT.

Ansonia, First Congregational Church,	34 00
Bristol, Cong. Ch., const. Dea. Frederick Allen, col. Edw. L. Dunbar, L. M's,	43 13
Chester, S. School, Cong. Ch., by Four Young Ladies, for Ships Library and const. Miss Ella S. Pratt, L. M.,	31 00
Columbia, Cong. Church, $10 from Daniel Holbrook, Ships Library,	21 00
Coventry, First Cong. Church (in part.)	5 00
Enfield, " " "	53 00
" Second " "	21 42
Griswold, First " "	26 00
" " " S. School, Ships Library,	12 00
Lebanon, Eleazar Huntington,	10 00
Morris, S. School, Congregational Church Ships Library,	12 00
New Haven, College St. Cong. Church,	63 05
" " Third Cong. Church, $20, from R S. Fellows, const. Saml. M. Fellows, L. M	117 71
New Preston, Cong Church, S. School (on the hill), Ships Library,	12 00
Norwich Town, C. W. Denison, Jr., for Ships Library,	10 00
Plymouth Hollow, Cong. Ch , const Rev. Jas. B. Pearson, L. M.,	30 60
" " S. School, L. M. Ships Library,	12 00
Ridgefield, Union S. Sch., Cong. & Meth. Churches. Ships Library,	10 00
Simsbury, Congregational Church,	18 04
Scotland, S School, Cong. Church, Ships Library,	12 00
Washington, First Cong. Church,	7 10
Watertown, S. School, Cong. Ch., Ships Library,	13 75
" Congregational Church,	50 55
Windsor Lock, Cong. Church,	26 20
Winsted, First Cong. Ch. (in part.),	15 95
Willimantic. Baptist Church,	7 45

NEW YORK.

Bridgehampton, Pres. Church,	20 84
Catskill, Pres. Church, additional,	30 00
Champlain, Congregational Church,	22 65
Chazy, " "	8 03
East New York, Refd. Dutch Church,	16 98
Fishkill, " "	36 50
" J. V. W. Vandervoort, Ships Library,	10 00
" S. School, do Ships Library,	10 00
New Paltz, Rev. C. H. Stitt,	5 00
New Hackensack, S. School Ship Libr'y,	12 00
New York City, A. Friend, const., John C V ndervoort, L. M.,	20 00
Madison Square Presh. Church,	253 95
Sale of clothes Sailors Home,	8 00
G. G Williams,	5 00
Cash,	1 00
"	5 00
Wm Curtis Noyes,	25 00
Wm. Alex. Smith,	25 00
D. Olyphant, additional to collection of Presb. Church, Morristown N. J.,	200 00
J. L. Merrill,	5 00
Jno. H Ormsbee,	5 00
J. H. Reed,	50 00
H. D. Carlile,	20 00
E. V. H.,	5 00
Cash,	2 00
Geo. A. Townsend.—Sub ,	5 00
Geo. W. Lane, additional to collection in Rev. Dr. Adams Church,	10 00
Cash,	2 00
P. Perit,	100 00
Cash,	10 00
Pokeepsie, S. School, Miss'y Soc'y, Second Refd. Dutch Church, Ships Library,	12 00

NEW JERSEY.

Newark, Friend, Ships Library,	11 00

PENNSYLVANIA.

Rev. J. R. Agnew,	1 00

IOWA.

Lorano, Jas. K. Barlow,	1 00
	$2,120 03

Robert Carter & Brothers, upwards of $50 worth of well selected books for Ships Libraries.
Barrel of religious papers and pamphlets for the Navy, from W. S. Hyer, Newburgh.
Bundle of New York Observers for S. Snug Harbor, from Miss Palmer, Newtown L. I.

For Sailor's Home.

From Miss M. C. Gay, Suffield, Connecticut, 1 quilt.
Mrs. Cloe Lamson, Jasper, N. Y., 12 prs. woollen socks.

Receipts into the Treasury of the Boston Seamen Friend Society.

J C. Tyler,	10 00
William Ropes,	10 00
H. Chickering,	10 00
A. Kingman,	20 06
Estate of Harriet Sherburne,	47 50
	$95 50

THE SAILORS' MAGAZINE.

Vol. 38.   JANUARY, 1866.   No. 5.

ANNO DOMINI,
ONE THOUSAND EIGHT HUNDRED AND SIXTY-SIX.

Through the Divine goodness, we enter with this number upon another year of christian work.

The one just closed has been wonderfully eventful. Its review is calculated to excite the devoutest gratitude, and to encourage a stronger faith in that word, which assures us that all human affairs are administered of God, in the interests of His Christ's kingdom.

Probably no previous year has sustained any closer relation to our national development. It is certain that none has ever equally disclosed the ability and resources of the Church for the work assigned her.

Students and writers upon the subject of prophecy have been singularly agreed in fixing on the present year as the beginning of a new spiritual era, the latter-day dispensation.

There is something significant in the wide-spread expectation among Christians of every name, that a time of refreshing is at hand. *Perhaps the Lord himself is at hand.* Not a few devout and scholarly men, in Great Britain as well as in this country, think so. In a sense, it is true for every one that "the Lord is at hand." Many who began the last year with a fair prospect of seeing its end, have been called to behold the King in his glory. Their work is done. It is not so with us. We are spared, because the Master who honors us in permitting us to serve him, and whom we love to serve, has something for us yet to do.

Without indulging in needless speculation, we should therefore come up to the particular work providentially allotted us, and strive to make, with God's blessing, the year whose threshold we stand upon the most useful year of our life.

Surely, the enlargement of commerce, incident to the happy return of peace in our borders, imposes the responsibility of corresponding effort, and a greater self-sacrifice in our endeavors to promote the temporal and spiritual welfare of the sailor. Prayer, also, should constantly ascend that, while quickening and accepting our charities, God would graciously bless the chaplains and missionaries of the Society, whether laboring in port or on shipboard, and use them in saving a multitude of souls.

Our work is one which God has deigned to regard with peculiar favor.

He is with us, not only by his promise, but according to his promise; and we have it to record, with thanksgiving and praise, that many a hardy son of the ocean has been led, through our agency, to the experience of a Saviour's love.

We rejoice, also, to know that the cause of God among seamen is gradually rising to its proper dignity and importance in the eyes of the Church.

May this year be one of conquest for the Prince of Peace; and from the abundance of the sea conversions be so continuous, as to keep the arches of Heaven ringing with the song of jubilant angels!

THE GIFTS OF COMERCE TO THE CHURCH.—A SERMON,

By Rev. J. E. Rockwell, D. D.,

PASTOR OF THE CENTRAL PRES. CHURCH, BROOKLYN, N. Y.

"And the daughter of Tyre shall be there with a gift."—Psalm 45.—12.

The forty-fifth Psalm is a celebration of the majesty, grace, and triumph of Christ, and a description of the glory of the Church in its union with him, as its head and Saviour, when he shall come to be admired of all his saints. This union is celebrated in all the glowing imagery and scenery of Oriental poetry, and is set before us with all the attendant circumstances of a wedding feast, when the friends of the Bride are present with their gifts and congratulations.

Among those who appear on this occasion to pay their tribute to the Church, is specially mentioned the "daughter of Tyre," (which in the Hebrew idiom is a personification of the *people* of that city.)

In the age of Solomon, Tyre was the symbol of commercial greatness, although it has now fallen to utter decay, and is a sad evidence of the results of sin in bringing down upon cities or nations the divine wrath.

But in the time when this Psalm was written, and the future glories of the Church celebrated, Tyre was renowned for its arts, manufactures and wealth, and its wide extended commerce. Its situation was such as to secure for it the traffic of the world. The sea washed its sides and front. The forests of Lebanon furnished timber for its navy.

Egypt was near at hand to supply it with sails and cordage. Its harbor was capacious and secure, and its fleets became the great means of transportation for the produce of the world. From the overstocked population colonies were sent forth, which made their way along the shores of the Mediterranean, and even passing beyond Gibraltar, it is said, discovered the British Isles.

As the natural result of their commercial enterprise, the citizens of Tyre became exceedingly opulent.— Their streets were lined with palaces and splendid works of art. Science and Philosophy there found a home. Artists and architects abounded, and were often called upon to assist in the adornment of other cities, not yet so far advanced in civilization and luxury.

Hence when Solomon was about to erect a magnificent temple for the worship of Jehovah, he sent to Tyre for the men who should carry out his plans, and received from the king large and costly gifts to further his work.

Perhaps it was a recurrence to this fact, that led the Psalmist to speak of what commerce should do for the Church in the great day of her espousals, when she should be brought to the King in glorious apparel, and shine forth in the splendours of her royal state.

Nor is this the only hint which the Scriptures give us of the influence which commerce is to exert on the future enlargement and glory of the Church. Moses when he is setting before his people their destiny, as he looks down the tide of time, says of Zebulon and Issachar, "They shall call the people unto the mountain, there they shall offer sacrifices of righteousness, for they shall suck of the abundance of the seas, and of the treasures hid in the sand." This Zebulun was he of whom Jacob has declared "he shall dwell at the haven of the sea, and shall be for an haven of ships."

Thus have we set before us a commercial people, mingling with all nations, and calling them to the mountain of the Lord, for the purpose of sacrifice and worship, and thus aiding the Church in its mission of spreading abroad the knowledge of the Lord.

The gifts of commerce were thus early given to the Church, and it is evident that even in the time of Solomon the close connection between the mariners of Zebulon and their maratime friends resulted in giving to them some knowledge of Jehovah, and of his laws, and thus in exerting a healthful influence upon them and the world.

And the influence of commerce in aiding and enlarging the Church is pointed at in other portions of the Scripture with such plainness as to leave no room to doubt what is the meaning of the phrase—" the daughter of Tyre shall be there with a gift."

The prophet Isaiah in his magnificent description of the future glories of the Church, addresses to her such language as this: "Then thou shalt see, and flow together, and thine heart shall fear and be enlarged, because the abundance of the sea shall be converted unto thee." And, again turning her eyes towards the sea upon which vast fleets are sweeping towards her like clouds, he adds: "Surely the isles shall wait for me, and the ships of Tarshish first, to bring thy sons from far, their silver and their gold with them, and to the name of the Lord thy God, and to the Holy one of Israel, because he hath glorified thee." The import of such passages cannot be mistaken, and we can see in them, and in similar ones from the word of God, that in the coming glory prosperity and enlargement of the Church, it is the design of its great head, to make commerce largely tributary thereto, and to use all its mighty resources of wealth and men in extending its influence, in promoting all the great interests of religion, and in spreading over all the earth, the light, knowledge, and blessings of the Gospel.

When the Church shall be publicly recognized as the Lamb's wife, and is set forth in all her beauty and grace before the King, the daughter of Tyre shall be there with a gift. Commerce shall bring her rich treasures all sanctified and appropriated for the glory and enlargement of the Church.

We will not pause to consider among these gifts, the *wealth* which is even now poured in upon the Church from those who are engaged in commercial enterprises, and adding, perhaps, beyond any other one class of men to the opulence of Christian nations. Though even this fact is worthy of consideration, the Church feels as much as the nation the results of a prosperous and enlarging commerce. Even now there are multitudes of her sons who are laying upon her altars the gifts which they have brought up from the sea; and with an enlarged benevolence and increasing ability are nobly consecrating to the Church, and its interests, the wealth which God is giving them.

And, as the spirit of Christ is more largely diffused among the men who are touching the great springs of commercial life, these gifts will be amazingly increased, as the Church comes to be loved and honored as God's instrument in the conversion of the world, and as the chosen bride of the King of Kings.

But aside from all this, let us notice, among the gifts of commerce to the Church:

1st. The binding together the nations in a common brotherhood.

It is recorded of Alexander the Great, that he esteemed the cultivation of commerce to be useful not merely " because she was the procurer of luxuries, but that the interchange of commodities might produce a reciprocation of sentiment and affection, and that the free, equal and unobstructed communication among men of different countries, might remove the local prejudices which prevented them from viewing each other as brothers."

Who can doubt that this is the natural result of commerce, and that the nations are thus yearly brought nearer and nearer to each other, and the prejudices and barriers which have separated them, thus broken down?

And, it is to this end, that the promises of God's word all point, revealing to us as the grand result of the spread of the Gospel to all nations, the establishment of a common brotherhood among them.

We are seeing the development of this fact every year, as commerce enlarges the sphere of its operations. We cannot walk the streets of our own metropolis without seeing the representatives of almost every nation of the globe. They come hither for the purposes of business or pleasure, and they return to their homes again, having with them new impressions of what Christianity can do for a people. And so, too, in all the great marts of commerce in Asia, and Europe, and Africa, and the islands of the sea, may be found the representatives of all Christian nations, mingling for purposes of business or curiosity, with the people of China and India, and Egypt, and sharing with them the influences of a common Christianity. Now the result of all this intercommunion of nations cannot but be for the furtherance of the Gospel. It follows commerce and its extension is thus largely aided.

2d. Commerce is to aid largely in carrying to the nations of the earth the influences and appliances of the Gospel.

Before the final conquest of the world by the Head of the Church, the Gospel is to be preached to all nations. The word of God and the teachers of our holy religion, are to be distributed over the earth.

But, between the mighty continents and the islands of the sea, which are the dwelling places of man, vast oceans are rolling which cover nearly two thirds of the earth's surface. These form the great highways of commerce, and over them she holds an undisputed sway. None pass over them without her consent and aid. Her servants are the masters of the sea; her swift ships bear the products of every clime, the manufactures of every people, and are the channels through which all the great currents of emigration ebb and flow. To her, then, is the Church to look as the agency by which her sons and daughters are to be brought from far, and their silver and their gold with them. It was a ship of commerce that bore the first missionaries of the Gospel from Palestine to Italy. By the same means was Paul borne along the coasts of the Mediterranean, preaching Christ to the Heathen, and so enlarging the bounds of the Church.

And to this same powerful agency is the Christian religion now indebted for the spread of its missionaries and its varied means of instruction over the world.

And with the growth of commerce has there been a proportionate enlargement of the misionary work. The opening of traffic with any nation prepares the way for the entrance of the Gospel. It follows in the track of commerce, and every new avenue of trade, is a gift of a new people to the church of God. It opens a new field for its operations, and the ships of the merchant must soon bear thither the living teacher and the varied auxiliaries that he needs in his work. Thus does commerce become the handmaid of the Gospel, and as it becomes more and more permeated with the spirit of Christianity, will it confer larger and nobler gifts upon the Church, which shall be for its glory and enlargement among nations now sitting in the region and shadow of death.

And we may believe, in this connection, that all the great appliances of commerce for her extension and convenience are gifts which are preparing, in the providence of God, to be laid at the feet of Christ and his Church.

The telegraphic wire that now thrills to every thought that is connected with public interest; the press that now teems with the varied records of human affairs; the vast systems of roads now groaning beneath the fierce tread of the iron horse, and the pressure of freight and passengers; the immense fleets that are covering our seas, lakes and rivers, and whitening every sea; the complicated operations of the financial world with its stocks, and banks, and insurances; the growing powers of manufacturers, with the hundreds and thousands who are identified with them; all these vast and varied interests of commerce will be her gifts which she will at length consecrate to Christ and to his Church.

Even now we can see here and there an earnest of what she can do as one and another of her sons come and lay their gifts upon the altar.

But when Christ shall come in his glory to subdue the nations to himself, and when the Church shall be recognized as his chosen and honoured bride; when his light and glory shall be seen in her, and the day of her recognition as the Lamb's wife shall come, then will commerce lay these gifts at her feet as the wedding present which the daughter of Tyre bestows upon her.

All her wealth and the means and appliances of her power shall then be consecrated to the glory of Christ, and the interests of his church, and a sanctified commerce shall become one of the noblest instrumentalities for the extension of Christ's kingdom, and the promotion of peace on earth and good will among all nations.

3d. Again, among the gifts of commerce to the Church, will be that of men, fearless earnest and devoted to Christ and his cause.

The evil influences which have been exerted upon the heathen by means of godless and unprincipled men who have visited their shores for the purpose of traffic, show what may also be done for this same class when they shall be brought under the power of the Gospel. Among the most untiring and earnest of Christ's followers whom he called to the ministry, were those whom he chose by the sea shore, the hardy sailors of Galilee. The same fearless and adventurous spirit which they had acquired by long familiarity with danger and toil, they bore with them into the apostleship. And this fact affords us a hint of what aid the Church is to expect from commerce when the abundance of the sea shall be converted unto God. Her offerings then will be not merely the gold and the silver, but her own brave and hardy sons, who will be found consecrated to the glory and extension of the Church. And, whereas, once they aided in introducing vice and misery and crime among the people where they found entrance, they will then as earnestly engage in making known the Gospel of Christ to the heathen.—Their influence will and must be great either for good or for evil. What ever they do, they do earnestly, and the sailor carries his ideas into his Christian course when his heart has been renewed by the Holy Spirit. Accustomed to scenes of peril, that require steadiness, energy, obedience to command, fearlessness and sleepless vigilance, he carries into the Christian life, these peculiar habits of thought and action.

And who can estimate the good the sailor may accomplish when under the influence of divine grace, he gives up his life to the work of extending the Church?

There are now, probably, nearly four millions of men engaged in a sea-faring life. They visit every shore and clime, are intimate with all peoples and nations, and when commerce shall bestow all these gifts on the Church, and consecrate them to her glory and advancement, who shall estimate the rapidity with which the light and blessings of the Gospel shall be communicated to all nations.

In the work which is even now being accomplished under the influence of Christian sailors, we may see a presage of what is yet to be done. And it is strange that the Church has been so slow to recognize the usefulness of this class of men in spreading among the heathen a knowledge of the Gospel. But drawing our instruction from divine revelations as already interpreted in the light of history, we may confidently anticipate the day when the Church shall find in commerce, one of her noblest auxiliaries in the spread of the Gospel among nations.

When that day shall come, and every ship shall be a Bethel, and every sailor a true and devoted missionary of the cross, as he leaves his home, he will carry with him his Bible and his closet; and as he reaches lands now lying in darkness, he will bear with him the light and sacred influences of our blessed religion. In him the missionary already seeking to bring the heathen to a knowledge of the truth, will find a faithful auxiliary and living epistle, known and read of all men. To him he can point as an illustration of the power of the Gospel, and he will become the trusty agent of the Church in its blessed mission of evangelizing the nations.

We may, therefore, look forward with confidence, to the day, when at the wedding feast of the Lamb, the daughter of Tyre shall come with her gift, and commerce shall lay her offerings before the Lord, her noblest present being that of millions of faithful men who shall labor for the conversion of the world to God. They will be found on every sea, and in every land, earnestly laboring to spread the knowledge of Christ. The islands of the Pacific will welcome them, the shores of China and India will hail them as the active coadjutors of the missionary in his blessed work. They will form the living links of a chain which shall bind all nations in a common brotherhood. They will bear aloft the banner of the Cross, and shout aloud to the dwellers in distant lands the news of salvation, and the glad tidings of peace on earth, good-will toward men. They will watch for the dawn of the latter-day glory, and its rising beams streaking the ocean, will be the harbingers of peace and joy to the nations, who, taking up the chorus, shall bear it over the earth, " Hallelujah, for the Lord God omnipotent, reigneth."

These considerations should teach the Church the vast importance of that work which has for its direct object and tendency, the conversion of the abundance of the sea to God.

They seem to direct attention to one of the most important auxiliaries which is to be used in the spread of the Gospel among the nations of the earth

The work to which we are thus invited claims the interest, attention and sympathies of all who value the Church, and hope for the coming of the latter-day glory on the earth.

Any work that cares for the temporal and moral wants of the sailor, deserves our heartfelt sympathy. He is an immortal being, and his soul is infinitely precious. He is surrounded by peculiar dangers and trials, both by sea and land. He belongs to a class of men who are continually undergoing fearful hazards and perils for the comfort and happiness of society. Art, science, literature, and social and political life, are alike indebted to him for the means of intellectual culture and personal enjoyment. Even common gratitude would claim a share in our kind thoughts and active benevolence,

" For the brave men that climb the mast,
 When to the billow and the blast
 It swings and stoops with fearful strain
 And bind the fluttering mainsail fast,
 Till the tos't bark shall sit again,
 Safe as a sea bird in the main."

The sailor forms a distinct and special class to which the word of God often alludes in terms there is no mistaking, and which leave us in no doubt as to the part he is yet to perform, when the day of Millenial glory shall rise upon the Earth.

Catching the spirit, then, of the word of God, and taught by his Providence, let us do our duty toward those who do business upon the great waters.

Let us furnish them with chapels, and comfortable homes where they shall be free from the terrible temptations which have hitherto beset them. Let us teach them how to husband their hard earned wages, which vice is urging them to squander in riotous living. Let us follow them upon the sea with the blessed influences of Christianity, supplying their chests with religious reading, and sending after them earnest prayers, that God would have them in his holy keeping. Let us provide for them religious instruction, and kind and faithful chaplains, who shall meet them on foreign shores and give to them a brother's welcome even in a land of strangers. They claim this at least from our hands. And what is thus done for them, will be repaid a thousand-fold in the influences they will exert upon the world.

It is the duty of the Church to see that commerce is sanctified, and made to lay its tribute at the feet of Jesus. Its work in this respect is hopeful. What has already been accomplished, is an earnest of what may be done when Christians awake to the vast importance of this great work. Every sailor converted to God, is henceforth a distributor of tracts, bibles, and religious influences from clime to clime, from shore to shore. Every such heart, filled with the grace of Christ, beats with a love that prompts to efforts for the Church, which stop at no sacrifices and faint at no labor nor perils.

And in this connexion I can most appropriately speak to you of the American Seamen's Friend Society:

I am persuaded, that aside from the great special work of the Church in the direct preaching of the Gospel, there is no agency so well calculated to effect wide and lasting good, as this society. It is Catholic in its spirit; and its aims and influences are worldwide. It needs a larger and nobler support from churches and ministers than it has ever yet received. Here and there a congregation does its duty in this respect, yet by many the cause is seldom if ever noticed; and yet there is not a town or hamlet that is not indebted to the sailor, or that has not some personal interest in him. We need more chaplains and homes. Even our own city, so long distinguished as a city of churches, has no suitable and decent provision made for the sailors who are now finding here a temporary home. We need an attractive chapel, with its bethel flag, and a preacher of recognized ability, who can address the sailor earnestly and lovingly, and in such language as shall attract his attention and enlis his sympathies. Our docks are now lined with ships. Commerce invites the sailor to our wharves and boarding houses, but the Church extends him no hand of greeting or fellowship. Surely it is not too much to ask of these who are in their commercial pursuits, adding largely to the wealth of our city by means of the sailor, that they aid the Society in finding for him (and that speedily,) a suitable chapel in which to worship God. Shall not the daughter of Tyre present this gift to the Church? Am I too sanguine in believing that our noble and generous citizens, who have never faltered at any sacrifice for the good of the country, or the prosperity of our city, would heartily respond to an appeal, which should ask them to provide for the sailors who throng our streets, a home and a house in which they may pay their vows to the God, whose is the sea, and by whose watchful providence, they have been kept amid its perils. The work is worthy our earnest and practical sympathy. Let us *do it*, and do it *now*.

Lights and Lighthouses.

At a very remote period, when the early mariners of the world first ventured to extend their sea-voyages beyond the few hours of daylight, or of moonlit nights, the want must have been felt of warning and guiding lights, and the more especially as those primitive voyagers, who were the first pioneers of commerce, must have perpetually "hugged" the shore, their chief fear being, that they should be carried away by an "offshore" wind into the great unknown region of waters extending they knew not whither.

There can be no doubt that all the earlier lights were simply fires of wood. The Tour de Corduan, when completed in 1610, was provided with an iron chauffer or cage, in which faggots of wood were burned; and in Great Britain, where coal is more abundant than in most others, open coal fires were sometimes adopted, a light of which description was actually in use at the Isle of May, on the coast of Scotland, from the time of the erection of its light tower, in 1636, until so late as the year 1816, when a new tower was built, and was provided with oil-lamps and reflectors. No less than 400 tons of coal were latterly burnt each year in maintaining this light.

The disadvantages of this primitive mode of illumination were manifold. The degree of intensity, size, and even color of the light must have been very variable, the distance at which it could be seen being equally so; it did not admit of any distinctive marks by which one light could be distinguished from another; the quantity of fire consumed was enormous, and its supply must, in proportion, have involved great labor and expense; while the waste of light was likewise great, since it shone in all directions, towards the land as well as towards the sea, and upwards to the sky. It is, however, recorded of the wood and coal fires as an advantage, that, in wet and foggy weather, their reflection was distinguishable high up in the air when they were not themselves visible.

The next change appears to have been first adopted at the Eddystone, at which, from its isolated position, being several miles from the land, it would have been very difficult to maintain a sufficient supply of fuel in the winter months. Its illuminator was accordingly composed of twenty-four wax candles, surrounded by a glass lantern, but without reflectors, or any other artificial means of increasing or concentrating the light; and insignificant as it must have been, compared with the splendid lights of the present day, the plan was yet a considerable step in advance of the open fires.

The next great improvement in sea-coast lights was the adoption of reflectors, which, like many other improvements in the various departments of art, science, and manufactures, appears to have been the immediate result of accident rather than of deliberate design and forethought.

Before, however, proceeding to describe the successive advances in the science of pharology, or the branch of "Optical Engineering," as it has been termed, which applies to sea-coast illuminations, it will be desirable that, without going deeply into optical details, we should briefly explain the principles on which science is made available to produce such truly valuable practical results.

Rays of light travel through space in all directions, and in straight lines, unless diverted therefrom by reflection from the surface of an opaque body, such as silvered glass or polished metal, or by refraction in passing through transparent bodies, as glass or water. If then two diverging rays of light, or bundles of rays, can be thrown, either by reflection or refraction on one point, thus occupying the space of one ray or bundle of rays, the intensity or brightness of the light on that point will be doubled: if twenty rays are thus made to converge into the space of one ray, the brilliancy at the point of convergence or focus will be increased twentyfold. A familiar instance of this principle, by refraction, exists in the common glass lens, vulgarly called a "burning-glass," which, by throwing a large number of rays of light on one point, produces an intense light and heat, capable of exploding gunpowder and igniting inflammable bodies. In the same manner, the shape of a mirror or reflector may be so arranged as to collect the rays of light emitted on one side of a luminous body, and to throw them forward, so that they shall converge in a point, or series of points, on the opposite side, and thus being added to the direct rays, increase the intensity of the light on that side.

A concave mirror, the curve of which is a parabola, is found to be the necessary form to effect the object in view, and a series of such reflectors, attached to lamps suitably adjusted, thus collect the useless rays of light from above, below, and behind, and throw them forward in a horizontal direction. As stated above, this system, which has been denominated the catoptric or reflector system, from the Greek word signifying a 'mirror,' was the first that was employed in the improvement of beacon lights. It is essentially the English system, both from its having been originated and been longer retained here than in other countries. The credit of first introducing it has been claimed both by England and France. Undoubtedly, however, the earliest application of reflectors was made in England, whilst to France belongs the honor of very greatly improving them.

Somewhere between the year 1763 and 1767, Mr. WILLIAM HUTCHINSON, the dockmaster at Liverpool, first applied a parabolic reflector to his flat-wicked lamps. The idea is stated to have thus originated. A convivial company of scientific men met at Liverpool, when one of the company present wagered that he would read a book by the light of a farthing candle, at a distance of 200 feet from it. The wager was won by means of a wooden bowl, lined with putty, in which facets of looking-glass were embedded, forming a reflector. Hutchinson was present, and seizing the idea, utilized it for his lighthouses. His reflectors were formed of tin plates, or of wood lined with looking-glass, the largest, 13 feet in diameter with six feet focus, being placed behind a "spreading burner mouth-piece" 14 inches broad. The Ridstone, Hoylake, and Leasowe light-houses were thus illuminated, and they were undoubtedly excellent lights for the period.

In the year 1786, the Northern Lights Board fitted reflectors and lamps of a similar description at the Isle of May and Cambrae Isle Lighthouses in the Firths of Forth and Clyde. These were said to have been the invention of Mr. Thomas Smith, the engineer to the Board; but whether or not he was aware of similar reflectors having been adopted elsewhere is not known.

On the other hand, in France, a M. Tealére, a member of the Royal Corps of Engineers of Bridges and Roads in that country, is said to have first proposed the use of parabolic reflectors; and the celebrated Corduan light-tower was illuminated in that manner, about the year 1780, by M. Lenoir, under the direction of the Chevalier Borda. The reflectors were made of sheet copper, plated with silver, and the lamp then just invented by M. Argand, of Geneva, since known as the Argand lamp, was adopted.

These great improvements then became general in other countries, and at once advanced the system of lighthouse illumination into a science.—The reflectors of the present day are made precisely in the same manner as M. Lenoir's, of copper thickly plated with silver, very highly polished, and, like his, lit by Argand burners, having a cylindrical flame of about one inch in diameter. The form of those now in use is that calculated by Captain Huddart, an Elder Brother of the Trinity House, in 1791. They are very durable, many of the reflectors still used remaining unimpaired after 30 or 40 years' continual service.

The size adopted by the Trinity House is 21 inches diameter for lighthouses, their sectional area being 346·3 square inches, and 12 inches diameter for light vessels, with an area of 113 square inches. Some reflectors are said to multiply the brilliancy of a light as much as 450 times. Catoptric lights are capable of nine distinct variations, viz., fixed revolving white, revolving red and white, revolving red with two whites, revolving white with two reds, flashing, intermittent, double-fixed, and double revolving. The first exhibits a steady and uniform appearance. The reflectors used for it are of smaller dimensions than those employed in revolving lights, and which is necessary in order to allow of their being ranged round a circular iron frame, with their axes inclined at such angles as to enable them to illuminate every part of the horizon. The revolving light is produced by the revolution of a frame with three or four sides, having reflectors of a large size grouped on each side, with their axes parallel; and as the revolution exhibits a light gradually increasing to full strength, and in the same gradual manner decreasing to total darkness, its appearance is extremely well marked. Eighteen, twenty, and even thirty reflectors are thus arranged on the faces of the revolving framework.

The succession of red and white lights is caused by the revolution of a frame whose different sides present red and white lights, and these, as already mentioned, afford three separate distinctions, viz., alternate red and white, the succession of two white after one red, and the succession of two red after one white. The flashing light is produced in the same manner as the revolving light; but, by a different construction of the frame and greater quickness of the revolution, a totally different and very striking appearance is produced. The brightest and darkest periods being but momentary, the light is characterized by a rapid succession of bright flashes, whence it derives its name. The intermittent light is distinguished by bursting suddenly into view, and continuing steady for a short time, after which it is eclipsed for many seconds, ordinarily in English lights for about half a minute. Its peculiar and striking appearance is effected by the perpendicular motion of circular shades in front of the reflectors, by which the light is alternately concealed and displayed. The double lights, which are commonly only used where there is a necessity of a leading line, for taking some channel, or avoiding some danger, are exhibited from two towers, one of which is higher than the other, and the two lights, when seen in one vertical line, form a direction for the course of shipping.

Missionary Statistics.

The whole number of Protestant missionary operations in the world, as carried on by American, British, and Continental Christians, is 48 societies, 9,418 agents or missionaries, etc., 518,000 church members, 235,000 pupils in the different schools, and an annual income of $4,481,000.

With such a machinery for operation in readiness and at active work, what is needful but the Holy Spirit to be poured out mightily from above, to go with the word, thus scattered abroad on its way to all the world and to every creature? Ask, and ye shall receive.—*Christian Instructor.*

A Magnificent Spectacle.

(From Hall's Arctic Researches.)

The day had been fine, with a moderate wind from the northwest. When the sun went down behind the ridge of mountains limiting the bay, a perfect calm followed, with a sky absolutely cloudless. At 4 P. M., there had been seen one solitary and peculiar cloud hanging in the heavens to the north about fifteen degrees above the horizon. This at last disappeared, and the night set in, still beautiful and mild, with myriads of stars shining with apparently greater brilliancy than ever.

I had gone on deck several times to look at the beauteous scene, and at nine o'clock was below in my cabin, going to bed, when the captain hailed me with the words, "*Come above, Hall, at once! The world is on fire!*"

I knew his meaning, and quick as thought, I re-dressed myself, scrambled over several sleeping Innuits close to my berth, and rushed to the companion stairs. In another moment I reached the deck, and, as the cabin door swung open, a dazzling, overpowering light, as if the world was really ablaze under the agency of some gorgeously colored fires burst upon my startled senses! How can I describe it? Again, I say, *no mortal hand can truthfully do so.* Let me, however, in feeble, broken words, put down my thoughts at the time, and try to give some faint idea of what I saw.

My first thought was, "Among the gods there is none like unto thee, O Lord! neither are there any works like unto thy works!" Then I tried to picture the scene before me. Piles of golden light and rainbow light, scattered along the azure vault, extended from behind the western horizon to the zenith; thence down to the eastern, within a belt of space twenty degrees in width, where the fountains of beams like fire-threads, that shot with the rapidity of lightning hither and thither, upward athwart the great pathway indicated. No sun, no moon, yet the heavens were a glorious sight, flooded with light. Even ordinary print could have been easily read on deck.

Flooded, with rivers of light. Yes, flooded with light; and such light! Light all but inconceivable. The golden hue predominated; but, in rapid succession, *prismatic colors leaped forth.*

We looked, we saw and *trembled*; for, even as we gazed, the whole belt of aurora began to be alive with flashes. Then each pile or bank of light became myriads: some now drooping down the great pathway or belt, others springing up, others leaping with lightning flash from one side, while more as quickly passed into the vacated space;

some twisting themselves into folds, entwining with others like enormous serpents, and all these movements as quick as the eye could follow. It seemed as if there was a struggle with these heavenly lights to reach and occupy the dome above our heads. Then the whole arch above became *crowded*. Down, down it came; nearer and nearer it approached us. Sheets of golden flame, coruscating while leaping from the auroral belt, seemed as if met in their course by some mighty agency that turned them into the colors of the rainbow, each of the seven primary, three degrees in width, sheeted out to twenty-one degrees—the prismatic bows at right angles with the belt.

While the auroral fires seemed to be descending upon us, one of our number could not help exclaiming:

"Hark! hark! such a display, almost as if a warfare was going on among the beauteous lights above—so near—seems impossible without noise."

But no noise accompanied this wonderous display. All was silence.

After we had again descended into our cabin, so strong was the impression of awe left upon us that the captain said to me:

"Well, during the eleven years which I have spent mostly in these northern regions, I never have seen any thing of the aurora to approach the glorious vivid display just witnessed, and to tell you the *truth*, friend Hall, *I do not want to see the like ever again.*"

Mining Under the Sea.

Mining can hardly be a pleasant occupation. The absence of sun and all natural light, the dripping sides of the shaft, and danger of explosion from the fire-damp, of jutting rocks and numerous other perils, invest it with vague terrors to active imaginations. But when the shafts run under the sea, and the swell of the ocean is distinctly audible, it must suggest many fears to the diligent miners. The following graphic description is taken from an English paper:

"We are now four hundred yards out under the bottom of the sea, and twenty feet below the sea level. Coast-trade vessels are sailing over our heads. Two hundred and forty feet below us men are at work, and there are galleries yet below that. The extraordinary position, down the face of the cliff, of the engines and other works on the surface, at Bottallie, is now explained. The mine is not excavated like other mines under the earth, but under the sea. Having communicated these particulars, the miner tells us to keep silence and listen. We obey him, sitting speechless and motionless. If the reader could only have beheld us now, dressed in our copper-colored garments, huddled close together in a mere cleft of subterranean rock, with a flame burning on our heads, and darkness enveloping our limbs, he must certainly have imagined, without any violent stretch of fancy, that he was looking down upon a conclave of gnomes.

"After listening a few minutes a distant and unearthly sound becomes faintly audible — a long, low, mysterious moaning that never changes, that is full on the ear as well as heard by it, a sound that might proceed from incalculable distance, from some far invisible height, a sound unlike any thing that is heard on the upper ground, in the free air of heaven, a sound so sublimely mournful and still so ghostly and impressive when listened to in the subterranean recesses of the earth, that we continue instinctively to hold our peace as if enchanted by it, and think not of communicating to each other the strange awe and astonishment which it has inspired in us from the very first.

"At last the miner speaks again, and tells us that what we hear is the sound of the surf lashing the rocks a hundred and twenty feet above us, and of the waves that are breaking on the beach beyond. The tide is now at the flow, and the sea is in no extraordinary state of agitation, so the sound is low and distant just at this period. But when storms are at their height, when the ocean hurls mountain after mountain of water on the cliffs, then the noise is terrific; the roaring heard down here in the mine is so inexpressibly fierce and awful that the boldest men at work are afraid to continue their labor; all ascend to the surface to breathe the upper air, and stand on firm earth, dreading—though no catastrophe has ever happened yet—that the sea will break in upon them if they remain in the cavern below.

"Hearing this, we got up to look at the rock above us. We are able to stand upright in the position we now occupy; and flaring our candles hither and thither in the darkness, can see the bright, pure copper streaming through the gallery in every direction. Lumps of ooze, of the most lustrous green color, traversed by a natural net-work of thin, red veins of iron, appears here and there in large irregular patches, over which water is dripping slowly and incessantly in certain places. This is the salt water percolating through invisible crannies in the rock. On stormy days it spurts out furiously in thin continuous streams. Just over our heads we observed a wooden plug, of the thickness of a man's leg; there is a hole there, and that plug is all we have to keep out the sea.

"Immense wealth of metal is contained in the roofs of this gallery throughout its entire length, but it will always remain untouched; the miners dare not take it, for it is a part (and a great part) of the rock which is their only protection against the sea, and which has so far been worked away here that its thickness is limited to an average of three feet only between the water and the gallery in which we now stand. No one knows what might be the consequence of another day's labor with the pickaxe on any part of it."

Theory of the Earth.

Mr. John Calvin Moss, of England, contests the much vexed theory that the center of the earth is a mass of fire and molten rock, over which a crust has formed, proportionately a mere shell, on which we live. "The idea that the interior of our globe is a vast fiery ocean doubtless arose," says Mr. Moss, "from the idea that heat was a material substance, and would have to pass off into space before the earth could cool; whereas the modern researches of science show that heat is no more a material substance than motion, gravitation or magnetism, but that it is merely a condition of matter; and that, in the case in question, instead of passing off from the earth, it would only become by a gradual chemical action fixed or latent.

"But even supposing that cooling would or did take place, it is a well known fact that all substances — water in the stars of ice alone excepted —increase in density or weight as their heat is diminished, so that the cooler portions would be the first to sink from the surface toward the center. Is it not quite evident that those substances most difficult of fusion and possessing the greatest specific gravity would, therefore, be the first to find their way to the centre? Now gold, platinum, and a few of the precious metals possess these qualities in a high degree above all others known substances, and though we believe them to be scarce on the surface of the earth we have no assurance that they are not abundant in Nature. I believe that the interior of the earth is abundantly supplied with, if not mainly composed of them."

The specific gravity of the earth has been variously calculated at 4.95, 5.54, 5.48 and 6,56; while that of platinum at 2.15 and gold 19.3. The specific gravity of the rocks which mainly compose the crust, which is under our observation, does not exceed 2.5; and supposing that the average density of all the constituents of the earth, except the metals named, is no higher, about one-fifth of the earth may be composed of gold and platinum—a globe four or five thousand miles thick. The value of such a deposit may be dimly imagined when it is remembered that five million dollars will go in a box two and a half feet cube. Certainly no safer place for such a deposit could be found than the heart of the earth.

The Army and Navy.

President Johnson, in his most admirable message, presents the condition of those two departments as follows, viz:

DEPARTMENT OF WAR.

In the report of the Secretary of War, a general summary is given of the military campaigns of 1864 and 1865, ending in the suppression of armed resistance to the national authority in the insurgent States. The operations of the general administrative bureaus of the War Department during the past year are detailed, and an estimate made of the appropriations that will be required for military purposes in the fiscal year commencing the 30th day of June, 1866. The national military force, on the 1st of May, 1865, numbered 1,000,516 men. It is proposed to reduce the military establishment to a peace footing, comprehending 50,000 troops of all arms, organized so as to admit of an enlargement by filling up the ranks to 82,600, if the circumstances of the country should require an augmentation of the army. The volunteer force has already been reduced by the discharge from service of over 800,000 troops, and the department is proceeding rapidly in the work of further reduction. The war estimates are reduced from $516,240,131 to $33,814,461, which amount, in the opinion of the department, is adequate for a peace establishment. The measures of retrenchment in each bureau and branch of the service exhibit a diligent economy worthy of commendation. Reference is also made in the report to the necessity of providing for a uniform militia system, and to the propriety of making suitable provision for wounded and disabled officers and soldiers.

THE NAVY.

It appears, from the report of the Secretary of the Navy, that while, at the commencement of the present year, there were in commission 530 vessels of all classes and descriptions, armed with 3,000 guns and manned by 51,000 men, the number of vessels at present in commission is 117, with 830 guns and 12,128 men. By this prompt reduction of the naval forces the expenses of the government have been largely diminished, and a number of vessels, purchased for naval purposes from the merchant marine, have been returned to the peaceful pursuits of commerce. Since the suppression of active hostilities our foreign squadrons have been re-established, and consist of vessels much more efficient than those employed on similar service previous to the rebellion. The suggestion for the enlargement of the navy-yard, and especially for the establishment of one in fresh water for iron-clad vessels, is deserving of consideration, as is also the recommendation for a different location and more ample grounds for the Naval Academy.

The Staunch old Ship.

"Sail on, sail on, Oh ship of state;
Sail on, Oh Union, strong and great!
Humanity, with all its fears,
With all the hopes of future years,
Is hanging breathless on thy fate.
We know what master laid thy keel,
What workmen wrought thy ribs of steel;
Who made each mast, each sail, each rope;
What anvils rang, what hammers beat,
In what a forge and what a heat
Were shaped the anchors of thy hope.
Fear not each sudden sound and shock,
'Tis of the wave, and not the rock;
'T is but the flapping of the sail,
And not a rent made by the gale.
In spite of rock and tempest roar,
In spite of false lights on the shore,
Sail on, nor fear to breast the sea:
Our hearts, our hopes, are all with thee.
Our hearts, our hopes, our prayers, our tears,
Our faith triumphant o'er our fears,
Are all with thee, are all with thee."

LONGFELLOW.

Sea Depths.

The Baltic, between Germany and Sweden is 120 feet deep, and the Adriatic, between Venice and Trieste is 130 feet. The deepest part of the Channel between France and England is 300 feet deep. Off the south-west coast of Ireland, in the open sea, the depth is 2000 feet. The narrowest part of the Strait of Gibraltar is 1000 feet, and a little to the east of this the depth is 3000 feet. On the coast of Spain the depth is 6000 feet; 250 miles south of Nantucket no bottom was found at 7,800 feet. West of the Cape of Good Hope 16,000 feet have been measured, and west of St. Helena 27,000 feet.

The New Webster.—A New Work.

We have commended this edition warmly already, on the faith of our first examination of it. It has grown upon us, in every day's farther study. We did not, at first, comprehend how entirely new a work this is, as compared even with the last preceding edition; and how important had been the etymological revision which it has received, making it, for substance, a rewritten volume, with all that was admirable and superior in the previous contributions of a generation to its pages, preserved and augmented by a thorough concentration upon it of the best skill and widest research of the present. As it stands,—in its etymologies, in its definitions, in its synonyms, and in its (real) illustrations,—it is far in advance of any other manual which offers itself to the aid of the student of the multiferious wealth of the composite English tongue.

The man who will buy and habitually and properly use Webster's Unabridged Illustrated Dictionary, in its latest and noblest form, has no excuse for not using the English language with intelligence, accuracy, and force

It is not a sectarian dictionary. We do most sincerely believe that all sects will find their especial phrases of faith more exactly, and fairly, and fully given in Webster, than in any or all others put together.—*Boston Congregationalist.*

We most cordially endorse the above notice. When the "New Webster" first came out, about a year since, we had leisure for its, careful examination. From that time until now, it have grown upon us, as an *indispensable* book.—We shall speak of this matter again. ED. MAG.

THE SAILORS'. MAGAZINE,

AND

SEAMEN'S FRIEND.

THE CHRISTIAN SAILOR.

A SERMON PREACHED IN THE CENTRAL PRESBYTERIAN CHURCH OF BROOKLYN, IN BEHALF OF THE AMERICAN SEAMEN'S FRIEND SOCIETY.

BY REV. J. E. ROCKWELL, D.D.

MATTHEW IV.; 18, 20.—And Jesus, walking by the Sea of Galilee, saw two brethren, Simon, called Peter, and Andrew, his brother, casting a net into the sea, for they were fishers. And he said unto them: Follow me, and I will make you fishers of men. And they straightway left their nets and followed him.

We have in these words, and those which immediately follow them, the history of the calling of the apostles who were to bear a prominent and important part, in the preaching of the Gospel and the establishment of the Christian Church. Our Saviour, in his Divine omniscience and power, had the wisdom and ability to select, from all classes of society, those who should be his immediate followers and disciples, and, had he chosen to do so, might have surrounded himself by the wise and the noble as well as by those who were poor and despised.— We cannot doubt that the same grace which made Peter and John his willing servants, could have turned the hearts even of Cæsar or Herod, or the priests of the Jewish Church, toward himself, and to have made them, as he afterwards made Saul, chosen vessels to declare his glory. Yet he did not thus lay the foundations of his Church. Not many wise or mighty were called. Here and there one like Nicodemus, or Joseph of Arimathea, sought him, and sat at his feet, and believed his words. Yet those whom he selected to be his apostles, on whom the great work of establishing his Church was to be laid, were men who, for the time, were unknown to the world, but who were fitted by their habits to endure hardness, and toil, and privations, and promptly and boldly to defend the religion which he well knew would be everywhere spoken against.

Among those whom he thus called, and who were destined to act the most prominent part in the work assigned them, were Peter and John, whom he found with their brothers, engaged in their work as fishermen along the shores of the Galilean Sea. There is a wondrous significance in this choice, which, when viewed in the light of the promises and the Providence of God, serves to point out to the Church one of the great moral agencies which it is to use in the conversion of the world to God. In many of the most remarkable prophecies which point to the latter day glory, we find the future prosperity and increase of the Church, connected intimately and inseparably with those "who do business upon the great waters." When the kings of the earth are to come and present their offerings at the great marriage feast of the Lamb and his bride, the daughter of Tyre (the symbol of commerce) is to be there with a gift. When the Church is called to look forth upon the multitudes which are coming up with their treasures to add to her power and glory, she is pointed to the sea, and beholds the navies of the world flocking to her 'as a cloud,' bringing her sons from afar, their silver and their gold with them. When the abundance of the sea is converted to God, the forces of the Gentiles are also brought to submit to his authority. Thus do we find the sea and its inhabitants identified in prophecy with the coming glory and prosperity of the Church; and, interpreting the words before us in the light of these promises, we may see the uses which Christ is yet to make of the sailor in the extension of his kingdom and the upbuilding of his Church.

1. In the first place, the sailor is peculiarly susceptible to religious influences and impressions. Notice the promptness with which the fishermen of Tiberias left their nets and followed Christ when they were made aware of his Divine claims, and heard his summons that called them to be his disciples. There was no hesitancy — no questioning of doubt and unbelief — no conferring with flesh and blood. Observe their conduct when amid the storm and darkness which shut in upon them while tossing upon the waters of the Sea of Galilee, they beheld a form walking upon the waves, and at length heard the voice of Jesus saying, "It is I, be not afraid." With what readiness did they acknowledge his divine claims. They had no doubt that he was God manifest in the flesh, and at once fell down and worshipped him. Nor are they any less disposed to receive the truth now when it is presented to them; and when they have fully embraced, they are bold to profess it, and prompt in making it known to others. The character of Peter and John and their brethren has often been reproduced in the sailor who has felt the drawings of this love of Christ. He is not the stolid and unthinking wretch that many fancy him to be. He is, like all men, a sinner. He needs, as do all men, the grace of Christ and the renewing influences of the Spirit.— He is exposed to peculiar temptations, and under them is often led into gross sins. Yet perhaps no one will so gratefully welcome the hand that is stretched out to save him from ruin, no one more readily listen to the counsels of a Christian friend who warns him of his guilt and danger, and points him to the means of his recovery therefrom. Use with him the imagery with which he is most familiar; speak to him of the blessed Jesus, "who once pressed a sailor's pillow, and can feel a sailor's woe," and you have a direct communication with his heart. He listens with a fixed attention, and is at no pains to conceal the tears that tell you how deep is the feeling that is stirring within him. Secure his attention

when it is his watch below, and draw out from him the history of his life, and in all probability you will find in his heart the traces of early religious impressions, or the memory of a mother's love and prayers, which time and temptation have never effaced, and which will afford you arguments and motives with which to make your most potent appeals to his heart and conscience. You will often find that, however far he may have drifted away from his mooring upon the great sea of life, and however fearfully the waves of temptation and sin have risen around him, there is an undercurrent of gentle influences, of warm affections, of grateful and tender memories of childhood and home, which will greatly aid you in your efforts to lead him back to the paths of virtue and safety, and to bring him to Christ.

2. And again, the character and habits of the sailor are such as to wonderfully qualify him to take an active and important part in the extension and upbuilding of the Redeemer's kingdom. The choice which our Saviour made by the Sea of Galilee, of hardy fishermen to be his disciples, was significant, as pointing to one of the great instrumentalities he is to use in the conversion of the world to himself. Those men who so promptly left their nets and their ship at his intimation were bold and fearless, full of warm and generous impulses, and they brought to their work all the ardor and energy, and noble daring and love of toil which marked their former course of life.—He often left them, to see that without him they could do nothing. He often rebuked their misguided zeal, and showed them the better way, but he never discouraged their noble and daring traits of character. Even when the impulses of Peter had been subdued and chastened by his sad experience of his own weakness, and by the aid of divine grace, he exhibited still the same manly and fearless qualities which marked him while following his early profession. His hasty zeal gave way to a wonderful dignity and firmness of purpose; to great sagacity; to an earnest love of active labor; to patient and self-denying toil; and to a fearlessness of danger and suffering which left the impress of his character wherever he went. He became a bold and courageous herald of the Gospel; planted churches over all the land; and was the first to break over the ancient prejudices of the Jewish mind, and to preach to the Gentiles the unsearchable riches of Jesus Christ. He who had in his early life often braved the perils of the sea, and faced a thousand dangers, had in those years of toil acquired a fearlessness which projected itself into his after life, and enabled him, with the early companion of his seafaring life, to say to the Jewish Sanhedrim, when they would forbid them to speak in the name of Jesus, "We ought to obey God rather than man. The God of our fathers raised up Jesus, whom ye slew and hanged on a tree. Him hath God exalted with his right hand to be a Prince and a Saviour, for to give repentance unto Israel and forgiveness of sins. And we are witnesses of these things, and so also is the Holy Ghost, whom God hath given to them that obey him." And how nobly did the early habits of the fishermen of Galilee indicate themselves in their unflinching courage as they went forth from the Jewish Council yet smarting with their wounds, rejoicing that they were counted worthy to suffer shame for the name of Jesus.

And it is evident that they who are to bear the most important part in the work which yet lies before the Church must possess these same elements of promptness, obedience, fearlessness, and self-denial, which are the certain results of a life spent amid the duties and perils of the sailor. There is that in his life, habits, and work which seems eminently to qualify him, when grace has made him a new creature, to do a noble work for Christ and his Church. It is no overstrained utterance which one of Nature's great limners put into his lips, as his own soul felt the inspiration of the scene, with which he is familiar:

"And I have loved thee, Ocean! and my joy
Of youthful spirits was on thy breast to be
Borne like thy bubbles onward. From a boy
I wantoned with thy breakers; they to me
Were a delight; and if the freshening sea
Made them a terror, 'twas a pleasing fear.
For I was, as it were, a child of thee,
And trusted to thy billows far and near,
And laid my hand upon thy main, as I do here."

When a man thus bold and daring becomes a servant of Christ, he goes forth, not tamely to check and conceal his feelings, nor to deny his professions, but bravely and nobly to bear testimony to the grace that hath saved him from sin and hell, made him a child of God, and renewed his nature, and called him to be an heir of eternal life.

3. Nor are we left simply to vague conjecture, or analogical reasoning as to what the sailor can do when his heart has been subdued and moulded by the influences of the Gospel and the grace of God. Divine Providence as well as the Holy Scriptures has pointed to him as one of the important instruments yet to be used in the conversion of the world. He forms the great connecting link between the nations, which but for him would be as widely separated as though occupying different worlds.—He bore the first messages of the Gospel to the Gentiles. He still is the agent by which the Bible and the Missionary is carried to the heathen. Nor has he been a silent and uninterested actor in this work. Converted sailors have been everywhere making their interest felt, in distributing Bibles and tracts, and in making known the Gospel of the grace of God. The efforts which have been put forth for the salvation of those who go down to the sea in ships have met with a success which has attended no similar effort towards the evangelizing of the world. It may be safely declared that, when we consider the amount of the agencies employed in behalf of sailors, and contrast them with those which are used for the conversion of heathens or the spread of the Gospel at home, the work of benefitting and saving seafaring men is every way the most encouraging. It is now about a half century since the first organized effort was made for the benefit of this class of men. Fifty years ago the first Bethel flag was raised as the signal for the assembling of the seamen of the Thames for religious worship. A society for the moral improvement of sailors had already been established in America, though it was short-lived. It was not long before a deep and powerful work of grace commenced, and sea captains and sailors were heard speaking of the wonders which God had wrought for them; while on many a vessel far out upon the sea, worship and the voice of prayer and praise was heard. And, though it can never be known until the histories of life shall be all summed up in the eternal world what an amount of

good has been accomplished by converted sailors, as they have passed around the world in their arduous and dangerous profession, yet we may form some idea of what they have done, and may accomplish, by considering the few facts which have come to our knowledge. It was a sailor in one of Captain Cook's ships who first told the Sandwich Islanders that their idols were vain things, and that by-and-by men would come to tell them of the God in Heaven who alone claimed their worship. A Christian sea captain, as he passed down the coast of South America, distributed Bibles and tracts as he had opportunity, and thus sowed good seed, which may be reaped after many days. A sailor, ordained as a preacher, organized a church with eighty or ninety converted Catholics upon an island on the South American coast. When the priest came to reclaim them, he was met with arguments which he could not gainsay or answer. Three converted sailors formed a prayer-meeting upon their ship, at which six of their mates were converted; and when they reached their destination in India, continued their services, at which sailors from other vessels found peace in believing. Among the heralds of the Cross, some of the noblest and most successful preachers have been converted sailors, who have brought to their work all the promptness and energy, and courage and deathless zeal which entered into their characters "while doing business upon the great waters."

A single fact, recently brought under my own observation, while passing over the great lakes which form the northern boundary of our country, will serve to illustrate the power for good which such men possess, and the results they may achieve:

At the point where the waters of Green Bay unite with those of Lake Michigan, stands a cluster of islands of singular and romantic beauty, known as the Washington Group, which have for years been the resort of fishermen, and which, in the increase of their business, have become filled with a population now amounting to more than a thousand souls. For years these hardy and enterprizing men have lived in these wild scenes, without any form of religious instruction, and, as a natural result, spent their hours of leisure in idleness and dissipation. The money which they obtained in the summer during the fishing season was spent in the winter in drinking and gambling, and the whole population seemed debased and ruined by vice. Among the men who occasionally stopped for business at these islands was an old sea captain, in command of a lake vessel, who had for many years been a servant of the Lord Jesus. The condition of these people so affected the heart of Capt. Kitwood that he made an appeal in their behalf to the agents of the Western Seamen's Friend Society, and requested them to appoint a chaplain for this post. After an earnest but fruitless inquiry for a minister whom they might send thither, it was suggested to the captain that he should himself undertake the work. The call came to him like the voice of Providence and his answer was as cheerful and prompt as that of the disciples who were henceforth to become fishers of men. He had received only the ordinary rudiments of an education, but had long been a learner in the school of Christ, and he resolved to do what he could for the salvation of that people. When he appeared among them, and made known his determination to remain with him, and preach to them the Gospel, he was met with bitter hostility, and even with threats to take his life. They consulted together what should be done to arrest him in his purpose. Some counselled to drown him, and others to set him on the nearest mainland, and thus rid themselves of him and his religion. But their threats of violence could not move him from his purpose, and he assured them that he intended to remain among them and preach the Gospel. Gaining the ear and the confidence of one of their number, whose natural virtues had not wholly been marred by intemperance, he prevailed upon him to give him the use of his house for religious service; and when this was known, threats were made to burn the house, if preaching were allowed therein. Yet all these things did not move him from his purpose. He was a bold and resolute man, whose former life and habits had prepared him to meet danger, and to face his enemies with a bold front. With his own hand he prepared some rude seats for the service, and sent out an invitation for the people to attend religious service on the coming Sabbath. A few women and children accepted the invitation; but the men, like the sons of Belial of old, gathered their dogs together in front of the house, having stimulated themselves by the free use of whiskey for their work of disturbing the worshippers within. When the captain began to preach, they set their dogs to fighting, and at the noise which they set up, most of the people left the house. When the fight was over they returned again, and the captain, who had patiently waited for them, resumed his discourse, and invited them, at its close, to meet again on the next Lord's day. During that week, he visited the mothers of the island, and talked with them plainly concerning their duties to their children, and invited them to bring them together, and form a Sabbath-school upon the next Sunday. They came together at the appointed time, and their children were arranged into classes and provided with books and papers. Gradually did the opposition to his work die away, as the people saw his earnestness and zeal, and felt the power of his kindness and love, and saw what he was doing for their children. One and another of those who had met him with threats and abuse dropped in to hear him preach, and some

"Who came to scoff, remained to pray."

Among the first who began to feel the power of the truth, was the man in whose house he had first held religious worship, and soon he and his wife were hopefully converted to God. Before the close of the summer, a work of grace commenced among them by which a goodly number were awakened, and brought to a saving knowledge of the truth. The place where they had met had already become too small for them, and a large saw-mill was fitted up for worship, and filled every Sabbath with a crowd of eager attentive listeners.—Under the auspices of the Western Seamen's Friend Society, a church was organized, and Captain Kitwood, having been ordained, at a meeting of the Methodist Conference, by a bishop, who recognized in him one who, though not regularly educated for the ministry, had been evidently called of God, was fully and duly set apart to his work. A score or more of persons, who had been converted under his short ministry, were organized into a church, among whom was a man sixty-five years of age, with his wife and five children; and an aged woman, who had already attained the age of four-score years ere she had found a Saviour.

It now became desirable to erect a suitable chapel; and although it was in the midst of the fishing season, these hardy and earnest men, though wholly unacquainted with architecture, went into the forests, and cut down the timber and hewed it into shape, and erected the frame of a commodious building. Just before it was fully set up, and when they were wondering how to obtain the materials for its covering, a vessel loaded with lumber passed by the harbor, when it was caught in a heavy gale of wind, and in order to save it from destruction, was lightened of its deck load, which floated ashore within half a mile of the site of the new chapel. Everything that was needed was thus by a remarkable Providence landed upon the island, and was sold to the people by the agent who came in search of it at a price scarcely one-tenth of its market value. A mechanic was sent for from below, who completed the edifice; and so a plain and comfortable chapel, which only needs a tower and bell to perfect it, was before the winter finished, and dedicated to the worship of Almighty God.

Just before the close of navigation, and when these islands are shut in by a vast sea of ice, and all travel is necessarily suspended, Captain Kitwood visited Green Bay, where he was met by a business man, who was leaving the islands for the winter, as was his custom, who expressed his surprise at his determination to return and winter among that rude and vicious people. Though himself a careless and irreligious man, he had been interested in the captain and his work; and when told that the only obstacle which he then feared was a number of barrels of whiskey, which were then going on board his boat for the islands, promptly ordered them on shore, adding, in a half jocular way, "We are going to try the Gospel at the Washington Islands this winter, and if that does not succeed, then we will go back again to the whiskey."

The captain returned to his people, and the winter was passed in almost continuous services, either in the chapel or from house to house. With the absence of intoxicating drinks, disappeared the gambling and the quarreling which had for years disgraced these islands; and better than all, the Holy Spirit was manifested in their midst, and many precious souls were converted to God. Three years have now passed since this work commenced, and the reformation is so complete and undoubted, that the most sceptical must see in it the mighty power of God.

As, during my recent summer vacation, I was passing down from Buffalo to Green Bay, we came to this beautiful group of Islands at the close of a calm and lovely Sabbath, which had been spent on board the steamer in public religious services, and in delightful converse with Christian friends, from whom I heard the story of God's work among this people. As we landed on the wharf, we were met by a crowd who had come down to welcome some of their Christian brethren, and it was my pleasure to grasp by the hand the Christian sailor by whose efforts this great work had, by God's blessing, been accomplished. I heard among them not a profane word. I was assured that so great had been the change on the island, that in three years the amount of strong drink which was needed for the supply of the people had been reduced from fifty barrels to less than one. I spoke with a number who had been the subjects of this work of grace, and felt assured that they understood the language of Zion.

Guided by Captain Kitwood and one of his people, I visited the chapel, which stands in the midst of a forest, and whose white walls were shining in the light of a cloudless moon. I was struck as I walked by the side of that brother, and heard his story, with his simple faith, and his deathless zeal, and untiring energy; and I felt a freshened interest in the work that cares for the sailor, and that looks to him as one of the instruments to be used in the conversion of the world. It is a work whose results are not uncertain. It is one which has its claims upon all classes of society. Who is not indebted to the sailor? He it is who brings to us the luxuries and the various products of other lands. The fruits of the tropics, the fabrics of India and China, of France, and Holland, and England, the gold and ivory of Africa, the spices of Ceylon, the carvings of Italy, the lore of every land, are all brought to us by the sailor. He defends our coast, and guards the honor of our flag. He is the great link that binds the nations together; and with our obligations to him, shall we not care for his moral and religious wants, and remember that he has a soul to save, and that the same promptness, and energy, and fearlessness which he exhibits in his profession will, if sanctified by the grace of God, do a noble work for Christ and his Church.

I thank God for the light which is dawning upon him, and for the wholesome laws which are now giving him a measurable protection from the harpies who have long fed upon his very life-blood. It is a matter of gratitude that legal provision has been made by which the vile men who for years have boarded every ship as it entered our port, and have seduced him to enter their dens of infamy, are now restrained in their operations, and prevented by severe penalties from engaging in their work of ruin. Let us, then, with fresh ardor and zeal, engage in the blessed enterprize of elevating seamen by religious influences, and bringing them within the reach of the light and blessing of the Gospel. This we may best do through the agency of the Seamen's Friend Society. Its sole work is to care for the sailor. It does this by means of chaplains and homes, and religious reading placed on board the vessels which leave our ports. God has blessed these means to the salvation of many souls. Let us aid it in its work by a generous and noble supply of the means essential to its success, and by earnest and importunate prayer to God without whom all our efforts are vain, that he would cause the abundance of the sea to be converted to Him.

STEAM AROUND THE WORLD.

The beginning of the new year will witness the inauguration of unbroken steam communication around the globe, to be thenceforth prosecuted as regularly as the arrival and departure of European steamships at our wharves. The steamship Henry Chauncy which sailed on the 11th of December, for the Isthmus; will connect with the Golden City, for San

Francisco, and from San Francisco, on the 1st of January, the steamship Colorado will sail for Yokohama, in Japan, and Hong Cong, in China. If, arrived at the latter port, the passenger wishes still to journey westward, he can proceed by the boats of the Peninsula and Oriental Company to Bombay, and onward through the Red Sea, to the Isthmus of Suez, which, crossed by rail, conducts to the British line of Mediterranean steamers, touching at Malta and Gibraltar, and arrive in England, where a few hours of railway will enable passage to be taken in one of the dozen lines of steamships for this country—the supposed point of departure.

So wonderful are the achievements of our busy age, and such is the progress of a century which bears every progress along with it. It is now barely 365 years since the Cabots discovered North America; only 353 since Vasco Nunez de Balboa

—— "With all his men,
Stood wondering on the heights of Darien."

as the Pacific was first revealed to European eyes, and but 345 years since Magellan first crossed the Pacific and sketched its gigantic proportions. It is, indeed, but a day in the chronology of nations since this country, which unites the extremes of the old world, was organized, and hours count the period since Fulton found the power which is about being applied to such important results. And now we are at the very threshold of an event which is among the wonders of the ages, and which, coupled with the progressing Russian telegraph, is annexing Asia to our western borders as the same instrumentalities have already annexed Europe to our eastern.

What results will grow out of the enterprise so soon to be inaugurated remains to be seen. Congress has believed them to be valuable and important enough to warrant a heavy subsidy to the line which is being begun. The country has believed them to be useful, and has watched the progress of the undertaking with extreme interest. The Pacific Railroad, so rapidly building, and of which a new section is even now being formally opened at the eastern end, while the western end is advancing, and the interior being graded at several points, acts on and is acted upon by this Asiatic correspondence, so that all who have an interest in the railroad have a proportioned interest in the steamships, the two, indeed, being but parts of one harmonious whole. The dawning manufactures of the Pacific slope see that they are involved, and our manufacturers at the East cannot avoid perceiving that now the door is opened by which they can assume to rival the business of Great Britain in the East. It is plain, too, that when the exchanges contemplated by this line have gone into effect, the commerce of all the American coast of the Pacific will be vitally affected, from Peru and Chili to Russian America, and that while their commerce will do much for the Asiatic, it will also in itself gain from it.

The important feature of the opening is, that it brings the exchanges of Eastern Asia to the American seaboard of the Atlantic, and makes New York and Philadelphia the accompting houses of the world's greatest trade, rather than London. All successful commerce, from the time of Tyre and Sidon, through the eras of Egypt, Greece, Rome, the Byzantine Empire, Italy, Spain, Portugal, Holland, England—all has been created or magnified by the grasp which it had upon Asia. There was the market for purchase—there for sale. Whatever nation could sell most into Asia, and draw most from it, has prospered most; and whenever, from neglect or defeat, a country which had grown in Asiatic trade lost it, then that country descended in influence and its successor arose. The fact is inscribed in every page of history, and needs no elucidation. We are now just beginning to realize these advantages. The newly opened opportunities will advance us more than they did our predecessors, because we are in a better condition for growth, and shall have a more vigorous hold, and because exceptional causes give us an advantage which others have not had. We hold no fear that any irruption of Asiatics will flood the West, but cannot doubt that our people will found "factories" in China, which will do as much as any of the long-established houses there.

Without entering, however, upon any of the details of what may be expected from this new opportunity, it is sufficient to observe that this enterprise is one which promises to head an era in our affairs—an era, too, which may be as signally successful as the one just passed. It begins with the close of the civil war, when we are prepared for unaccustomed exertions. It begins when a spirit of enterprise penetrates every class, and when our manufactures are so started that we shall be able to meet more and greater demands than ever; when our wants, too, are beginning to expand, and when, freed from many domestic risks, we can with safety make ventures which would have been dangerous before. Its growth and its end, if it ever comes, defy the dreams of the most visionary.—*United States Gazette.*

A STAR ON FIRE.

BY EDWIN DUNKIN, OF THE ROYAL OBSERVATORY.

About the middle of May last, astronomers were startled by the announcement that a new star of considerable brightness had suddenly burst forth in the constellation Corona Borealis (the Northern Crown).— Its increase of magnitude must have been extremely rapid, for on the 9th of May an observer, who was occupied on that day in scrutinizing that portion of the heavens, felt certain that no object comparable to it was visible. On the 12th, three days afterward, the star shone with the brilliancy of one of the second magnitude, or equal to three well-known stars in the belt of Orion. The important results obtained from the observation of this truly extraordinary astronomical object are sufficient reasons for our giving a brief and popular account of its short history, which we are sure will be duly appreciated by our scientific readers.

The first person who appears to have noticed this new variable star was Mr. J. Birmingham, of Tuam, Ireland, who observed it May 12th. Subsequently, it was seen on the 13th, at Rochefort, by M. Courbebaisse, and on the same day at Athens, by M. Schmidt; on the 14th it was noticed at London, Canada West, by Mr. Barker, and on the 16th, at Manchester, by Mr. Baxendell. These observers saw it independently, without any previous notification. Attention being now drawn to the star, it has since been regularly observed, either for position or for the inquiry into its physical constitution, at most of the public and private observatories in Europe and America. Its brightness rapidly diminished after discovery, but probably not in the same ratio as it had increased before. The relative magnitudes, determined by comparison with neighboring known stars, are as follows:

May 12, ... 2 magnitude.
" 15, ...3 5 "
" 18, ...4 8 "
" 21, ...6 7 "
" 24, ...7 8 "
" 30, ...8 8 "

Very little change had taken place from May 30 to June 22. On the evening of the latter day, the magnitude was reckoned as the ninth.

So far, this discovery would not, probably, have attracted any greater attention than that of any ordinary variable. The new star would most likely have been followed very closely only till the extent and period of its variability were satisfactorily established. Of such objects the firmament contains many extraordinary examples; stars which appear for a season and then disappear, again reappearing, performing in the mean time all their changes of brightness with perfect regularity. While there are some which complete their period in days, there are others occupying months, or perhaps years, between the intervals of maximum magnitudes. If our new star had been, therefore, simply one of this class, interesting though it might have been from the abruptness of its first appearance, it would merely have added one to the list of those known variables, which are to be found scattered here and there among the fixed stars.

But astronomical observations have unfolded other properties peculiar to this star, giving us an insight into physical composition different from that of others around it. This has been attained from the observation of its spectrum, as viewed through a spectroscope attached to an astronomical telescope.

On looking at an ordinary star through a spectroscope, its spectrum is seen with transverse dark lines across it, similar to Fraunhofer's lines in the solar spectrum. Some of these are common, or nearly so, in most stellar spectra; while each star has generally, in addition, its own peculiar dark lines. This would seem to show that, whereas certain metals or gases are indicated as being present in the majority of stars, each one contains materials peculiar to itself. Now, this marvelous star in Corona Borealis, which has so astonished us all, has not only the ordinary stellar spectrum with the *dark* lines across it, but there is also a second spectrum, apparently superposed upon the other, in which four or five *bright* lines have been observed. Mr. Huggins, who has devoted his whole astronomical attention to this class of observation, has, in conjunction with Dr. W. A. Miller, concluded that the light of the star is compound in its nature, and that it has really emanated from two different sources. Mr. Huggins remarks that "each light forms its own spectrum. The principal spectrum is analagous to that of the sun. The portion of the star's light represented by this spectrum was emitted by an incandescent solid or liquid photosphere, and suffered partial absorption by passing through an atmosphere of vapors existing at a temperature lower than that of the photosphere. . . . . The second spectrum, which in the instrument appears on the one already described, consists of five *bright lines*. This order of spectrum shows that the light by which it was formed was emitted by matter in the state of gas rendered luminous by heat." Independent observations, made at the Royal Observatory, Greenwich, principally by Mr. Stone and Mr. Carpenter; and at the Imperial Observatory, Paris, by MM. Wolf and Rayet, gave results confirmatory of those made by Mr. Huggins and Dr. Miller.

Such, then, is a brief account of the analysis of the light emitted from this temporary but brilliant visitor to our sky; showing, with little doubt, that, from some cause unknown to us, it must have been the subject of a terrible catastrophe, at a period perhaps distant; for it must be borne in mind that, owing to its immense distance from us, we may be only witnessing the calamity of a past age.— From the sudden blazing forth of this star, and then its rapid fading away, Mr. Huggins and Dr. Miller have suggested that, in consequence of a great internal convulsion, probably a large quantity of hydrogen and other gases were emitted from it, " the hydrogen, by its combination with some other element, giving out the light represented by the bright lines, and at the same time heating to the point of vivid incandescence the solid matter of the photosphere. As the hydrogen becomes exhausted, all the phenomena diminish in intensity, and the star rapidly wanes." That hydrogen gas in a state of combustion was present is very probable; for, by comparing simultaneously the bright lines of the stellar spectrum with those of hydrogen produced by the induction spark, taken through the vapor of water, it was found that two of the lines sensibly coincided. During a discussion on this star, at a meeting of the Royal Astronomical Society on June 8, the astronomer royal expressed his firm belief that this wonderful object was actually in flames.

If we were inclined to speculate on this unique astronomical phenomenon, or the probable consequences arising from such a sudden outburst of fiery gas, what au extensive subject for contemplation is opened to us. Astronomically, we have known this minute star for years without suspicion; it has been classified with others of similar magnitude; it has been one of many millions of such while now it will be remembered by all future generations as one of the most extraordinary among the most celebrated stars of the universe. Or let our speculations be carried a little further, and let us reasonably suppose this small and hitherto nearly invisible object to be an immense globe like our own sun, and surrounded probably with planets and satellites depending upon their center for light and heat, what would be the effect of this sudden conflagration on them? It makes one almost shudder at the idea of a system of worlds being annihilated at once without warning.— But such must doubtless be the fact. We, however, in this quiet world of ours, can scarcely, perhaps, realize such a catastrophe; but were our sun, which is only a star analagous to those in the heavens around us, to be suddenly ignited in a similar manner to this distant and unknown sun, all its attendant planets and satellites the earth included, would be destroyed.—*Leisure Hour.*

MAHOMMEDANISM OR CHRISTIANITY.

The Anthropological Society of London, the youngest and most pretentious of the so-called scientific societies of England, has lately been discussing the question of whether Mahommedanism or Christianity is better suited for the civilization and elevation of the African race. Mr. W. Winwood Reade, the author of *Savage Africa*, some time ago read a paper justifying Mahommedanism, polygamy, and slavery, and, as a matter of course, condemning Christian missions, as Christianity was altogether unsuited to the negro, whom it only made worse than he was when in a Pagan state. He was supported in his views by Captain Burton, the traveler.

At an adjourned meeting, an able reply to this attack was read by Mr. H. Bernard Owen, who vindicated the character of the Christian negro and his instructors, while at the same time, he pointed out how much the work of the missionary was thwarted, and the character of his converts deteriorated, by the conduct of the traders on the coast, who set both the faith and morals of the Gospel at defiance. He pointed to remarkable instances of mental and moral attainment among the maligned race. The case of Bishop Crowther is, he said, an effectual refutation of the assertion that the native African is incapable of being raised to a very high standard of intellectual advancement. Does the request of another native minister (Rev. G. Nichol) betray incapacity for education? He desired a friend to send him from England some books, foremost on the list of which was *Alford's Greek Testament*, next an *Arabic Lexicon*, *Maunder's Treasury of Universal Knowledge*, *Maunder's Biographical Treasury*, *Melvill's Sermons*, etc. To the Church Missionary Society he applies for two first-rate University men to superintend the studies of the African theological students, adding: "It will not do to send men of ordinary capacity now-a-days. Our students are too well taught in their Greek Testament not to catch their professor tripping, if he displays insufficient knowledge." That this assertion is not unfounded, the Freetown grammar school examinations in 1859 conclusively show. The Governor expressed his astonishment at the intelligence of the pupils. "I had no idea that you had such youths," said he; "they can learn anything."

Every part of the coast, from Sierra Leone to the Gaboon, can boldly proclaim the success of missionary enterprise. With regard to the assertion that the converts to Mahommedanism were much more numerous than those to Christianity, such a representation is not corroborated by official documents, for the Colonial Blue Book, issued in 1863, gives the returns from Sierra Leone under the census of 1860 as follows: Total population, 41,624; of these were liberated Africans, 15,782; born within the colony, 22,593. Of the whole population, only 3,357 remained Pagans; 1,734 were Mohammedans, 15,180 Methodists, etc., and 12,954 Church people; 11,016 children were taught in the schools in the year. The trade of the colony is steadily growing; the population is rapidly learning the general customs of civilized society, and in many instances amassing wealth, enabling them to vie with European enterprise. Sierra Leone is thus proving not only a refuge for those who are rescued from slavery, but a nucleus of civilization and school of Christian teaching.

Dr. Livingston replied very convincingly, though somewhat contemptuously, to the statements made by Mr. Reads and Captain Burton, at a meeting of the London Missionary Society. He alluded in the following terms to the statements concerning the sprend of Mohammedanism in Africa:

"Ever since I was a boy I have heard a great deal about the advance of Mohammedanism; and in my own pretty extensive travels, I have also been looking out for the advance of that wave of Mohammedanism which I was led to believe would soon spread over the continent of Africa. Now, I never happened to meet with a Mohammedan till two years ago, when I met two Arabs on Lake Nyanza, who were very busy slave-traders. They were building an Arab vessel to transport slaves across the lake toward the east, and they were at the same time as busy as they could possibly be transporting the slaves by means of two boats. One of their men understood the Makololo language. I found him to be very intelligent, and we could converse readily together. I was rather anxious to find out whether he had been made a convert. He was the servant of these Arabs, who had been there for fourteen years; but this poor fellow knew nothing at all about Mahommedanism, except that it was wrong to eat an animal if its throat was not cut. (Laughter.) Why, the people knew as much of our religion, as that in about three weeks after our arrival, for they would not go to hoe their garden on Sundays, because they were afraid that if they did they would have an unlucky crop. All the Mohammedan proselytism that has come under my observation, and all that I have been able to ascertain about their converts, is simply this, that occasionally in the west and north of Africa they make forays and capture numbers of people, and sometimes conquer large portions of territory. In doing this they gratify their own selfishness; they get slaves, land and other plunder; but I find lately, on making some inquiries, that the native Christians, the men whom our missionaries have converted in West and South Africa, and also in the West Indies, contributed upward of £15,000 annually to the support and spread of their faith. (Cheers). In the one case the Mohammedans gratify their selfishness; in the other the native Christians make large sacrifices for the propagation of their religion.— Now, I think the religion which teaches people to deny themselves and make sacrifices, must be divine; and for all that I can ascertain, the only religion that makes proselytes is the religion of our Lord Jesus Christ."

SAVING A WRECKED CREW.

A short time since, the schooner *Evelyn Treat* of Frankfort, Me., was wrecked off Nantucket. There were five men aboard. When seen she was 200 yards from shore, her decks under water, and the men lashed to the rigging. The manner of their rescue is thus given by the New Bedford Mercury:

The wind was blowing furiously, and the sea making a complete breach over her. A wrecking gang immediately proceeded to the shore, about two miles off, and took with them the gun of the Massachusetts Humane Society, with its apparatus. Cit:zens soon followed, and by the time the gun was ready for use, a considerable number had arrived at the beach. No life-boat could be launched, although one was at hand, and the masts, as they oscillated, showed that there was no time to be lost. The gun was loaded and elevated, and so skilfully that the line attached to it fell upon the rigging of the ill-fated vessel, so that the men, who were all in the rigging, got the small line, the end of which was carried by the ball beyond the vessel. After much delay by reason of their weakness, they hauled on board the larger line attached, and read the order sent with it to fasten it to the mainmast head. When this was done, a chair made for the purpose was run off on a hanging block, and one of the crew got in to be hauled on shore. When his weight began to press on the small line from the masthead to the shore, it began to stretch and to sink down towards the top of the raging billows beneath him. But everything was well rigged on shore, and the tackle on the shore end was gradually gathered in, which kept him from being drifted from his seat by the surges. When a litt:e more than half way to land, the small line from the vessel used to veer him along the line and to pull the chair back, got foul, and for more than an hour there the poor fellow hung, the line stretching, and the waves ready to swallow him in case it parted. At last enough was cleared to bring the man within a few yards of the nearest breaker, into which he was now dipping every time the vessel rolled towards the beach. Then was the time for fresh exertion. Three men went into the breakers up to their necks, got nearly under him and threw him a rope, with orders to lash it around him and drop into the breakers from the chair. This he did, and he was pulled through the surf and saved. The sailor was the son of the master, an old man still on board. The chair was hauled off again, and another of the crew with much delay landed in the same way, by the same three men rushing into the serf and giving him a line that he could drop overboard. The third man that came was the captain, who had been hurt when the vessel struck at midnight. He had another son on board, who veered him out the line, but unfortunately the line on board got more foul, and he hung for another hour where he could not be reached from the shore. The old man was dipping into the breakers as the vessel rolled, and seemed nearly exhausted. A crotch was set up under the line, which held him up some, when a young man offered to "shin" along the line and cut the small one leading from the vessel. This he did amid the cheers of the multitude, and at the risk of his own life, and soon the old gentleman was landed and taken to town. The other two were soon after rescued, and the people came away with a light heart.

INDIRECT INFLUENCE OF CHRISTIAN EFFORT.

BY REV. C. J. JONES.

During the great revival of 1858, many of our United States seamen were converted to God. At one time, there were over one hundred on board the receiving-ship North Carolina. In process of time these men were drafted to the various men-of-war then fitting out for foreign stations—some in one ship, and some in another—until there were representatives of the cause of Christ in a large number of vessels of our navy. These men became the centres of religious influence, and witnessed a good profession among their ungodly shipmates. The number of pious seamen was thus, during the next two years, very largely increased, and at the opening of our rebellion, in 1861, almost every vessel dispatched to blockade our coast carried with her a praying band, by whom prayer-meetings were established, and the gundeck, the berth-deck, the reef-deck, the fore-passage, the steerage, and even the "tops" and the "chains" became vocal with prayer and praise to God. On board one of these vessels on the Southern coast, the brethren who were accustomed to meet for prayer singled out one of their shipmates, and united their prayers in his behalf. He was reckless and careless, and absolutely repulsive toward those who would have done him good. Months rolled away. Their efforts were unavailing. He grew worse and worse. Prayer did not cease, though the subject of them seemed farther from God than ever. At this juncture, a letter was written by one of the brethren to the pastor of the Mariner's Church in New York, giving an account of the good work in progress on board the ship, saying nothing, however, about the young man who was the object of their solicitude. The letter was read in the Port Society's Mariner's Church at the montly concert of prayer. In the audience was a stranger, providentially led there that evening, who was the friend of the young man who had been so faithfully and so unsuccessfully importuned by his shipmates to turn to God. The intelligence affected the stranger, and he thought of his young friend on board that same ship, and wondered whether he had yielded to the mercy of God. He was induced to write to him, and to appeal to him to accept the invitation of Infinite Love. That letter was blessed of God to the conversion of his soul. He then joined himself to his praying shipmates, and revealed to them the blessed intelligence that he was "*born of God.*" thus they were permitted to rejoice with him, and to thank God that, indirectly at least, they were permitted to see the answer to their long-continued prayers.

Progress in Chili.

On the first Sabbath in January, the first Protestant church was opened in Santiago, Chili, the sermon being preached to a full and attentive audience by Rev. David Trumbull. Another Protestant church was also opened in Orsono for the Germans. The press noticed the event with pride of the liberality of their laws, which now permit Protestants to build churches and hold schools. The *Patria* of Valparaiso, the best daily paper in Chili, in a long article upon the inauguration of this Protestant church, says, "Liberty of worship in Santiago, until quite recently, was thought to be an idle chimera. That city was the general rendezvous of ostracism and the Jesuit militia. There idolatry and superstition, two insatiable monsters, set fire to the funeral pile, December 8, 1863, in which perished so much innocence and youth;" referring to the burning of the great church of the Jesuits, when over 2,000 females perished. "To-day, among this people, the Protestants raise their temples. Upon this soil is taking root and growing the tree of liberty. Is there not in this the most eloquent announcement, and the proudest testimony of the progress and civilization of the country.

Vol. 42.   FEBRUARY, 1870.   No. 2.

NOTICE.

If any LIFE MEMBER OR DIRECTOR fails to receive the MAGAZINE after this number, it will be simply because he has not asked for it. We send it upon "an annual request for the same."

Those who heretofore have received it as SUBSCRIBERS, will please remember, that, if they wish it continued, our terms are ONE DOLLAR A YEAR IN ADVANCE..

FEBRUARY, 1st, 1870.

"THE BELOVED PHYSICIAN."
IN MEMORIAM.
DR. THOMAS CLARKSON MOFFATT.
BY REV. J. E. ROCKWELL, D. D.

There are few sailors who have entered and left the port of New York during the last fifteen years, with whom the name of Dr. Moffatt is not familiar, as connected with the Seamen's Retreat on Staten Island; and there are thousands now scattered over the world that have personally experienced his tender care and surgical skill, who will hear with unaffected sorrow of his death, which occured on the 26th of December last.

He fell at his post in the fearless discharge of his duty, of the same disease which had already carried off three of his associates or predecessors in the hospital, typhus, or ship fever. As the hospital has been for many months free from any infectious disease, and is never permitted to retain such cases when they make their appearance, it is supposed that Dr. Moffatt must have contracted the fever from one who came to the Retreat evidently under its power, and whom he immediately sent to Ward's Island, directing him to be carried to the boat in his own carriage, in which he was constantly riding.

On the Sabbath preceding his death, Dr. Moffatt was in his wonted place in the Sanctuary, leading, as usual, in the praises of the House of God. In the afternoon he attended the meeting held for the children and their friends of the sabbath-school, and addressed them most tenderly and solemnly on the worth of the soul. On Monday and Tuesday he was attending to his ordinary duties in the hospital and elsewhere, though complaining of chilliness and occasional wandering pains. On Tuesday evening a heavy chill set in, and thenceforward the disease, which he seems to have suspected was in his system, rapidly developed itself, despite all the efforts of medical skill and science to arrest its progress.

The most eminent and skillful physicians of the Island were in attendance upon him from the hour that his disease assumed a serious and threatening aspect. Dr. Jordan and others of the medical profession were often in his sick room, and Dr. Walsher, his intimate friend, was almost constantly by his side, spending the night in watching and administering the medicine with his own hand. Loving brothers could not have showed more affectionate interest and more earnest and painful solicitude for him than did these gentlemen of the medical faculty. Could professional assiduity and human science and skill and devoted attention have turned aside the hand of disease and warded off the shafts of death, the sad record of Dr. Moffatt's decease would not now have to be made.

But despite all that affection and science could do for him, the terrible disease made unusually rapid progress, and finished its work even before it seemed to have reached its crisis.

Early on Thursday morning, I was summoned to his bedside and found him calm and cheerful, though he had already expressed his conviction that the fever would prove fatal. He complained of restlessness, and an inability to keep his mind fixed upon any one subject, or to follow out any consecutive train of thought. I knelt by his side in prayer and he responded with evident heartiness to such simple statements of the gospel as always gives comfort to the believer in times of affliction. Late in the evening of the same day I was again called to see him, and perfect some business which he had entrusted to my care. The fever had made rapid progress, but his mind was still calm. Upon the walls of his sick room had been hung a hospital chart, with the text: "What shall I do to be saved?" etc., turned into view, and the Hymn, "COME TO JESUS." These were the precious themes which he had directed to be set before his eyes, so as to enable him to fix his thoughts, and keep his mind from wandering. They were the subjects that enlisted his attention until reason lost its balance. On Thursday he passed into the delirum or unconsciousness of fever, and so continued until Sabbath afternoon, when he entered upon the rest and worship of the temple whose light is the Lamb. Just as the sun was going down, he beheld the glories of the city where there is no night, and breathed the air of the land whose inhabitant shall never say, "I am sick."

Few men like Dr. Moffatt are called to occupy such positions as he held. He was one of whom it may be said with truth, that he followed in the footsteps of Luke, the beloved physician. He could minister to the soul as well as to the body, and was ever ready to offer words of comfort and counsel to those who were brought under his professional care.

Dr. Moffatt was born at Bloomingrove, Orange Co., N. Y., in the year 1825, and was the son of godly parents, by whom he was instructed in the principles of the Christian religion, and trained up in the fear of God. Early in life he was led to receive Christ as his saviour, and to make a public profession of faith in him. In the year 1850 he graduated at the University School of Medicine, then under the care of the distinguished Dr. Mott, and in the following year was appointed one of the assistant physicians of the Seamen's Retreat. In the year 1854 he was placed at the head of the institution, a position which he filled with undoubted ability to the close of his life. In the year 1853 he married Miss Sarah A. Church, of Brooklyn, who, with the children that have been born to him, now lament his loss.

He was one of the passengers on board the steamer *Northern Indiana*, which was burned August 17th, 1856, while on the way from Buffalo to Toledo. In the midst of that fearful scene in which many lost their lives, he remained calm and self-possessed. He continued on board the burning vessel so long as there was a hope of saving any, and then putting on a life-preserver, and throwing his valise into the water, he leaped after it, and finding a floating spar from the wreck, clung to it until a passing steamer saved him.

Soon after he took up his permanent residence in Staten Island, he was elected an Elder in the Reformed Church at Stapleton, and when that was united with the Presbyterian church, was chosen to the same office in the new organization. He was also a most earnest and efficient worker in the sabbath-school, and ever manifested a deep interest in its welfare. It was always a pleasure to him, to meet the children in their Sabbath afternoon's service, to lead them in their songs of praise and to speak to them a word for Jesus and the soul.

In the arrangements made in the church for having reports upon the various departments of the missionary work, at the monthly concert of prayer, the cause of the sailor was naturally assigned to Dr. Moffatt, and the earnest and large hearted interest which he manifested in this important field of Christian enterprise, never failed to awaken a corresponding feeling in the minds of his hearers. They who were present at the last December concert, will not soon forget his allusion to the work of grace which had been quietly going on in the Retreat for the last two years, in which it is believed that over one hundred souls have been converted to God, and his tender and touching allusion to the dying sailor whose attention had been turned to his spiritual interests by the reading of the fourteenth chapter of John.

Dr. Moffatt was one who literally watched for souls. Often since the writer's connection with him as his pastor, has he been taken out in his carriage to see some patient who was in need of spiritual counsel and comfort. Still more frequently has he heard from him descriptions of cases requiring his attention, giving min-

sician when stricken down by disease. His presence by the bedside of a dying sailor was calculated to soften the harshness of the poor fellow's fate, his words of religious comfort spoken in accents of purest Christianity found an echo in many an obdurate heart. To say that his patients loved him would be but a weak manner of expressing their regard for him. The sick man has watched for his coming, and his countenance grew brighter when Dr. Moffatt's gentle hand touched his brow. There will be mourning in every clime in which the American flag waves when seamen hear of his death." Such is the testimony borne to the life and character of a Christian physician. It is impossible to estimate the good which such a man can accomplish. Who would not prefer him for ministrations in his family to a godless, pleasure-loving, or dissipated man of the world, however skillful he might be in his profession? He moves amid the sick and afflicted like an angel of mercy, and where human skill and science is powerless, can with a tender and loving heart, point the dying to the Great Physician, and comfort the mourner with words of Christian sympathy and compassion.

Such a man was Dr. Moffatt. All his knowledge was sanctified by religion. His noble profession was exalted by being made the means and occasion of doing good to the soul as well as the body. By a wise but inscrutable Providence, he has been called away from his work just when he seemed most necessary to his family and to society. His name will long be fragrant in the community where his life was spent. His memory will be blessed for it is the memory of the just.

It needed not the testimony of the dying hour to assure his friends that all was peace. Pleasant as it is to hear amid the whispered farewells of dying friends expressions of faith and hope, it is far better to be able to look back upon a life that has given its unvarying testimony to the value and power of the Gospel. And such is the comfort which they have who now weep over his death. Early in his sickness, when expressing his belief that he should not survive the fever, he also expressed his confidence in Christ as his Saviour, and his hope of seeing him as he is. His life had been given to him.

And when death came he had nothing to do but to die. It was of little moment to him whether his great change came amid the delirium or unconsciousness of fever, or while reason had her perfect or proper balance. His work of preparation had been made in health and his earlier years; and many, as they now recall his experiences and his exercises, feel that he has for many months been ripening for heaven and preparing for his great and last change. When he thought that probably a malignant and fatal disease was at work within him, he looked at the fact calmly and without pain. He knew whom he had believed, and was persuaded that he was able to keep that which he had committed unto him until the great day. Hence when he felt that his thoughts were already disposed to become confused under the influence of disease, he directed these words to be set before his eyes which most simply and clearly brought before him the plan of salvation. They recalled to him his needs as a sinner and his only help in Christ as an all-sufficient Saviour. It was the repetition in another form of the dying sentiment of the sainted Alexander: "All my theology is narrowed down to one point, 'Jesus Christ came into the world to save sinners.'"

It is a grateful fact to record the history of men of science and learning who have consecrated all their attainments to the glory of God and the honor of Christ. Such a history is full of instruction. Such a death re-echoes the closing sentiment of the Thanatopsis of our honored poet:

"So live, that when thy summons comes to join
 The innumerable caravan that moves
 To that mysterious realm, where each shall take
 His chamber in the silent halls of death,
 Thou go not like the quarry slave at night,
 Scourged to his dungeon, but sustained and soothed
 By an unfaltering trust, approach thy grave
 Like one who wraps the drapery of his couch
 About him and lies down to pleasant dreams."

May the thousands to whom Dr. Moffatt has ministered, remember his words of warning and counsel, and his godly example and life. And may God, who has the hearts of all men in his hand, raise up from the multitude of young men who are yearly entering the profession which he honoured, many who shall add to their science and skill, the humility, the faith, and the love to God and man which made him truly "a beloved physician."

At a meeting of the Board of Trustees of the SEAMEN'S FUND AND RETREAT, held at their office No. 12 Old Ship, on Thursday, January 10, 1870, the following resolutions were adopted:

Whereas, The Trustees of the Seamen's Fund and Retreat, having heard of the death of Thomas Clarkson Moffatt, M.D., which occurred on the 24th December ultimo, thereupon,

Resolved, That while we recognize in this event the hand of an all-wise but inscrutable Providence, and would bow with submission thereto, we can but mourn deeply over the loss of one endeared to us by long and intimate association with us in the care of the institution of which we have the oversight.

Resolved, That we hereby record our testimony to the value of the long and faithful services of our deceased friend as the Physician in Chief of the Seamen's Retreat, to his kind, tender and Christian sympathy with the suffering, and to his noble, fearless, and philanthropic efforts in behalf of the patients committed to his care.

Resolved, That we shall long bear with us the memory of his pure and exalted character as a citizen and philanthropist—his self-denying devotion to the good of others—his attainments in earnest devotion to his profession—his manliness, intelligence, prudence and wisdom—his warm and generous sensibilities—his high sense of honor and of right, and his noble exemplification of the virtues of a christian.

Resolved, That we are deeply sensible of the loss which the Institution has sustained to which he has so long ministered, and in whose service he was at his death.

Resolved, That we mourn with his bereaved family over their loss, and hereby tender to his afflicted widow and children our cordial sympathies and the assurance of our earnest prayers that the God of the widow and fatherless may sustain and comfort them.

Resolved, That these proceedings be published in our Annual Report, and be read by the chaplain upon the Sabbath in the Chapel of the Institution, and that a copy of them be forwarded to the family of the deceased.

NEW YORK, January 13, 1870.

A EUROPEAN HOLIDAY.

BY AN EYE WITNESS.

Yesterday was a great day in Antwerp. It will be memorable in the history of the port as the day on which the new dock, or rather, another section of the series of new docks which have been long in process of construction, was opened. The old docks were built by Napoleon the First, who contemplated making this port one of his chief naval stations, for which the harbor is so admirably fitted. But as these have proved quite inadequate to the increasing commerce of the port a series of new docks were projected some fifteen years ago. The king of Belgium, assisted in laying the corner stone in 1856. One section has been open for several years, and now another large section is completed and was opened yesterday with great *éclat*. Of course, the day chosen for this celebration, as for all public demonstrations, was the *Sabbath*. Active and expensive preparations for this great occasion have been going on for several weeks, and the work has been very much hastened by the clerical party in whose hands the city government now is, in order to bring on the celebration before the election, which occurs in a few days, with the hope of making political capital out of it against the rising power of the liberal party who hope to carry the day. Hundreds of flag staffs were planted along the basin, a most magnificent and celebrated series of fireworks was erected, preparations for a grand illumination along the whole course of the river were made, and the great guns were put into position. Kiosks for the music were constructed; two great triumphal arcs composed of boxes, barrels, bales and bags of merchandise were erected, and between them, an immense platform with seats for the city government and two or three thousand invited guests was prepared in front of the dock. Every thing was in readiness. The day could not have been more pleasant and beautiful. In the early morning ten thousand flags, of every nation, were seen floating in the breeze from the shipping in every quarter, and from the windows and housetops, and stretched across the streets throughout the neighborhood of the docks. The people were coming in from the country and gathering from all parts of the city to assist at the celebration. The crowd was immense. There could not have been less than 20,000 on the spot at 11 o'clock, the hour appointed for the inauguration, and probably, two or three times that number visited the scene of display in the course of the day and evening, and the *estaminets* and grog shops in the vicinity, having all laid in an extra supply of liquors for the day, did a most thriving business. Now the Burgomaster makes his speech; the commemorative stone is laid; the gates are thrown open; the cannons boom; the multitude shout and two large Belgian ships prepared for the occasion, accompanied by several others of different nations, all decked out with colors flying from every part and manned throughout all their spars to the very top, with the jolly sailors, dancing and cheering, with bands of music on deck,—glided through the gates from either side. Again the cannons roar and the multitude shout at the top of their voices, and wave their handkerchiefs and swing their hats,—and so the first act in the drama is finished at noon. In the afternoon, at 3 o'clock, there was music in the kiosks and a general jollification in the drinking saloons. In the evening the illumination takes place, and the whole is closed by a most magnificent display of fireworks from 9 to 10 o'clock.

Notwithstanding the enlargement of our hitherto commodious docks the accommodation is not sufficient for the increasing demands of this port. The authorities are hastening the completion of other docks, and still others and larger accommodation are projected. The city also has been greatly extended and improved during the past three or four years. I do not believe there is a city in Europe which is improving and increasing as fast as Antwerp. It is already the chief entrepot in Europe for the petroleum and the guano trade, and perhaps, also, for the trade in hides, wool and dye woods from South America. The merchants here expect it will soon be, in every respect, the leading commercial port on the continent. *But it is a very wicked port.* Its accommodation for seamen could hardly be worse, nor the temptation to intoxication and immorality greater than they now are. From my window I can count more than twenty grog shops within as many rods that are in full blast day and night and Sundays above all, and could I look round the corner—for our view is much obstructed, I could count three or four times as many more, and as you look into the doorways and windows of these ante-chambers of hell you will see girls serving liquor to scores of half intoxicated brutes. There is not one hour in the twenty four in which you will not hear the song of the drunkard and meet with drunken men reeling through the streets and lying along the side walks and in the gutters. The whole city seems to be possessed, both high and low, rich and poor, male and female, with this mania for drink, drink, drink—not for water—indeed the water here is not a fit beverage—but for something that will exhilarate—stupify or intoxicate. This leads to such exhibitions of gross indecency on every side in the public streets, that one cannot walk anywhere, especially if he has ladies in his company without confusion and shame!

"Sooner Hang Than Deny Him."

An old sailor recently rose in a prayer meeting and asked prayers for seamen. While up he told of his conversion. "I know (he said) what it is to profess Christ in a ship's crew of three hundred men on board of a man-of-war. And when they tried every way to drive me from my steadfastness, I told them at last that I would sooner hang at the end of the yard-arm than deny my Divine Redeemer, and then they *let me alone*."

THEORIES OF EARTHQUAKES.

Theories as to the cause of earthquakes are innumerable. Their primary cause, as well as their intimate nature, is no more known than their relations to the whole of atmosphero-terrestrial phenomena. The ancient philosophers attributed earthquakes to ordinary air which was blazing in the bowels of the earth. This air engulphed in the cavities of the earth is condensed into clouds, is compressed, accumulates, is loosed, revolves circularly, or in a whirlwind, and finding vent, escapes with a crash by terribly shaking the ground. Such is one of the first theories sustained by Anaximander Anaxagoras, Aristotle, and even Seneca, with others as renowned. All we can say at present is, that earthquakes naturally belong to dynamic phenomena, while in their origin, certain electro-chemical actions must play either a primary or secondary part. The ground is shaken by a system of waves of diverse kinds. According to the mode of first impulsion, these are sent from the interior to the outside of the earth's crust, and *vice versa*, as well as to a certain depth of the heated mass below. The idea of comparing the progress of earthquakes to sonorous waves was first proposed by Dr. Young, and sustained by Gay-Lussac.

Many philosophers of antiquity, and among them Pliny, compared earthquakes to subterranean thunders. Dr. Stukely read before the Royal Society of London in 1750, memoirs in which he held that electricity was the cause of earthquakes. Beccaria was of the same opinion. Hyacinthe Coggo, who compiled a journal of the shocks felt at Burges, held that they came from electricity condensed within the earth. Nicholson believed they were caused by discharges between the clouds and the earth. Abbe Bertholon held so strongly this idea that he invented earthquake rods and volcano rods to carry off as much as possible the fulminating matter stored up within the globe In 1855, M. Ferdinand Hoefer, appearing to be ignorant of the labors of his predecessors, compared earthquakes to true subterranean storms in a solid medium, as Pliny had done before him. Until the earthquake at Alba in 1771, Father Beccaria believed that electricity was the primary cause of the shocks; but from that date he attributed them specially to dissolutions of pyrites. Vassali-Eandi, a diciple of Beccaria, adopted, later, his master's theory, and held that the electricity developed in the fermentation of sulphurous pyrites extended its effects. Dr. Lister was of the same opinion. This theory deserves to be taken anew into notice, not exclusively from the point of the dissolution of the pyrites, but in connection with the electro-chemical actions and reactions taking place in the heart of the globe. No one is ignorant that there is in different strata of the earth's crust a rich deposit of substances produced by electro-chemical action; that there are liquids in circulation, and metallic masses, capable of exciting electric currents. As M. Becqueret has already shown, there exists in most terrestrial formations substances whose alteration by atmospheric agents and water produces electric effects like the water we obtain with zinc. Of all theories proposed on the subject, that of M. Alexis Perry seems to be the best founded and well observed. At the time when the Academy of Sciences in Paris, in 1854, made a favorable report on the labors of M. Perrey, this savant had collected and discussed seven thousand observations from the first half of this century. The conclusions from his work are these: first, that the frequency of earthquakes increases toward the syzigies (points in the earth's orbit nearest the sun); second, that their frequency increases also in the neighborhood of the moon's perigee (point of its orbit nearest the earth) and diminishes toward the apogee (the point of its orbit furthest removed); third, that earthquake shocks are more frequent when the moon is in the vicinity of the meridian than when it is removed 90 degrees. Every other cause which tends to diminish the enormous pressure suffered by the central mass of the globe may act equally, and at the same time with the action of the moon and sun. For example, the sun's heat by rarifying the atmospheric strata tends to diminish their pressure, and the centrifugal force of the cyclone of hurricanes tends equally to exercise an ascensional action on the central mass. Humboldt believed that we must attribute to the reaction of vapors submitted to enormous pressure in the interior of the earth, all shocks which agitate it.

From this rapid glance at the principal theories in relation to earthquakes, it is easy to see that they turn around a fixed principle of which the forms of interpretation alone vary. At present we say that theory reposes on one side, according to the researches of M. Perrey, upon the attractive force of the moon and the sun exerted on the central fiery mass of our planet; and on the other upon the chemical, or probably electro-chemical action produced by the contact of compounds, solid, liquid, or gaseous, in the center of the earth, influenced by atmospheric agents. In this respect, the late researches of M. Ch. Sainte Claire Deville upon the analysis of volcanic emanations have great value.

INTERESTING DEEP SEA DISCOVERIES.

A communication has been made to the Royal Society by Dr. Carpenter on the results of the deep sea explorations carried on during the past summer and autumn by himself, Professor Wyville Thompson, and Mr. Gwyn Jeffreys. On an application made by the Royal Society, the Admiralty placed her Majesty's ship Porcupine, Captain Calver, at the disposal of the explorers. In this vessel three expeditions have been made, and the sea-bed explored from the northern extremity of the Bay of Biscay to the Faroe Islands. Dredgings were obtained from a few fathoms near the shore to 2,500 fathoms, or nearly three miles, out at sea; and the mud brought up has been carefully examined for whatever of animal life it might contain. Deferring for a moment a notice of the animal forms discovered, we turn to the account of the temperature of the sea at the different depths. These determinations were made with the thermometer expressly devised for the purpose by Dr. Miller, of which we gave a description before the expedition started. The results obtained may be stated shortly as follows: At the surface there is a stratum of water, the temperature of which varies with the latitude and the season. When, however, this temperature is high, it declines rapidly, and is lost at about 100 fathoms. From this, in deep water, there is a rapid decline to about 1,000 fathoms, at which there is a tolerably constant temperature from 38 deg. Fah. to 36 deg. Fah. Abrupt variations in the level of the sea bottom occasion considerable local differences in temperature, by obstructing the current of cold water from the Arctic regions, but the result of the thermometric observations is to show the existence of a stratum of ice-cold water from 300 fathoms downwards; a stratum of warm water from 150 fathoms upwards; and a stratum of intermixture between the two. It should be mentioned that the lowest temperature found in these higher latitudes is above that of the deep sea water in the equatorial regions, which is accounted for by an uninterrupted flow of cold water from the antarctic regions. Turning from the temperature we come to the extraordinary fact that in the deepest abysses of the sea there is an abundance of animal life. It was once supposed that no animal could exist lower than 300 fathoms; but the question is now set conclusively at rest, for not only have the globigerinæ (comparatively low forms of life), but the echinoderms, molluscs, and crustacea been brought up from the profoundest depths of the ocean. What will most interest zoologists to learn is, that 127 species of molluscs were found, none of which were previously known to exist in British seas, and many of which are altogether new to science. Of echinoderms the number known to exist is now nearly doubled, while so many varieties of arenaceous foraminifera have been found that it will be difficult to find names for them. Many sponges altogether new have also been discovered, some fine specimens of which were exhibited at the second meeting of the Royal Society last Thursday. As regards the source from which these animals derive their food, Dr. Carpenter remarked that it resolves itself into the single question of the maintenance of the globegerinæ or chalk animalcules. They, it would appear, can live by themselves, and all the others can live upon them. The food of these animals is supposed to be the organic matter (the mysterious bathybius) which is everywhere diffused through deep sea water. But, it may be asked, bathybius whence? There are some who believe that inorganic matter may pass by a spontaneous change into a condition ready to become organized. There are probably others who will see in this deep sea organic matter only the result of animal decomposition, of which there must surely be enough in the ocean.

To conclude this brief review we may notice what is perhaps the most interesting of all the discoveries made, viz: that some of the animals brought up from a depth of 1,270 fathoms had perfect eyes, while the color of their shells indicated the influence of light. Thus it would seem that the deepest abysses of the ocean are not absolutely dark. Sir Charles Lyell suggested that the light in these depths is phosphorescent. On this matter we must wait for further information, and Mr. Gwyn Jeffrey held out the hope that, with the assistance of Sir C. Wheatstone, some steps might be taken in another expedition to ascertain the character and the intensity of light in deep ocean.

It is gratifying to learn that the results of this expedition are incomparably more important than any before obtained. Italians, Danes, Norwegians, Swedes, and Americans have also been busy sweeping the ocean bottom; and Russia is now preparing a dredging expedition. From all this we may expect that, in a few years, the world under water will be as well known as that above it.

THE PHOSPHORESCENCE OF THE SEA.

Every one recognizes the beauty of the singular phenomenon that we call the phosphoresence of the sea; and has watched the track of foam and diamond points of light, left behind as the steamer cuts the wave. For a long time the cause of the shining appearance was a puzzle to philosophers. But the naturalists finally came to the conclusion that it is produced by animalculæ, which are excited to luminosity when the water is agitated. It was also shown that the phosphorescence is brightest, and the sparks most numerous immediately preceding an atmospheric disturbance. Thus, the little animalculæ must be included in the long list of delicate organisms that feel the approach of bad weather.

The Professor M. Decharme observed this coincidence, and has been diligently studying the habits of the tiny creatures, and their shining propensities. He tells us as the result of his observations, that they are visible in the daylight with a glass magnifying about forty times. They are, under this magnifying power, of a lens-shaped form, and from seven to fifteen hundredths of an inch in diameter. They are of a transparent nature, more diaphonous in the centre than around the periphery of their little bodies. The specimens experimented on by the Professor, lived in a bottle for several weeks, and became very brilliant when the water was shaken or stirred, or whenever a small quantity of exciting fluid, alcohol or acid, was introduced into it. We shall look hereafter with increased respect upon these infinitesimal barometers, which, when fully developed, attain the size of from two to four thousandths of an inch! We wonder how many of them it takes to make the track of sparkling foam we have so often watched upon the ocean.

The Old Fisherman.

There was a poor old man
Who sat and listened to the raging sea,
And heard it thunder, lunging at the cliffs
As like to tear them down. He lay at night;
And "Lord have mercy on the lads," said he,
"That sailed at noon, though they be none of mine?
For when the gale gets up, and when the wind
Flings at the window, when it beats the roof,
And lulls, and stops, and rouses up again,
And cuts the crest clean off the plunging wave,
And scatters it like feathers up the field,
Why, then I think of my two lads
That would have worked and never let me want,
And never let me take the parish pay.
No, none of mine; my lads are drowned at sea—
My two—before the most of these were born.
I know how sharp that cuts, since my poor wife
Walked up and down, and still walked up and down,
And I walked after, and one could not hear
A word the other said for the wind and sea
That raged and beat and thundered in the night—
The awfulest, the longest, lightest night
That ever parents had to spend. A moon
That shone like daylight on the breaking wave.
Ah, me! And other men have lost their lads,
And other women wiped their poor dead mouths,
And got them home and dried them in the house,
And seen the driftwood lie along the coast,
That was a tidy boat but one day back;
And seen next tide, the neighbors gather it
To lay it on their fires.

"Ay, I was strong
And able-bodied,—loved my work;—but now
I am a useless hull; 'tis time I sunk;
I am in all men's way; I trouble them;
I am a trouble to myself; but yet
I feel for mariners of stormy nights,
And feel for wives that watch ashore. Ay, ay,
If I had learning I would pray the Lord
To bring them in; but I'm no scholar, no;
Book learning is a world too hard for me;
But I make bold to say 'O Lord, good Lord,
I am a broken-down poor man, a fool
To speak to thee; but in the book 'tis writ,
As I hear say from others that can read,
How, when thou camest, thou didn't love the sea,
And live with fisherfolk, whereby 'tis sure
Thou knowst all the peril they go through,
And all their trouble.

"'As for me, good Lord,
I have no boat; I am too old, too old;
My lads are drowned; I buried my poor wife;
My little lasses died so long ago
That mostly I forget what they were like.
Thou knowest, Lord, they were such little ones;
I know they went to thee, but I forget
Their faces, though I missed them sore.

"'O, Lord,
I was a strong man; I have drawn good food
And made good money out of thy great sea:
But yet I cried for them at nights; and now,
Although I be so old, I miss my lads,
And there be many folks this stormy night
Heavy with fear for theirs. Merciful Lord,
Comfort them; save their honest boys, their pride;
And let them hear next ebb the blessedest,
Best sound—the boat-keels grating on the sand.
"'I cannot pray with finer words; I know
Nothing; I have no learning, cannot learn—
Too old, too old. They say I want for naught,
I have the parish pay; but I am dull
Of hearing, and the fire scarce warms me through.
God save me, I have been a sinful man,
And save the lives of them that still can work,
For they are good to me—ay, good to me.
But, Lord, I am a trouble! and I sit
And I am lonesome, and the nights are few
That any think to come and draw a chair
And sit in my poor place and talk awhile.
Why should they come, forsooth? Only the wind
Knocks at my door, oh, long and loud it knocks,
The only thing God made that has a mind
To enter in.'"

Yea, thus the old man spake,
These were the last words of his aged mouth—
BUT ONE DID KNOCK. One came to sup with him,
That humble, weak, old man; knocked at his door
In the rough pauses of the laboring wind.
I tell you that one knocked while it was dark,
Save where their foaming passion had made white
Those livid, seething billows. What he said
In that poor place, where he did talk awhile,
I cannot tell; but this I am assured,
That when the neighbors came the morrow morn,
What time the wind had bated, and the sun
Shone on the old man's floor, they saw the smile
He passed away in; and they said, "He looks
As he had woke and seen the face of Christ,
And with that rapturous smile held out his arms
To come to Him!"

"The Debt is Paid."

Many persons who are anxious to know the Lord Jesus as their Saviour, find it difficult to understand in what way his sacrifice saves them, and so they get no comfort from it. The following true story of a poor woman who felt this difficulty, may be helpful to others, in showing them how this great blessing is received.

Betty was poor—very poor; and besides this so ill as to be confined to her bed. Sickness alone is no light trouble, nor is poverty; but when both come together, they do in truth make a heavy burden. Yet Betty had a heavier burden still—a burden of doubt and fear about the safety of her soul. She had heard over and over again about the death and merits of our blessed Saviour, and about believing in him; but she could not understand it, and her soul was sorrowful with the thought of being far off from God, and unable to find the way to him.

A lady who was in the habit of visiting Betty, tried again and again to explain to her the wonderful truth, that Christ had atoned for sin upon the cross—that he had paid the debt forever, and that we, being justified by faith in him, may have peace with God. But put it in what way she would, her poor friend could never take hold of it; and so, without finding any comfort for her soul, poor Betty grew worse and worse in body, till at length she lay at the point of death.

At last, one day, when the lady called, she found poor Betty in the deepest possible distress. She had drawn the clothes over her face, and was sobbing as if her heart would break.

"Poor Betty," said the lady, "what is the matter? What makes you so wretched to-day?"

"Oh, ma'am, they're coming to turn me out for the rent, and to take my bed from under me—and I shall die! I shall die!

Her anguish was so great that all that her friend could say gave her no comfort. How could it? for she had not a farthing, and the debt must be paid, or the bed would be taken from under her.

While the lady was trying to comfort her, a harsh knock at the door below was heard, which threw the poor creature into a fresh fit of anguish. Throwing the clothes over her head, she cried out:

"Oh, they're come! they're come!"

Greatly moved at the sight of her poor friend's distress, the lady slipped quietly down stairs, and found that, sure enough, two men were come to take the goods.

"Well, now," she said, when they had told their business, "the poor thing can't possibly pay the rent."

"Well, ma'am, we can't help that. If she can't pay the rent we must take her bed."

"But it would be dreadfully cruel. The poor thing would die. Indeed she is almost dying already."

"Well, ma'am, that's not our business: we must have the money or the goods."

"Then just tell me what is the sum you claim for rent?"

"It's thirteen shillings, six pence, and two shillings expenses."

"Here, then," taking out her purse, "here is a sovereign. Give me the change and write a receipt."

On receiving the receipt, the lady laid it between the leaves of her Bible, which she held in her hand, and went up stairs to relieve poor Betty's mind about the bed, little thinking that her act of kindness was to be used by the Spirit of God as a means of a better blessing to the poor thing's troubled soul.

She found her in deep agony, expecting every moment that the men would come up, and take away the bed to satisfy the rent.

She sat down beside her, and gently whispered, "Betty, don't trouble yourself."

"But, ma'am, I *must* trouble—for I shall die."

She whispered again, "But the debt is paid, Betty."

The poor creature drew down the clothes from her face, and looked up amazed. She could hardly believe her own ears.

Again the lady repeated her delightful words—"I assure you, Betty, you need not trouble yourself about the debt: I have paid it;" and opening the Bible, she showed the receipt, saying, "Why, Betty, here is the receipt for the money. Read it yourself, and be satisfied."

The poor thing spelled it out as well as she could, and then gazed at it with a strangely earnest look, as if some new and wonderful thoughts were working in her mind. At last her face brightened, she threw up her hands, and exclaimed—

"Ah! I see it now, ma'am—I see it now! and thank you a thousand times; and more than that; I see now all the meaning of what you've so often tried to teach me. I do see it now; I do see it, he has paid the debt. I'm delivered, and I can die happy!"

And so it was: she sank back gently on her pillow, and breathed forth her happy spirit into the hands of him who had paid the debt.

And now, reader, do you see it? Do you receive and own Christ as your Saviour? Do you believe he has paid *your* debt; and that *your* debt having been paid by him, you have not to pay it again? Can you say in the words of the hymn,

"Payment God will not twice demand,
First at my bleeding Surety's hand,
And then again at mine."

If this be the language of your heart, you give Christ glory. You honor him as your Deliverer; and you may rest assured that he is able to keep that which you have committed unto him.

The Land Breeze.

Here is an ocean memory to which Mr. Beecher lately treated the old folks of his congregation:

When, after the weary voyage that I first made across the ocean, sick, loathsome, I arose one morning and went upon the deck, holding on, crawling, thinking I was but a worm, I smelt in the air some strange smell; and said to the captain, "What is the odor?" "It is the land breeze from off Ireland." I smelt the turf, I smelt the grass, I smelt the leaves, and all my sickness departed from me; my eyes grew bright, my nausea was gone. The thought of the nearness of the land came to me and cured me better than medicine could cure me. And when, afar off, I saw the dim line of land, joy came and gave me health, and from that moment, I had neither sickness nor trouble; I was coming near to the land.

Oh! is there not for you, old man, and for you, wearied mother, a land breeze blowing off from Heaven, wafting to you some of its odors, some of its sweetness? Behold the garden of the Lord; it is not far away, I know from the air. Behold the joy of home. Do I not hear children shout? The air is full of music to our silent thoughts. Oh! how full of music when our journey is almost done, and we stand upon the bound and precinct of that blessed land! Hold on to your faith. Give not away to discouragement. Believe more firmly. Take hold by prayer and by faith. In a few hours visions of God, and of all the realities of the eternal world, shall be yours, and you shall be saved with an everlasting salvation.

Only.

Only one drop of water at a time that had found its way from the mighty ocean through the dyke, and was slowly wearing a little channel. Only one drop! Yet if that little child in her morning ramble had not noticed it, who can tell what the terrible results might have been. Only a stray sunbeam! yet perchance it hath pierced some wretched abode, gladdened some stricken heart, or its golden light found its way through the leafy branches of some wild wood, kissed the moss-covered bank where the tiny violet grew, and caused a rich shade of beauty to adorn its lovely form.

Only a gentle breeze! But how many aching brows hath it fanned, how many hearts cheered by its gentle touch!

Only one stray bullet that pierced the noble soldier-boy as he trod the lonely midnight round, faithfully guarding the precious lives intrusted to his keeping; yet the life-blood slowly ebbed out, and the morning sunbeam fell upon the cold face of the dead.

Only a sentinel! And yet one soul more had passed from its earthly tenement to meet its reward at the hands of a merciful God.

Only a drop of ink! And yet it carried the news of death to anxious ones at home, and caused the tear of anguish to trickle down the furrowed cheek of a widowed mother.

Only a frown! But it left a sad, dreary ache in that child's heart, and the quivering lips and tearful eyes told how sadly he felt it.

Only a smile! But ah! how it cheered the broken heart, engendered a ray of hope, and cast a halo of light around the unhappy present; made the bed-ridden one forget its present agony for a moment as it dwelt in sunshine of joy, and lived in the warmth of that smile.

Only a word! But it carried the poisonous breath of slander, assailing the character. O how it pierced the lonely heart!

Only one glass! And how many have filled a drunkard's grave through its influence! How many homes made desolate! How many bright anticipations of a glad and happy future blasted by its blighting influence.

Only a mound in the quiet churchyard, and yet it speaks volumes to the stricken ones. Some home has lost a light! some home-circle has a vacant chair!

Only a child, perhaps, yet "of such is the kingdom of heaven."

Only a cup of cold water given in the name of a disciple, but it is not forgotten. Then toil on, Christian; yours is a glorious work; hope on ever, for yours is a bright reward.

One soul snatched from the ways of sin and degradation through your feeble efforts, coupled with the grace of God, will add lustre to your crown of glory, and speak more for your happiness hereafter than a life of selfish works.

Only a prayer! And yet it calls to you for help. It calls for good raiment and food; and Christians, shall not we, through the grace of God, answer that prayer? God grant it in his mercy.

Only a lifetime! A short day in which to prepare for death, for "as death overtakes us, so judgment will find us." Let us then gird on the armor anew, and press on, the hope of a brighter hereafter being our talisman, using the weapons of prayer, lest we enter into temptation, and lose the rich reward of Him who is faithful even unto death.—*N. W. Presbyterian.*

(For the Sailor's Magazine.)

A Sailor's Autobiography.

I was born in the town of F——, in the state of Rhode-Island, in 1803. When I was about five years old my parents moved to Connecticut. My father was what would be called a man of the world. My mother was a member of the Church, and carefully trained her children (I had four brothers and two sisters) in religious things. She would gather us about her morning and evening, read a chapter in the bible and pray with us. On the Sabbath we attended church twice and occasionally three times, besides the sabbath schools, and after the second service had an exercise in the catechism. At the age of sixteen I went to live with Mr. G——, a country merchant, and after three years came to New York, where I obtained a situation. On leaving home my mother gave me a small bible, and entreated me to study it, which I promised to do, but I am sorry to say, I did not keep my promise long.

After a few months in the city, all the pious teachings of my mother were forgotten. I made bad associations, neglected my bible, and instead of the sanctuary, went to houses of debauchery, taking to strong drink and becoming very profane. Here I remained for a couple of years, when, being out of employment, I went to sea. I resolved at that time that I would not be a drunkard, and in a measure refrained from intoxicating liquors, but I continued fearfully profane. I

&c., &c., might do for the writer of "American Whalemen," but we very much doubt whether whalemen themselves would care about drawing a book. They don't take to such. The fact is, that experience in this work is the best possible teacher, and those who are engaged in putting up our libraries have been familiar with seamen, their tastes and their needs so long, that it is no venture with them, but the adapting of the means to an end, which every Christian prays for and confidently expects to see.

The public may be assured that "quality and not quantity is the governing principle in our selection. That a worthless volume is never put in a library knowingly, either because it costs little or even because it was a free gift," but that we are aiming to do a good work, *thoroughly*, so that it shall continue to have the blessing of God and the approval of such excellent men as Captain Robert C. Adams, when commanding the *Golden Fleece*, who said, "I assure you once more of my great interest in the efforts of your Society and my high opinion of the libraries," and of Capt. J. G. Baker of the *N. A. Eldredge*, who writes, "I think they are the best selection of books in regard to historical and religious matter that can be made for the benefit of seamen."

Dr. Rockwell.—Lady Aberdeen.

AN INTERESTING LETTER.

Rev. Dr. HALL, Sec., &c.

My dear Brother:—Among the pleasant things of my recent trip to Europe was the opportunity afforded me of seeing something of the field which our Society is cultivating, and of the work which it is doing.

On my passage over, I had the pleasure of meeting the venerable Bishop of Newfoundland, who is attempting for the sailors of his diocese, much such a work as we are accomplishing on a larger scale. Libraries are put on board every vessel that sails from St. Johns, where Rev. JAMES SPENCER is our Chaplain, and where kind, religious influences are brought to bear upon the seamen visiting that port.

In Scotland, as I had opportunity, I described our library work to the pastors who are laboring in Glasgow and elsewhere upon the sea board, and sought to call their attention to the importance of such a work for the temporal and spiritual welfare of British seamen. It was my pleasure to preach five times upon the ocean in going and returning, and my last sermon was a special address to sailors, from the text 'Which hope we have as an anchor of the soul.' On one occasion, I held a service upon the deck, and having a few tracts with me, and some copies of a little work of my own, for sailors, called the 'Sheet Anchor'—distributed them to the men of the forecastle, and was pleased afterwards to see them busily and seriously engaged in reading them.

I am greatly indebted to the Board of Trustees for the privilege afforded me, as their representative, of visiting the COUNTESS OF ABERDEEN, to whose munificence we are indebted for a noble contribution to our library fund, in memorial of her son, who was lost at sea, January 7th, 1870.

A note addressed to her at Haddo House, was promptly answered, from London, where she was temporarily residing, and a cordial invitation extended me to meet her there. Soon after my arrival in the city, I called upon her and presented her with the specimen library which you sent her by me, and placing in her hands also the minute adopted by our Board, expressive of their sympathy with her in her bereavement, and their gratitude for the memorial gift which she had made, through them, to those who go down to the sea in ships.

I shall long remember that pleasant interview with her, and with the ladies whom I met at her table. She expressed great interest in the library work of our Society, and was much affected with the fact I related to her, that the first case of books given out upon the donation she had made, was presented to the captain of a ship bound for California, who had known her son when sailing from Boston, and who, though unconscious of his noble birth, had loved and admired him as a gentleman and a friend. We spoke together of the remarkable history of her son, and of the inscrutable Providence that had removed him when he seemed just entering upon a life of usefulness and honor. Happily she has learned by the teachings of Infinite Wisdom, that God does all things well, and has found that even afflictions are graciously made to "work out the peaceable fruits of righteousness."

I was happy to learn elsewhere, that her younger son, who now bears the title and rank of her distinguished and godly husband, is following in his footsteps, and that the husband of her daughter, Lord Polwarth, whom I had the pleasure of meeting at the General Assembly, in Edinburgh, is also making his influence felt for good as an elder of the Church of Scotland.

I regretted that the departure of friends with whom I had arranged to visit the Continent, rendered it impossible for me to enjoy again the kind hospitalities of her house. At the hour when I had hoped to have dined with her, we were at Dover awaiting the departure of the steamer for Ostend.

Yours truly,
J. E. ROCKWELL.

Acknowledgment.

Our thanks are due to the Managing Agents of the White Star Steamship Company, for their kindness in sending to Liverpool, a sick and destitute sailor, upon our hands, at the Sailors' Home. An application in his behalf from the Superintendent of the HOME, Mr. Alexander, was cheerfully granted, and by this time, the poor fellow—a confirmed consumptive—is at home and among his family friends.

A similar acknowledgment is due to Messrs. Borden & Lovell, Agents of the O. C. B. B. Co., for transportation furnished a party of sailors who arrived at this port last week, having been picked up at sea, from the Provincetown Schooners *Mary E. Simmons* and *Arizona*. Their names are as follows, viz.: Schr. *Mary E. Simmons*, Ed. Flood, Geo. Randall, Francis Quinn, Thos. Mulcahy.

Schr. *Arizona*, Wm. Bagley, Frank Patterson, George Leavitt.

These men state that both schooners were off Cape Hatteras, hunting whales. That four boats left the vessels, on the 24th August, for that purpose, and in pursuing the whales they got out of sight of their respective vessels. The weather became dirty, and at four o'clock on the morning of the 25th instant, a squall came up, making matters worse for them. They searched in vain for the schooners, and while in this dilemma they fell in with the schooner *Hettie Card* and got aboard of her. After the lapse of two days they were transferred to the bark *Diadem*, and finally carried into the port of Beaufort. They went before United States Commissioner Thompson and made a statement of the above facts. They came here because it was believed that they would have a better opportunity of getting home. They are apprehensive as to the fate of their vessels, not being sure that the persons left aboard could navigate them.

Kittery, Me.

A correspondent of the *Congregationalist*, who signs himself *Vacation*, says: "Sunday, Aug. 23d, an interesting Seamens' meeting was held in this old port. The wind of Saturday forced some thirty sail of fishermen and coasters to seek refuge here; ten or twelve of them remaining at the Point over Sunday. Early in the morning an old sea captain, a member of the First Church, rowed out to invite the men to church. In the afternoon service was held on board the *William Butler*, of Wellfleet, where, in response to an invitation given to the fleet, forty or more sailors gathered for worship. A portion of the fifth chapter of Luke was read by a lay brother, and after his remarks the pastor followed with a happy and impressive lesson on the scene of our Lord's work, and his call to the fishermen of the lake of Galilee. Here, beneath the open sky, the brave mariners listened to the blessed and comforting words of our dear Lord and Master, words of warning and of hope to guide and cheer them on their way. Upon asking them what success they had in fishing, they told us they had been out for nearly three weeks, after mackerel, and caught but twenty-five barrels. On the Sunday previous, the captain said, they came upon a large school, and could have filled the deck in half an hour; but he had been in the business seven years and never fished on Sunday, and did not mean to begin. If he could not make a living without fishing on Sunday, he would go home without it. How few of us realize the sufferings and losses of these toilers of the sea. One of the men to whom we spoke commanded a vessel last year. It was dashed upon the rocks in the great gale, when so many went down, but the part of the mast to which he was clinging when the vessel struck, broke and fell upon the shore. Many a one can tell of shipwreck, loss of men, vessel, and a season's catch. A friend tells me of the wreck of one hundred and fifty sail, and the loss of three hundred men, in a storm out of which he with great difficulty escaped. Some friends of his suffered shipwreck then, and again a month afterward. When we remember what we all owe to the sailor, should any of our churches fail to pray and to work for those who go down to the sea in ships, that do business in great waters.

Brooklyn, N. Y.

One of our missionaries, when visiting a sick person, found her father avowedly sceptical, and a non-attendant upon church. After a kind conversation upon the subject, he began to attend quite regularly. Upon being taken sick some weeks later, he sent for the missionary, and desired to be taught more fully the way of salvation, stating that he had changed his views, and wished to become a Christian. In due time he gave evidence of conversion, and said: "I feel that I have peace with God." Taking the missionary by the hand, he asked him to be present at his funeral, and tell the people that "I do not die an infidel, but believe in Christ as my Saviour." He passed away in this blessed hope.

Capt. Davis' Book, and Books for Sailors.

This story about "American Whalemen," will fascinate many in spite of its extravagant statements and rhetoric. Whaling and whalemen may almost be said to belong to the past. The number of American whalers at sea is 129, so that if their crews be allowed an average of 23 men, the whole number engaged in the business of whaling would only be 2,967, one-third of whom are probably foreigners. Capt. Davis' book therefore, relates to what used to be rather than to what is. But what is in in it on this subject that is really true, when separated from its abounding Munchausenisms, is hardly enough to justify regarding it either a treatise or a history.

Sailors will laugh over its "yarns" artistically illustrated as they are with a most vigorous fancy, and wonder if there are any land-lubbers actually green enough to swallow them.

The *Christian Intelligencer* of September 17th, in a discriminating notice of this "Nimrod of the Sea," quotes Capt. Davis' commendatory statement in regard to Rev. Mr. DIEL, for many years, and at the time of his death in 1841, a chaplain of the AMERICAN SEAMEN'S FRIEND SOCIETY at Honolulu, S. I.

Mr. DIEL was succeeded by the Rev. S. C. DAMON, a man of like earnest spirit who for the past twenty-four years has been serving at that port, with a fidelity that has greatly endeared him to the seamen of the South Pacific.

Probably no man lives whose usefulness has been greater, or who is more extensively known among seamen, or more deeply loved by them for acts of personal kindness and friendship, both on ship-board and on shore, than Chaplain DAMON.

It argues badly for Captain Davis that he does not appear to know that there is an admirably managed Sailors' Home at Honolulu, and that he does not seem even to have heard of Chaplain DAMON, nor to have shared the hospitality either of his popular Bethel or his attractive Christian Home.

The fact that those excellent men, Rev. Titus Coan of Hilo, and of late, the Rev. Frank Thompson, himself a sailor, have always sought to befriend the seamen visiting that port, and that the same friendly offices are exercised toward them by Chaplain Rowell of San Francisco, and by Rev. Dr. Trumbull and his helper, Mr. Muller, of Valparaiso, shows what provisions are made for the welfare of our seamen on the west coast of America. And no doubt, more would be done in that direction if the means were at hand.

Captain Davis evidently has had an unfortunate experience with what he calls, "a scant ship's library of uninteresting books provided by some Seamen's Friend Society."

We cannot answer what may not have been intended to refer to the libraries sent out by this Society, but it is proper to say, that our libraries reaching to nearly 5,000 afloat to-day, have been selected with a conscientious regard to the work they are designed to accomplish.

The character of these libraries is most carefully considered, and while this has been improving with the facilities afforded us for selection and purchase, there never has been one sent out with the imprint of the Society which deserves to be spoken of in the disparaging terms used by Capt. Davis. The books are of a kind calculated to interest, entertain and instruct. They are not all strictly religious books by any means, but each library contains (with a copy of the Bible) more or less that are evangelical and designed to lead the sailor to the Saviour; and this doubtless accounts for their great acceptability and usefulness.

A library made up according to Capt. Davis' suggestion, "showing poor Jack that Providence planted the succulent cactus, and created the water bearing terrapin on the Scoria of the Gallipagos,"

THE SAILORS MAGAZINE AND SEAMENS FRIEND.

Vol. 46.   JANUARY, 1874.   No. 1.

THE REFLEX INFLUENCES OF THE SEA AND LAND.

A SERMON PREACHED IN BEHALF OF THE AMERICAN SEAMEN'S FRIEND SOCIETY, IN THE FIRST PRESBYTERIAN CHURCH OF EDGEWATER, STATEN ISLAND,

BY REV. J. E. ROCKWELL, D. D.

ECCLESIASTES, 1 : 7. "All the rivers run into the sea; yet the sea is not full: unto the place from whence the rivers come, thither they return again."

The wise and royal preacher of Jerusalem is presenting some illustrations of human mutability as found in the changes and unrest of Nature. The sun is in constant motion, rising and setting and hasting round its great annual circuit, by which day and night and the alternating seasons are produced. The wind is perpetually changing its course and motion, and life itself presents to us in the passing away of successive generations, the same law of unrest and change. It is in this connection that we meet with the words of our text, which are the simple statement of a well-known fact in the natural world. The vast torrents of water which, from every continent are pouring their tribute into the ocean, never cause it to overflow, nor are the rivers ever exhausted or dried. By a wise permission of Nature, the waters are made to return again to the springs from which they issued, and so they keep up their ceaseless flow. This is a most wonderful process, which in all its marvellous details as science has spread them before us reveals the infinite wisdom and goodness of him who created all things, and who has thus made the waters in their ceaseless motion to be the source of health, and not the very emblem and pregnant cause of death as they would have been were they inert and moveless. The sea gives back to the earth all that it receives from it of what is pure and wholesome, so that every spring and fountain, however remote or hidden, that sends forth its waters to the ocean, receives them back again, when they have fallen in refreshing showers upon the land, and have revived the corn, and supplied every tree and shrub, and spear of grass with needed moisture. This process of Nature is most amazing and instructive. One who stands by the cataract of Niagara, whose leaping waters have come down more than a thousand miles from their great reservoirs in the northern lakes, might think that the mighty torrent must eventually exhaust its springs, or cause the ocean to overflow. And the wonder increases when we remember that more than a hundred similar rivers on the eastern and western continents are in like manner giving their tribute to the sea. Yet all these vast floods return again, by the simple process of evaporation, to their sources among the hills. All that they leave in that vast reservoir are the salts and alkalies which they have caught up on their way to the ocean, and even these are taken up by the coral insect and the unnumbered tribes of animalculæ and fish, and turned to shell or bone, or reared up into vast piles of rock which form the foundations of islands, and become the abode of man and the home of vegetable and animal life. Such is the reflex influence of the sea and land. And what is true in regard to the physical world of waters, may be applied also to the great currents of life which are ebbing and flowing along these great highways of the nations.

I.—Even in the immensity and grandeur of the sea, we find a counterpart in the multitudes that are passing over it, or are making their home upon it. How ceaseless is the current of life that comes from the land to the ocean, and that returns from the sea to the shore. We have but to stand by our own beautiful harbor to see an illustration of the magnitude of the commercial interests of the world. The tide of life flows on without an ebb. Swift ships are going and coming literally as a cloud. An endless stream of vessels are passing in and out of port. We ascend the hills and look outward upon the ocean, and find that the horizon is always filled with ships either approaching the land or fading from the sight. We go out upon the ocean and see the same vast procession of maritime life. We enter foreign ports and find their endless tides all pouring into the sea. Three millions of men are permanently engaged in moving the commerce of the world. And yet this number only gives us an imperfect formula with which to estimate the vastness of the currents of commercial life.

We take up our morning papers to look over the lists of arrivals and departures, when we have parted with a friend or expect his return, and when we have patiently toiled through hundreds of names in the search, find at the end those numbers increased by nameless thousands who have come or gone in the steerage. And so they go and come, and ebb and flow. The land gives them to the sea, and the sea bears them back again to the shore. Sometimes, indeed, even as it keeps to itself the salts and earths which the rivers bring into it, it swallows up, until the sea shall give up its dead, a ship with its living freight. Yet, usually it gives back what it takes, even as it yields to the clouds the moisture which they carry back to the fields and hills and valleys and springs.

And every land is yielding this mighty tribute to the sea, and pouring into it its countless millions of treasure and life, with all their currents and counter currents, with all their wealth of mind and soul and thought and affection and social influence and commercial and national and moral power. They come from every hamlet and state and nation, mingling in one vast sea of life, meeting, and parting, going and returning, leaving home and visiting distant scenes and shores, and coming back to go over again the same course, to leave behind them influences for good or evil, and to receive in turn saving or destructive impressions and principles, which shall make themselves and the world either better or worse. Such elements as these cannot be safely left out of the account when we would estimate the influences that are at work in the world either for good or evil, and especially when the church sits down to sum up its duties, or to see what are its appliances for carrying forward its great work of converting the world to Christ.

II.—Again, we find an illustration of the reflex influence of the sea and land in the results of their motions one toward the other. Were the rivers to cease their flowing, the currents of the ocean permanently arrested, the sea to be forever calm and motionless, and the clouds no longer the carriers of its moisture back to the land, the world would become the grave of all that dwell therein. Disease and death would reign with uninterrupted sway. The forests would wither and fade, the green hills become verdureless, the broad prairies would be a solemn and awful scene of desolation, and the valleys the shadow of death. Health and life, fertility and food, are the results of all these ceaseless ebbings and flowings, these currents and tides, these winds and fogs and storms which are connected with the flood of waters that run into the sea and that return again to the places from whence they came. Every river that pours its tribute into the ocean bears with it untold masses of vegetable and earthy matter, which become food for the countless inhabitants of the deep, and they in their turn become food for man. The salts and alkalies which are caught up by the rushing waters are taken by myriads of insects and wrought into fairy homes, that, in the lapse of ages rise to the surface and by accretions of earth and vegetable matter are fitted to be the abode of man. And these coral islands, blossoming with beauty, covered with perennial verdure, shadowed by the broad spreading palm, and fruit-bearing groves, and resonant with the songs of birds, are bearing witness to the wisdom and goodness of him by whose command all the rivers run into the sea. And then again, the sea sends back their waters purified by the sun and air, which, borne upon the wings of the wind in chariots of mist and cloud, are dropped upon the highest mountain peak, distilled on every plain and valley, and emptied into every bubbling spring, and so the forests are nourished, and the corn is revived, and the ripe and golden harvests wave over a thousand fields, and the rich pastures give food to the living herds, and the bleating flocks, and the whole earth smiles in beauty and verdure. And what is true of the world of waters may be said of the multitudes who make their home upon them. Where would be commercial life, or national growth and progress, but for the sea and those who do business upon it. We send forth men in their swift and staunch ships, freighted with all the products of the land, but we receive back at their hands a full return. Even those who are engaged in fisheries bring in yearly about $12,000,000, while the value of the products that are annually moved by sea-faring men is estimated at two hundred millions of dollars. What a spring does this vast amount of treasure give to all the activities of life. How the sea and the land alike share in its influence, and re-act, the one upon the other. What perfect isolation would there be amid all the nations of the earth were the seas to have impassable barriers between them, or were there no brave or hardy men who were willing to pass over it at the behests of commerce. What a change would be witnessed in our busy seaports, now full of life and energy, were the ocean no longer to be the great highway of nations. How lonely and desolate would the forests and plains of this western continent have remained, if no adventurous sailors had ever trusted themselves to the deep and opened the way thither for the teeming millions of the old world. It is the interchange of the products of our nation for those of others, that gives to it life, that stimulates its industries, that builds up its cities, that develops its resources and gives to it strength, symmetry and power. Athens was for ages the centre of wealth and refinement and political influence, because she sent forth upon the sea her works of art and taste and mechanical skill, and brought back the products of the nations that were about her. And her genius was most renowned, and her orators, and poets, and philosophers, and schools, most numerous and famous, when her commerce had reached its highest stage, and her ships were known in every port of the eastern world. What she gave to the sea, the sea brought back to her in full. And when her commerce declined, and other cities and nations wrested it from her, they also reaped the benefits and grew in wealth and power, proportionate to the ventures they sent forth upon the deep. And what was true of Athens, and Carthage, and Alexandria, and Tyre, is pre-eminently so in the present day. The sea gives ample returns to all the nations that use it as their great highway and connecting link with the commercial world.

The delta formed out of the slime and sand brought down by the Rhine, the Meuse, and the Scheld, grew up into the powerful and wealthy kingdom of Holland by means of commerce. So, out of the vast lagoons of the Adriatic, grew up Venice, throned on her hundred isles, who sent forth her ventures upon the sea and received back wealth and splendor, and political power. Such, too, has been the history of England, France, and America. They have found the ocean their great harvest field of wealth.

And the social and intellectual influences of the sea are as great as their commerce, and they in like manner act and react upon the land. If you take a map of the world and mark down the nations that have made the least progress, that retain with most persistency the bigotry, customs, morals, and institutions of past ages, and that are the least open to healthful reforms, you will find them to be the countries that have no sea coast, and hence, no commerce. There it is that bigotry, superstition, and despotism, hold the people in an iron bondage, and that custom and caste keep them rooted fast to old and effete institutions, while the rest of the world outstrips them in intelligence, education, and virtue. Were there no sea, there could be no intercourse between remote nations, no interchange of ideas, and no improvements by adopting customs and institutions which other people have found to be beneficent and wise. The spirit of commerce is the spirit of growth and progress in inventions and art, and science, and social and moral life. It is the spirit of peace, and friendship, and fraternity. It binds the nations together in bonds of amity and mutual good will and common interest. It breaks down international prejudices. It prepares the way for the entrance of light, and knowledge, and truth, and social and moral advances among nations that have long sat in darkness.

III.—And this brings us to the consideration of the influence and uses of the sea in the subduing the world to Christ. The word of God reveals to us in a most clear and remarkable manner, how the church is to use the sea in its great highway in carrying the gospel to every creature, and how the ocean is to send back to the shore its waters of truth, and love, and christian activity. If we look over the prophecies, we find that the ocean is clearly identified with the land in the offerings it brings to the church, and the part it is finally to perform in the final triumphs of the gospel. The conversion of its abundance precedes immediately the coming of the forces of the Gentiles. Its isles wait for God's law. Its ships bring his people, and their silver, and gold with them. They fly as a cloud to witness and aid in the triumphs of Christ, and in that day of glory the daughter of Tyre, the very symbol and embodiment of maritime power and wealth, comes with her gifts. So also, messages of wondrous import are sent to the land of nestling wings, to visit remote nations with her swift ships and bear tidings of love, and grace, and mercy.

And what appears in prophecy is amply fulfilled in the history of Providence and the church. Hardy sailors inured to toil and danger were selected by the Saviour to be his choicest and ablest ministers. The sails of commerce became the wings of the gospel. The ships of the merchant bore the embassadors of Christ to their varied fields of labor, and carried christianizing influences to the nations that had long sat in darkness. The history of Paul as a missionary is a record of scenes and events which are largely connected with the sea, and shows how largely the sailor is associated with the work of the church in preaching the gospel to every creature. The great apostle to the Gentiles was often found upon the decks of vessels that traded along the eastern coast of the Mediterranean. He entered Rome only after a long and dangerous voyage across the waters of the great sea, during which he had acted as chaplain to the sailors, was flung ashore from a wrecked Alexandrian vessel, became for a while a missionary among the barbarous people of Milita, re-embarked in the ship *Castor* and *Pollux*, and was at length landed at Puteoli, whose ruins still have a deep interest to the christian traveler as he enters the splendid bay of Naples. Thus the church has used, and must continue to use, the sea in the prosecution of its great work of subduing the world to Christ.

But, aside from this obvious truth, we may observe the intimate relations of the sea and land in the moral influences of the sailor himself. He may become a messenger for good, even as he has long been the subject agent of vice and immorality. And what he is to be or do, depends largely upon the influences exerted upon him by the dwellers on the land. What the world contributes to the ocean, in the way of truth or error, of virtue or vice, comes back to it again and is felt everywhere for good or evil.

The sailor who has spent his money and time, while on shore, amid the pest houses of crime and vice that are open in every port, carries with him to the sea and to other lands the demoralizing influences to which he has been subjected. He who has spent his time at his own home, or in the homes which christian benevolence has prepared for him, especially if he has learned to pray, and has felt the power of the gospel in his heart, carries with him to his ship and to other lands the spiritual treasures which he has received. He is a prompt and fearless man, inured to toil, familiar with danger, and obedient to authority. When he becomes a christian he carries with him into his new life all the qualities that mark him as a man. He seems to see upon the flag of his great Captain, the words: Christ expects every man to do his duty. He never thinks of being ashamed to confess him, he never dreams of shrinking from any task he imposes upon him. And it is such men that the church needs in its work of carrying the gospel to every creature. It is such men that the world needs in the behests of peace, and order, and civilization, and commerce. If it sends forth its navies on ventures that are demoralizing, it receives its demoralization in return. The history of the slave trade, of piracy, of the importation and exportation of intoxicating drinks, afford us ample illustrations of this statement. If commerce becomes the servant of vice, and its mighty floods that enter the sea are defiled with sensuality, and greed of gain, and profanity, and lust, and immorality, the returning tide not only, but the very atmosphere, is saturated with vice and crime, that comes back from the ocean. If commerce sends forth men of integrity and virtue, with ventures that it need not blush to own, then will come back clouds of healthful and blessed influences that shall make the whole land to rejoice.

In 1620, the *May Flower* brought to the rock-bound coast of New England, a precious freight of living, earnest, thinking, and godly men, and who sought "Freedom to worship God," and the influence of that venture is felt to-day, and will be felt for good in ages yet to come. In the same year, a Dutch trading vessel brought to Jamestown, a cargo of slaves, and the bitter harvest of that venture has been reaped by the whole nation in long years of sorrow, and trial, and blood.

The law is universal, "that whatsoever a man soweth that shall he also reap." Here, then, we have set before us the duty of the church, and the only source of safety to the world. Commerce is to be purified, and so to become the handmaid of truth, virtue, and religion. It is not simply in the work of the church that the SEAMEN'S FRIEND SOCIETY is engaged when it seeks to provide for the sailor christian homes, and Chaplains, and Bethels, and other religious influences. It is doing a work for the country and the world. It is seeking to purify the streams that must surely come back again to the lands whence they issue. It recognizes the great law announced by the wise man in the words of our text, and knowing that every ship that leaves or enters our ports is filled with sailors that are a power for good or evil, endeavors to throw around them the restraints and fill them with the blessed principles of true religion. It preaches to them, by its Chaplains and Missionaries, while on shore. It looks after their temporal interests.

It seeks to protect them from their enemies, whose influence is only demoralizing and ruinous. It places in their ships, libraries of well selected books. It provides friends for them in foreign lands. It constantly seeks their present and eternal good.

The work it has already accomplished is incalculable in its benign results. Many a sailor has become the servant of Christ. Many a ship has become a bethel. Many a community and land beyond the seas has felt the blessed power of christian sailors.

The Society that cares for seamen asks and deserves the help of every class of men. It comes alike to the merchant and the artizan, the farmer and the mechanic, the citizen and the christian, and claims from all, their aid in carrying on its work. Where is the community that is not indebted to the sailor for benefits conferred; where is there a hamlet that has not some association or relation to those who go down to the sea in ships. To all such the Society comes and asks that the sailor may be remembered in their prayers and offerings. Its plans are simple but effective. It can point with thankfulness to grand results already accomplished, to harvests already reaped, to souls already saved from sin and death, and to blessed influences for good everywhere recognized as the results of its labors.

A single example of its work may show better than any general statement what the Society is doing for the sailor. In a recent number of *Harper's Magazine*, there may be found a notice of a work of Mr. Nordhoff, on the Sandwich Islands, in which, honorable mention is made of the Seamen's Chaplain at Honolulu. The mention of the name connected with it brings back to my mind the class that left Amherst College in 1836, while I was yet an undergraduate. Among them were men whom it was even then evident would make their mark upon the world. One of them became in after years the Governor of Massachusetts, another represented his native State in the National Legislature, another is an able and distinguished Professor in one of our Theological Seminaries, another is a leading mind in the Southern Presbyterian Church, and others are doing a noble work at the bar, on the bench, in the medical profession, and in the ministry. Among this band of young men thus destined for usefulness and honor, was the present Chaplain at Honolulu, Rev. S. C. DAMON, D. D. Robust in health, a good scholar, possessed of strong, practical, and common sense, cheerful, hearty, social, earnest in whatever he undertook to do, overflowing with good humor, always friendly, manly, and genial, sincere and unostentatious in his piety, he was just the man for a lifework among seamen. Thirty years ago he left for the Sandwich Islands via Cape Horn. He went then not as a missionary to the heathen, but as a chaplain and friend of the sailor. The Islands were already showing the rich fruits of christian labor among the aborigines. But the influence of the crews which were constantly arriving there were fearfully counteracting the labors of the missionaries. The church was trying to teach the people the gospel. But commerce was sending its sailors there to practice vice and sow the seeds of immorality and death.

Mr. DAMON began his work in a chapel which had been carried thither in sections from America. He invited the sailor upon his ship. He cared for him while in port. He overlooked the work of providing for him a home. He preached to him in the house of God. He followed him with his kind offices, warning him of danger, rebuking his sins, reasoning with him of righteousness, repentance, and judgment to come. He edited a paper which was devoted to his interests. He showed himself every way to be his sincere friend. He gave him help in distress, counsel and comfort when sick and in trouble. Hence he is known and loved by thousands that annually visit the port of Honolulu. They call him Father Damon. They attend his chapel when there, and they carry away with them the books and papers he has provided for them, and the memory of all his kindness and attention.

Contrast such a work with that which is done for the sailor in too many a seaport, where he is tempted and robbed and demoralized, and then carried back to the sea with all his hard earned wages in the hands of publicans and harlots, and say which is best for society, commerce and civilization.

And it is this work of caring for the sailor and surrounding him by associations and influences that shall save him and make him a blessing that the SEAMEN'S FRIEND SOCIETY is doing at home and abroad. Will you aid it by your prayers and contributions, and so help to speed the day when the abundance of the sea shall be converted to God, and when all the rivers that run into the sea shall bear to it rich blessings that shall return in due season to refresh and beautify the earth and make it as the garden of the Lord.

Sympathy.

SAILOR! we will think of thee,
On thy lone pathway o'er the sea,
When the storm is darkly gathering
And the winds are wildly sweeping,
  We will think of thee.

Sailor! we will pray for thee
To him whose voice hushed Galilee.
When we seek his blood-bought dower
The Holy Spirit's saving power,
  We will pray for thee.

Sailor! we will give to thee
Our warm and earnest sympathy;
The thought will cheer thy midnight watching,
That memories fond and prayers are reaching
  Across the deep to thee.

SHARON, CT.   E. N. T.

LIFE-SAVING SERVICE.—REPORT OF THE CHIEF OF THE BUREAU.

TWO HUNDRED AND THIRTY-FIVE LIVES IMPERILED, AND ONLY ONE LOST—AN EXTENSION OF THE SERVICE CONTEMPLATED—THE STORM SIGNAL AND LIFE-SAVING STATIONS CONNECTED.

We here present our readers with an interesting document from the Treasury Department. It is but a few years since the Government entered upon any systematic attempt at Life Saving, and Mr. Kimball's report will show a most gratifying progress in this humane work. Any appropriation necessary to extend the arrangements proposed should be cheerfully made.—ED. MAG.

To the Hon. WM. A. RICHARDSON, *Secretary of the Treasury.*

The Life-Saving Service, as at present constituted, comprises 81 stations on the coasts of Cape Cod, Rhode Island, Long Island, and New Jersey. There are three districts—the coast of Cape Cod, from Race Point to Monomoy, forming the first; the coasts of Rhode Island and Long Island, from Narragansett Pier to Coney Island, the second, and the coast of New Jersey, from Sandy Hook to Cape May, the third. The following lists show the situation of the stations, the numbers by which they are designated, and the names of the persons in charge:

DISTRICT NO. 1—COAST OF CAPE COD.
Benjamin C. Sparrow, East Orleans, Mass., Superintendent.

No.	Station.	Keeper.
1.	Race Point,	Lewis A. Smith.
2.	Peaked Hill Bar,	David H. Atkins.
3.	Highlands,	Edwin P. Worthen.
4.	Parmet River,	Nelson Weston.
5.	Cahoon's Hollow,	Wm. C. Newcomb.
6.	Nauset,	Marcus M. Pierce.
7.	Orleans,	Solomon Linnell.
8.	Chatham,	Alpheus Mayo.
9.	Monomoy,	George W. Baker.

DISTRICT NO. 2—COASTS OF RHODE ISLAND AND LONG ISLAND.
Henry E. Huntting, Bridgehampton, N. Y., Superintendent.

No.	Station.	Keeper.
1.	Narragansett Pier,	Benj. Macomber.
2.	Block Island,	Samuel Allen.
3.	Montauk Point,	Jonathan Miller.
4.	Ditch Plain,	Samuel T. Stratton.
5.	Hither Plain,	Geo. H. Osborn.
6.	Napeauge,	Elijah M. Bennett.
7.	Amagansett,	Charles J. Mulford.
8.	Georgica,	Jonathan F. Gould.
9.	Bridgehampton,	Baldwin Cook.
10.	Southampton,	Charles White.
11.	Shinnecock,	Lewis R. Squires.
12.	Tyanda,	Edward H. Ryder.
13.	Quogue,	Mahlon Phillips.
14.	Tanner's Point,	Franklin C. Jessup.
15.	Moriches,	William Smith.
16.	Fargo River,	Sidney Penny.
17.	Smith's Point,	Joseph H. Bell.
18.	Bellport,	Geo. W. Robinson.
19.	Blue Point,	Daniel A. Nevens.
20.	Lone Hill,	Edmund Brown.
21.	Point of Woods,	Geo. W. Rogers.
22.	Fire Island,	Leander Thurber.
23.	Oak Island, E. End	Henry Oakley.
24.	Oak Island, W. End,	Prior Wicks.
25.	Jone's Beach, East End	Augustus C. Wicks.
26.	Jone's Beach West End,	Townsend Verity.
27.	Meadow Island,	Leander Lozee.
28.	Long Beach, East End,	Daniel W. Smith.
29.	Long Beach, West End,	Charles Wright.
30.	Hog Island, W. End,	Joseph Langdon.
31.	Rockaway Beach, East End,	Daniel Mott.
32.	Rockaway Beach, West End,	Isaac Skidmore.
33.	Sheepshead Bay,	Cor. Van Nostran.

DISTRICT NO. 3—COAST OF NEW JERSEY.
W. W. Ware, Cape May City, N. J., Superintendent.

No.	Station.	Keeper.
1.	Sandy Hook,	C. W. Patterson.
2.	Spermaceti Cove,	Samuel Warner.
3.	Seabright,	Charles West.
4.	Monmouth Beach,	Edward Wardell.
5.	Long Branch,	Hamilton Taber.
6.	Deal,	Abner Allen.
7.	Shark River,	Wm. A. Harvey.
8.	Wreck Pond,	Samuel Ludlow.
9.	Squan Beach,	E. H. Jackson.
10.	Point Pleasant,	John C. Clayton.
11.	Swan Point,	James Numan.
12.	Green Island,	Wm. P. Chadwick.
13.	Tom's River,	Wm. N. Miller.
14.	Island Beach,	K. F. Reed.
15.	Forked River,	John Parker.
16.	South End Squan Beach,	D. D. Herring.
17.	Barnegat,	Saml. Perine, Jr.
18.	Loveladic's Island,	Charles Cox.
19.	Harvey Cedars,	Charles Martin, Jr.
20.	Ship Bottom,	Henry Lamson.
21.	Long Beach,	W. H. Crane.
22.	Bond's,	Thomas Bond.
23.	Little Egg,	J. B. Rider.
24.	Little Beach,	W. P. Shrouds.
25.	Brigantine,	W. Holdzkom.
26.	So. Brigantine,	C. A. Holdzkom.
27.	Atlantic City,	Burton Gaskill.
28.	Absecom,	Thomas Rose.
29.	Great Egg,	John Bryant.
30.	Beazely's,	Richard B. Stiles.

Vol. 47.   JANUARY, 1875.   No. 1.

THE MISSIONARY ELEMENT IN CHRISTIAN WORK FOR SEAMEN:

A SERMON.

BY REV. J. E. ROCKWELL, D. D.,

Pastor of the First Presbyterian Church, Edgewater, Staten Island, N. Y.

DEUT. 3:19.—They shall call the people unto the mountain; there they shall offer sacrifices of righteousness, for they shall suck of the abundance of the seas, and of the treasures hid in the sand.

This prophesy was uttered by Moses in his final interview with the people whom he had led out of Egypt. It was the blessing which he pronounced upon Zebulon, and served to give emphasis and meaning to the words of the dying Jacob, "Zebulon shall be a haven for ships." By their natural position this tribe of the Israelitish people was especially devoted to commercial pursuits, and had dealings with all the nations lying around the great sea, which was then the centre of the world's commerce. Although it is impossible to define their exact limits during its early history, yet we are assured by Josephus, that they reached from Lake Gennesareth on the East, to Mount Carmel and the Mediterranean on the west, and that it was the great thoroughfare by which the vast commerce of Damascus and the regions around made its way to the sea, so that this people were brought into constant and busy contact with the merchants of Syria, Phœnicia and Egypt. Such intercourse while it adds breadth and spirit and intelligence to any people, affords also opportunity for the spread of truth in all its forms. It cannot be supposed that the men who were constantly brought into social contact and business relations with a people who were devoted to the worship of Jehovah, could fail to gather from them new ideas of religion, and new views of the method in which man is to worship and serve God. The heathen who had come from scenes, where idolatrous rites and services often of the most degrading character, were offered to stocks and stones, must have received most solemn and important lessons in regard to the nature of God and the spiritual worship which He required when they came in contact with a people who were governed by a law whose first words were: "Thou shalt have no other Gods before me—thou shalt not make or worship any graven image." And anticipating this result of their intercourse with the people around them, Moses says of the tribes of Zebulon and Issachar, "They shall call the people unto the mountain, where they shall offer sacrifices of righteousness." There had undoubtedly been a partial fulfillment of this prophecy as early as the days of Solomon. The ships which he built upon the Red Sea were manned with sailors of Tyre, whose king was a worshipper of the God of Israel, and between whom and himself the warmest friendship existed. If it be asked how this knowledge of the true God had come among a people who for ages had been marked and distinguished as idolators, we may find the solution in the intimate relations which had existed between Tyre and Sidon, the haven of the sea at which Zebulon dwelt. Between these two ports there was constant communication, and if the sailors of Zebulon were faithful to their own religious obligations, as it was foretold they would be, it would have been no strange or difficult thing to make known the truth to the Syrian seamen. There were times when these idolatrous men must have witnessed scenes which were new to them, and which must have deeply impressed them as being wholly the reverse of what they witnessed in their own land. They saw no idols to which the sailors of Zebulon bowed in worship. They heard them speak with reverence and awe of the one only living and true God, whose name they honored and whose commands they obeyed. Three times in the year they saw them leaving their homes and their business and going up to Jerusalem to keep the solemn feasts which commemorated God's goodness to them and their fathers. In many ways they heard from them the story of their separation from all other nations as a distinct people; and of the hopes they cherished of a coming Messiah who should redeem his people from their sins. Thus it was that in the intercourse which Zebulon had with other nations through its commerce, the people were invited to the mountain of the Lord, and were taught the nature of the service which He required and the worship to be offered to Him.

Here, then, we have presented to us a class of men who by the very nature of their employments, should have remarkable opportunities of spreading abroad the knowledge of God, and under whose influence they who were hitherto ignorant of His worship, should be invited to engage therein, instructed in the truth and led to an enjoyment of the blessed hopes of the Gospel.

And this fact opens to us a most important view of the influence of a Christianized Commerce upon the moral destinies of the world, and shows to us *the missionary element in the work of the church for seamen*.

Who can estimate the power for good which is possessed by a single crew of sailors, whose hearts are all alive to the hopes of salvation, and whose souls are permeated with the love of Christ as the Saviour of lost men? What has been the influence of commerce when unsanctified—what has been the power for evil of seamen whose characters have been debased by crime and passion, is too well known to need proof or illustration? Thus far, the heathen world have learned little else but evil, through the men who have come to their ports and coasts from nominally Christian countries. What ideas can we suppose have been formed by idolatrous nations of a religion which has had its representatives in men whose characters have ever been stained by lust and intemperance and every debasing crime? What notions could they entertain of Christianity which its missionaries have represented to be peaceful and honest and pure, when they have seen the very men who have brought them thither, practising the most degrading vices, plundering the helpless and destroying the innocent? Can we wonder at the comparatively little progress which the missionary enterprises of the church have made, when we recall the tremendous influences against which they have had to contend in the opposing drifts of crime, sensuality, fraud and violence, which have set in upon them from the commerce of Christian countries? One of the most fearful hindrances to the progress of the Gospel in heathen countries, has been found in the sailors who visit them, and bring with them the vices and demoralizing influences of their new civilization.

On the contrary, we can hardly estimate the power for good which Christian sailors possess, who carry with them wherever they go the spirit of the Gospel of Christ, believing its truths and practising its virtues.

While we cannot over estimate the importance of what is known as the special work of foreign missions, which consists in the establishment of churches, schools and all the varied instrumentalities essential to the spread of the Gospel among the heathen, we are in danger of undervaluing the power of the Christian sailor in aiding this work. Nay, is it not true that the church has scarcely recognized this agency as of any essential value in the accomplishment of Christ's command to preach His Gospel to every creature? Its missionaries are numbered by hundreds only, while three millions of men are toiling upon the sea and visiting every nation and tribe whose lands border upon the ocean, and if properly prepared might be of eminent service in aiding the church to do its work. We are learning in the developments of divine providence, that while the church and the world need an educated ministry, men of ordinary training and abilities if filled with the spirit of God and the love of Christ, may wield a mighty influence for good and be effective in saving men whom an educated ministry might be unable to reach. A Christian layman has often accomplished incalculable good among his fellow men by his godly example, and his loving words of warning and instruction spoken at the fitting time, and which have been like apples of gold in pictures of silver. Men even of little intellectual ability or culture have sometimes been instruments of good to many a soul by their simple, direct, affectionate and fearless appeals made to the heart and conscience. It needs surely only a practical knowledge of the Gospel to be able to tell men the simple story of the Cross and of salvation through Jesus Christ. Why then need the church wait until it can send forth bands of educated men to every island and nation before it enters upon its work of evangelization. What if it press the sailor into its work, and empower and commission him to say to every man who is bowing to idols that Jehovah hath said: "Thou shalt have no other Gods before me," or to tell to the poor and wretched the story of Christ's great love for sinners, and of his death on the Cross for lost and guilty men. Who can doubt the fidelity with which such a message would be given, when he knows the promptness and fearlessness with which the sailor meets the demands of duty. What if every ship that sailed from the ports of Christian nations was manned and officered by men who felt the power of the truth in their own souls, and who were supplied by the church with Bibles and tracts written in the language of the people whom they were to visit; who can doubt that such reading would if placed in the hands of thinking and intelligent men, open to them the knowledge of the way of salvation, and be at least the means of preparing the way for the missionary of the Cross. Is not the experiment worth the trial? It was said by one of the early missionaries to the Pacific Islands that the readiness with which those people received them, was owing to a few words which had been dropped by one of the sailors of Captain Cook, who when he saw them worshipping idols, told them that they were not thus to expect to secure the favor of God, and that bye and bye men from England would come and tell them about God and how to serve him. These words were treasured up among the traditions of the Islanders, and when the early missionaries from America came among them were recalled, and served to secure a welcome for those who came to tell them of the way of salvation.

Why then may not the sailor be used in helping forward the missionary work of the church? What is needed to make the attempt hopeful is such an earnest and persistent effort for his spiritual good as shall by the divine blessing secure his conversion to Christ and his consecration to the work of spreading abroad the knowledge of the truth as it is in Jesus.

One or two simple facts will serve to show the power of the sailor for good when his heart is under the influence of the Gospel. The late Dr. C. S. Stewart, once a missionary to the Sandwich Islands, and for many years after a chaplain in the U. S. Navy, gave a most striking testimony to the influence of Christian seamen in a brief notice of the voyage of the steamer *Niagara* when bearing homeward the Japanese Embassy, whose visit to our shores many will remember.

"We have" (he wrote) "regular worship at which the whole ship's company attend on the quarter deck every morning and evening, as well as the public services of the Sabbath, when congregational singing, by the officers and crew, and a sermon are added to prayer.

The worship is open to the free observance of the Japanese, and is regarded by them with worshipful attention and interest. At first, the princes when on the deck at the time the ship's company were thus assembled, retired to their apartments, but of late they often remain as spectators.

The professing Christians among the sailors, a dozen in number, hold a prayer meeting on the berth-deck every evening. It was commenced the first night we were at sea after leaving New York. Many of the fifty servants of the embassy have been attracted to the vicinity of this, by the singing of hymns, and no doubt have informed themselves of the nature and meaning of this new aspect to them of the religious observances of Christians. The ambassadors and their suite are frequently remembered in prayer at these meetings, and as I have seen one and another of the Japanese stand and look with seeming wonder at the group of sailors bowed down upon the deck in prayer, I have been moved more than once to tears by the simplicity and earnestness with which these converted sailors have interceded with the Saviour in their behalf, that the light of His truth and the power of His grace might be manifested among these pagans, and in the nation to which they are returning."

What a testimony is this to the character of the work that sailors might perform were they fully interested in the service of Christ. Nor is this an isolated fact. Many a similar testimony might be adduced to show the power for good which lies in the sailor when he has had an experience of the love of Christ in his soul.

Several years since, a sea captain engaged in a coasting voyage on the Pacific, disposed of over a hundred Bibles, besides many religious tracts in the ports at which he stopped. A sailor who had been ordained as a preacher established a church with more than eighty members, mostly converts from Catholicism on an island near the coast of South America.

Two converted seamen once shipped from Boston to Calcutta. An impenitent shipmate who thought piety in a sailor was a matter of mirth and ridicule, and who expected to make himself and his comrades merry at the expense of these Christian men, said to a stranger after they had sailed: "Well, I learn that there are a couple of pious fellows in our crew." The stranger looked up with a meek glance, and replied: "Yes, sir, and I hope I am one of them." A second stepped up promptly, and said: "And I hope I am another." "My sport" (said the scorner when afterwards relating his experience) "was all over. Surely, said I to myself, these men are Christians of the genuine kind—they are not afraid to show their colors." This man was thus led to reflection, and then to Christ. These three established a prayer meeting in the forecastle, and before the voyage was ended, six others were rejoicing in hope. Moreover, while they were in India, sailors from other ships attended their meetings, and several of them also were converted to God. Like the men of Zebulon, these earnest sons of the sea called the people unto the mountain of the Lord, and there offered their sacrifices of righteousness. With such facts before us and with many similar ones which might be readily mentioned, who can fail to see what immense power for good is garnered up in the commerce of a Christian nation when it is sanctified to Christ and the church.

Is it not a matter of wonder that in the agencies to be used for the conversion of the world, so little attention has been paid to the men who in the very nature of their calling are brought most in contact with every nation, and who if they were in full and hearty sympathy with the work might be constantly exerting an influence that should be for the furtherance of the Gospel and the bringing of the world to the knowledge of Christ. Without dwelling at length upon the points which show the power of the missionary element as it exists in a Christianized and sanctified commerce, we may mention a few obvious facts which may set the matter before us.

1st. The sailor is a citizen of the world. He is to-day at home among the influences of Christianity and civilization, and in a few weeks in India or China or Japan or Africa, or the Islands of the sea —the very fields the church is seeking to cultivate, and the people whom it desires to convert.

2d. The sailor is a bold and fearless man. He learns from the experiences of every day to face danger wherever duty summons him. He is in constant contact with perils and inured to hardships. He never shrinks from the work which is laid upon him, though it is to be performed amidst storm and darkness, though it call him to climb the swaying masts amid blinding flashes of lightning or the flying spray that freezes as it falls. Such a character surely is one that is needed in the work of missions, and that eminently qualifies the Christian to engage in its arduous duties.

3d. Again, the sailor has learned the necessity of prompt and cheerful obedience to orders. He knows that the commands of his captain are law, which he is never to question, but must at once perform. He never thinks of doubting their propriety or neglecting their fulfillment for a moment. What then may we believe will be his conduct when he enlists under the great captain of our salvation, and with his heart full of love for Him, hears His command: "Go preach my Gospel to every creature."

Lastly, the sailor is frank and generous and free hearted, and thus endowed with the very qualities that would lead him, were he a Christian, to just such a work as might be of essential service to the church in its great duty of evangelizing the nations. With such qualifications, what an agent for good might he become were he but duly prepared by the grace and Spirit of God to devote himself fully to the service of Christ.

And did not the Master Himself give a hint and a lesson to the church as to its work, and its agencies, when He selected four of His most eminent apostles from the sailors of Galilee, and said: "I will make you fishers of men." Is it not strange then that the church has seemingly lost sight of this instrumentality, among all the agencies it has sought to employ for spreading the Gospel over the world? When has the sailor ever failed in fulfilling a trust committed to him? Commerce has placed in his hand its untold treasures, and has grown and flourished through his fidelity.

Nations have employed him to defend their honor and guard their coasts, and he has nobly and manfully accomplished his mission. Science has used him in her task of gathering together the facts and phenomena on which she makes up theories and systems, and he has essentially aided her in her work. He has brought to her the secret treasures of the sea—has marked its currents—observed its motions—traced the course of the winds—visited the regions of eternal winter—pushed his way through vast seas of ice—sounded the mysterious depths of the Ocean—and laid from shore to shore the electric wires that thrill with the thought, and bear the tidings of commercial and social life from continent to continent.

Yet the church seems almost to have overlooked him when seeking for agents to do her work of carrying the news of salvation to the nations it has sought to enlighten and bless.

Hundreds of Christian congregations while contributing their benefactions for the cause of missions, have forgotten to aid the society that is seeking to fit the sailor to be a most important element in the missionary work. In our larger seaports it is true, Bethels and churches have been established for seamen. Yet this is only one item in the work which must be done for his spiritual welfare. He needs books for his quiet and leisure hours at sea. He needs religious influences in foreign ports. He needs a home that shall be free from the terrible temptations with which he is usually surrounded when he enters a sailor's boarding house. He needs the watch and care of a pastor or chaplain when he lands on a foreign shore—that he may be visited upon his ship—invited to the house of God—warned of his dangers and temptations, and pointed to the Saviour. What the treatment has been which the sailor has received in return for his perils and labors encountered at the behests of commerce and science and national and social interests, is too well known to need more than a simple and passing allusion. He has been met on his return from sea by the throngs of men whose only object has been to plunder him of all his hard earned wages, and set him adrift again, with health undermined, and character gone. He has been the victim of the most systematic efforts to defraud and degrade and ruin him. He has been often entrapped into dens of vice and infamy, when in a few days the gatherings of months have disappeared, when he has been drugged by strong drink, and has only known the full extent of the evils he has suffered, when he has waked up, far at sea, upon some ship where he has been placed by the wretches who have made merchandise of him and have received the wages he is yet to earn, as a part of their nefarious business.

And nations that have grown great by means of his perils and work, have looked coldly on and failed to step in to help and defend him. And when wise and humane laws have been passed for his protection, the most persistent efforts have been made to defeat their due execution, and to send the sailor back into the hands of the vile combinations for his destruction.

Against these unhappy influences the AMERICAN SEAMENS' FRIEND SOCIETY seeks to defend the sailor, and to throw around him safeguards, and spiritual and social agencies that shall ensure his temporal and eternal well being.

It is the agent of the Christian Church in caring for three millions of men who need to be followed, at home, and upon the sea, and in foreign lands, with the influences and appliances of the Gospel. In the prosecution of its work, so far as it is successful, it is preparing a most important missionary agency for the evangelizing of the world—it is aiding the church to fulfill the command of Christ, "preach my Gospel to every creature."

Facts which are continually coming to the knowledge of those who are engaged in the management of the society, are clearly revealing the missionary element of its work. Its chaplains and agents—its libraries, which are now numbered by thousands, and its Christian homes whose establishment it is aiding, are all so many auxiliaries to the church in its great mission. On many a ship that goes forth at the behests of commerce, are Christian sailors, who are earnest and faithful servants of Jesus Christ. On some of our noble lines of steamers every sailor is shipped with the understanding that no spirituous liquors will be furnished him, except on case of actual sickness and by the direction of the surgeon. This statement I know is true in regard to the line, in whose ships I recently crossed and re-crossed the Atlantic, and the effect on the character and conduct of the crew was most marked and noteworthy. In many a ship's cabin the crew are now regularly gathered for religious services, and in many a forecastle prayer meetings are held, and the Bible read, and souls re-freshed and saved.

A single fact will illustrate the work that is going on among those who do business upon the great waters.

A few months since the Trustees of the SEAMENS' FRIEND SOCIETY received a letter from the COUNTESS OF ABERDEEN, in Scotland, expressing her wish to place in their hands a sum of money for the purchase of a number of libraries, which should be sent forth in her name as a memorial of her son who was lost at sea. In the course of the correspondence which ensued the following facts, were learned in respect to this noble young man. On the death of his beloved and honored father, LORD HADDO, in March, 1864, he succeeded to his title, and for nearly a year and a half remained at home comforting his widowed mother, and being the centre and source of happiness in the household. Early in the year 1866 he sailed for New Brunswick as a passenger. During the voyage, as the captain had no religious services on board, he used to meet with the sailors on Sundays, reading to them portions of the Word of God, and using for prayer the collects which were found in an old Catholic book of devotion. After making a tour in the United States, he went to Boston, and laying aside his title and concealing his rank, under the name of GEORGE H. OSBORNE, shipped as a common sailor on a voyage to the Canary Isles, partly from a love of the romance of sea life and partly from an idea that his health might be benefited thereby. He no sooner was engaged in the duties of the merchant service, than he became deeply interested in the welfare of seamen. A sight of their wrongs and hardships so enlisted his sympathies, that he turned his thoughts to the best methods for improving their condition—determined to remain at sea long enough to obtain a full knowledge of a sailor's life, and then to return to his home and endeavor to bring about needed reforms in the mercantile marine. For a period of nearly four years he spent most of his time at sea, mingling freely with sailors, and exerting among them a noble Christian influence, which has made his memory precious and fragrant. Though his rank and position at home were unknown to his associates, yet his accomplished manners—his studious habits—his high moral character—his regular attendance at church when on shore—his uprightness and purity of life, and his constant efforts to lead his associates to a knowledge of the truth, were remarked by all with whom he came in contact, and were affectionately remembered, when, after his death, inquiries were made concerning his career and history as a sailor. He seldom lost an opportunity to do good, or to leave some moral and religious influence upon his associates. In the cause of temperance he was a faithful worker, and he sought in every way both by precept and example to lead men to the practice of this Christian virtue. When on land he sought out some church where he might worship God, and often took with him his companions whom he desired to interest in the sanctuary, and to bring within the reach of the means of grace.

A man of such intelligence and moral worth could not long remain a common sailor. He was soon promoted to the position of an officer, where he had still higher opportunities of usefulness, which he continued to improve for the benefit of the sailor, in whose cause his whole soul was interested. It was only his brief experience at sea that prevented his being placed in charge as captain of the missionary ship, which left Boston for the Islands of the Pacific.

On the 27th of January, 1870, while doing his duty as first mate on a vessel bound from Boston to Melbourne, his feet became entangled in some of the rigging, and by a sudden lurch of the ship he was thrown overboard. Every possible effort for his rescue was made at once, but all in vain. He had sunk to the sailor's grave amid the fathomless depths of the ocean, and his last cry for help was heard only by his shipmates and by Him who once walked upon the waters, and whose ear is ever open to the prayer of the needy, and in whose grace he had trusted for salvation.

It was while the agents of his family were searching after some clue to his fate, after long waiting for their customary letters from him, that his noble mother became acquainted with the work of the SEAMENS' FRIEND SOCIETY, through whose aid the missing links in his history were found. Anxious to have some memorial which was befitting her son's career, she offered a generous gift to the society for the purpose of sending forth libraries, which should bear his name and remind his brethren of the sea, of his love and sympathy for them.

It was my privilege on a recent visit to Europe, to carry to his bereaved mother, the COUNTESS OF ABERDEEN, from the Trustees of the Society, their expressions of gratitude for her munificent gift, and of sympathy with her in her sorrow, and to place in her hands a model of the libraries which were to bear her son's and her own name. It was a fact worthy of notice which I had the pleasure of stating to her that the first library given out on her donation, was placed in the hands of a captain bound for California, who had known her son intimately, who though ignorant of his rank and title had loved and honored him as a Christian gentleman and a noble sailor, and who was most deeply affected on being told from whom and in whose memory the gift had come to him.

Such is an example of the influences which are at work among the men of the sea. And it is in behalf of a Society that has in it so many elements of the missionary cause, and connected with which are a thousand facts that show the importance of caring for the sailor, that we ask the aid of all who love the Master and who would seek the welfare of mankind. We would place a chaplain in every port where our seamen are found. We would give to every ship a library for the use of its officers and crew. We would encourage and aid the establishment of Christian homes for the sailor when he reaches the land.

We would surround him by moral influences that would help him to resist the fierce temptations that beset him on every hand. The work is one that appeals to all who desire to see our common Christianity extended over the world. Every sailor converted to Christ becomes an agent for the spread of His Gospel. Every influence that is used for his salvation is also exerted through him upon nations yet to be given to Christ as His inheritance, and the islands that wait for His law.

THE ABERDEEN MOTTO.—" HE HATH MADE THE DEPTHS OF THE SEA, A WAY FOR THE RANSOMED TO PASS OVER." Isa. 51: 10.

[For the Sailor's Magazine.]
THE SEA-WARD DRIFT.

BY REV. CHARLES J. JONES, *Seamen's Chaplain.*

Sometimes a vessel when nearing the land, as night approaches, is becalmed. The coast is a strange one. The captain's fears are excited, lest in the coming darkness she may drift too near the unknown coast. He paces the deck, and through the long hours of the night, anxiously wishes for the land breeze, which will enable him to stand off shore. But, when the day breaks, he finds that his fears were all premature. The set of the current has borne him seaward, and given him the offing he craved.

To the eye and heart of the sailors friends, the good ship—the CHURCH—has seemed to be thus becalmed, and when they would have her moving forward to their aid, she has appeared motionless. But as the night shadows flee away, we find that she, too, has been drifting sea-ward—insensibly borne onward by the currents of prayer. What may we not anticipate then, when, instead of thus listlessly drifting, her sails shall be filled with the breathings of the Divine Spirit to bring her with all her resources to our rescue? Then will she indeed

" An emblem yield to friends and enemies.
" How the Great Teacher's doctrine, sanctified
" By truth, shall spread throughout the world dispersed."

To drop the figure. We may well "thank God and take courage," as we notice that the tendencies of the church to-day, have a sea-ward drift. She is looking "toward the sea." There have been, here and there in the church, since the first fourth of this century, men who have seemed to appreciate, in some measure, the agency of the sailor in the great work of carrying the Gospel to the nations. But even these seem scarcely to have risen to the dignity of the subject. They appear to have considered the sailor rather as the common carrier, than as the "living epistle," and conceived the idea of sending the Word of God *by* him rather than *in* him. Note the guarded language of Rev. Charles Gutzlaff, in the journal of his labors in Siam and China, written but a quarter of a century ago: "While representing Christianity as the only effectual means of establishing a friendly intercourse, I would not reject the efforts of commercial enterprise to open a trade with the maritime provinces, but rather regard them as the *probable means* of introducing that Gospel into a country to which the only access is by sea." We should be thankful that there is less of timidity, and a more cheerful and hopeful ring in the church's tone to-day. "The times are changed, and we are changed with them." Testimonies are now more pronounced in favor of these men of the sea than ever before. As an evi-

GOD'S PROPRIETORSHIP IN THE SEA.

A SERMON

BY REV. J. E. ROCKWELL, D. D.,

PASTOR OF THE FIRST PRESBYTERIAN CHURCH OF EDGEWATER, STATEN ISLAND, N. Y.

PSALM 95; 5.—The Sea is His and He made it.

The Ninety-fifth Psalm is a call upon the people to worship God, for which act two especial reasons are given—his greatness and his goodness. Under the first head is placed his proprietorship of the depths of the Earth and of the mighty and towering mountains—and to this is added that he is both the owner and maker of the Sea. This is not the only reference to the ocean which the Scriptures make when setting forth the power, wisdom and glory of God. Hundreds of similar texts may be found in which the sea is alluded to, not simply as a grand and magnificent work of Jehovah, but as bearing a most important part in the accomplishment of his purposes concerning this world, in which he has made the grandest displays of his wisdom, power and love. There is then a special emphasis in the words "the sea is His" which may be marked and felt as we look over the sacred oracles, and notice how much is said of the sea and its inhabitants, as associated with God's plans in reference to his church, and the highest interests of the human race.

There is a wondrous significance in the words which describe the sea as first appearing when the light had broken upon the chaotic world and the waters which were under the firmament were divided from those which were above. How simple yet how sublime is the story as told by the sacred historian. "And God said let the waters under the heaven be gathered into one place and let the dry land appear, and it was so. And God called the dry land Earth, and the gathering together of the waters he called Seas; and God saw that it was good." While as we read, subsequently, the beasts and fowl were brought by the Lord to Adam that he might give them names, the sea, which is his own, God named himself, as though it were his own special work and property, and to be his own favorite agency in accomplishing his wise and beneficent purposes and showing forth his own glory. It is to many a matter of wonder that he who created the world should have made two-thirds of it a simple waste of waters. They ask, where is the wisdom of thus appropriating so much space to seas and oceans which might have been used as the domain of man, and turned into fruitful fields waving with golden harvests, or into populous towns filled with life and teeming with busy and active inhabitants? It is a sufficient answer to the devout mind, that it pleased him "whose ways are not our ways nor his thoughts our thoughts" to set these vast waters as natural boundaries between the nations. Yet we may find a sufficient solution to the inquiry, if we reverently search for it, amid the same records that reveal Jehovah to us as the wise ruler of the universe, that assure us that the sea is His and He made it.

I. It is worthy of notice, in the first place, with what an almost affectionate interest God himself speaks of the sea, as his work not only, but as mirroring forth his sovereignty, power and glory. When He would set before Job and his friends his divine majesty he introduces his argument by the question, "Who shut up the sea with doors when it brake forth as if it had issued from the womb, when I made the cloud the garment thereof and thick darkness a swaddling band for it, and brake up for it my decreed place and set bars and doors, and said hitherto shalt thou come, but no farther, and here shalt thy proud waves be stayed?"

When he would open to his people their contempt for his authority, he presents to them the sea as his obedient servant, and asks with wonder, "fear ye not me, and will ye not tremble at my presence which have placed the sand for the bounds of the sea by a perpetual decree that it cannot pass, and though the waves thereof toss themselves, yet they cannot prevail; though they toss themselves, yet cannot they pass over?" When the Psalmist would set forth God's wondrous works and power he says, "thy way is in the sea and thy path in the great waters." When he would describe his glorious attributes, the sea appears as a fit mirror of his omnipotence and omnipresence. It is he who gathers its waters together; who stills its raging, who controls its power, and who is mightier than its waves.

There is that in the sea which speaks to the thoughtful and devout mind most impressive lessons of the natural attributes of Jehovah. It is a

> "Glorious mirror where the Almighty's form
> Glasses itself in tempests; in all time
> Calm or convulsed, in breeze, or gale, or storm,
> Icing the pole, or in the torrid clime
> Dark-heaving, boundless, endless and sublime.
> The image of Eternity—the throne of the Invisible."

No one who loves to contemplate God's works and whose soul is capable of being stirred by deep and strong emotions can fail to find in the sea abundant evidence and illustrations of the wisdom, immensity, power, majesty and glory of him whose is the sea and who made it. To the thoughtful mind the ocean always has its solemn lessons which seem as the voice of God itself. Who can ever look forth upon it and not think of him who gave the sea its bounds, and who measures its waters in the hollow of his hands? What a lesson it reads to us, in all its vast appearings and the wild roar of its billows, of God's wisdom and power and glory. What an image it is of his immensity and eternity. Through how many ages has it rolled on unchanged. The storms that have swept over it have left no trace of their fury. Time has been busy, but though the marble monument has crumbled beneath its touch, the strong fortress fallen, and cities and palaces are in ruins, and the earth itself shows signs of age and decay, the sea is unwasted and unchanged. Generation after generation has stood by its shores and listened to the music of its ripples or the thunder of its surf, and has passed away, yet its dark waters still ebb and flow, and its wild billows sing their requiem over the dead.

> "Time writes no wrinkles on its azure brow;
> Such as Creation's dawn beheld, it rolleth now."

Who can stand and look upon the sea and feel no emotions of wonder and awe, and no reverence for Him who made it? What lessons it teaches us of our own weakness and of God's greatness and power, of our littleness and his infinitude and grandeur. In all its moods of rest or storm, of peace or wild commotion; it tells us that he who made it is almighty and eternal.

II. Again, the ocean is one of God's great instruments in exerting his providential care and control of the world. Science is every day bringing to us fresh illustrations of the influences which the sea exerts upon the land. Out of its mighty waters rise the mists and clouds that roll backward over the broad fields and lofty mountains of the earth and leave there the moisture that gives fertility to the land, that fills the springs and pools, and swells the rivers that are flowing onward to the ocean. Its currents bear the heat of the tropics to islands and continents that would otherwise have an arctic climate and sterile soil. Its countless inhabitants are food for man. Its storms, even, are sources of health. They sweep over every land, and bear before them the miasmas and poisons that might otherwise prove destructive of life. Its tides keep in constant and healthy motion all the inland waters that flow into its bosom. Its restless waves, as they beat upon the shore, accomplish mighty geological changes, and leave their undoubted records in stony leaves which are turned and read by the student of Nature in succeeding ages, unveiling to him the vast revolutions by which the world has been built up and made the habitation of man. Thus does He who when he pleases can bring to pass his purposes by the most insignificant agencies, use also the mighty ocean as his servant in executing His providential will towards the world which he has built and peopled, and over which he reigns as sovereign.

III. Again, the sea is God's agent in separating and bounding the nations of the earth. The Scriptures, although they do not pretend to instruct us fully either in natural or political science, yet have frequent reference to the fact of the separation of the nations by a special ordinance of God. While he hath made of one blood all that dwell upon the face of the earth, yet he did not intend there should be any such uniformity as would allow only a single family or nationality. It was a part of his plan that there should be distinct races, who, while having all the essentials of a common brotherhood, should yet be so widely diverse as to require separate residences and governments. Hence we read, "When the Most High divided to the nations their inheritance, when he separated the sons of Adam, he set the bounds according to the number of the children of Israel." And again it is written of the people, "He hath determined the times before appointed and the bounds of their habitations." It was by his own direct agency that after the flood the people, who were of one language, were prevented from forming one nation through a confusion of tongues, and so forever separated, not only into different nationalities, but into different climates and countries—divided not simply by mountains or deserts, but by rivers, seas and oceans. It was thus that he solved the problem of the peopling of the whole world through the family which he had made in his own image, and to which he had given the task of subduing the earth. And he who has studied with the least care and attention the history of the world has surely seen what infinite wisdom and benevolence was concerned in this separation of the nations. The experiments which Alexander, Xerxes and the Cæsars made of stretching one government over the world were but magnificent failures. Even the vast empire of Rome was the scene of constant collision between the distinct nationalities it embraced, and at length broke down by its own weight. Out of this vast sea of revolution arose separate governments, each after its own kind and order—each in its own way unfolding its power, and moving forward for the fulfillment of some of God's wise and beneficent purposes. And those nations which have been most insulated have made the most decided progress in civilization, and social and intellectual science and culture. England, though its people were barbarians when Rome was in the zenith of her splendor and power, rose in a few centuries like another sun in the firmament and shone on when Italy's light was quenched in blood and revolution. Cut off from the rest of Europe by a cordon of waters, and shut up to art and commerce, she became the great bulwark of law and the temple of science and religion. Her insulated position enabled her to gather strength and power, not as the tributary of some adjoining nation, but as an independent government working out her own ends and destiny. It was the surrounding of these straits and seas, hemming her in to her own resources and developing her energy, thrift and virtue, that gives meaning to the song of her poet:

> "Britania needs no bulwark,
> No towers along the steep;
> Her march is on the mountain's wave,
> Her home is on the deep."

And how manifestly can we see the same divine wisdom that divided the nations of the old world, engaged in separating from it the western continent by two vast oceans, and leaving here full scope for the development of some of the grandest problems which the human race has ever solved. Fifteen centuries passed after Rome had reached the highest point of her power before the existence even of a western continent was known, and when it burst like a new world upon the sight of the adventurous explorers of Europe, a whole century pregnant with mighty changes passed away ere these vast forests began to disappear before the advancing tread of civilization, and these broad prairies and fertile hills were filled with an earnest and industrious and hardy population. And now, severed by two mighty oceans from either Europe or Asia, the people of America have been left at liberty to work out the grand experiment of independence and self-government, while side by side have arisen separate nationalities, each developing some peculiar phase of civil or religious principle, and illustrating its excellence or its evil.

It would seem then that God had made the seas to be boundaries of nations, and so to separate them that all might be left to work out his plan for the welfare of the race, and for the upbuilding of his kingdom, which is to stretch from sea to sea and from the river to the ends of the earth.

IV. Again, God made the sea as a highway of the nations, and a means of intercourse and correspondence between the inhabitants of the earth. We can hardly imagine what would have been the state of the world had there been no ocean to be the path of commerce, and had all the intercourse of the earth been carried on over immense plains thousands of miles in extent. Over those vast distances travel would have been necessarily difficult, and communication infrequent. Commerce would have been carried on only between adjacent nations, while the knowledge of more remote people would have been but a confused, indistinct and overdrawn picture, the rudest and wildest work of the imagination. We may see illustrations of this thought by casting our eyes over the nations that are most remote from the great tracks of commercial enterprize. What barbarism and ignorance exist among the tribes that skirt the great deserts of Africa. How little progress is made by the nations of Asia that have no sea coast. There it is that bigotry, superstition and despotism hold the people in an iron bondage, and that custom and caste keep them rooted to old and *effete* institutions, while the rest of the world outstrips them in intelligence, education, and all the grand ideas of an enlightened and advancing civilization. Were there no sea there could be no intercourse between remote nations, no healthful interchange of ideas, and hence no improvements by adopting customs and institutions which other people have found benificent and wise. The spirit of commerce is the spirit of growth, and of progress in invention, art and social sciences. It is the spirit of peace, of friendship and fraternity. It binds the nations together in the bonds of unity, good will and common interests. It breaks down international prejudices. It prepares the way for the entrance of light and knowledge and truth, Hence, while the ocean separates, it unites; while it isolates nations, it brings them together; while it leaves each distinct nationality free to work out its own destiny, it enables each to impart to others its influence and to assist them in the progress of our common humanity in what may elevate and enlarge and bless. All this is a part of God's great purpose, and he who built the earth made the sea also, and gathered its mighty waters together that they might serve as his agents, and carry forward his wise and benificent plans towards the great family of man.

V. And this leads us to notice, as a last and most important consideration, that the sea is set before us in the word of God as intimately associated with the final subjection of the world to Christ. It is wonderful how much the ocean is introduced into the prophecies as connected with the conversion of the nations and the bringing in of the latter day glory. Even the histories of the church which are given in the Old Testament and the New, seem to point to the uses which will be made of the sea when the glory of the Lord shall cover the earth. When God was bringing forth his people from the iron bondage of Egypt he used the sea as the instrument of salvation to his church, and of vengeance upon his enemies. When Christ was selecting his apostles, he found his most earnest and faithful servants by the sea, and called them from toils and dangers to be fishers of men. And then if we look over the prophecies we shall find the sea associated with some most glorious triumphs of the Gospel. When the Psalmist would set forth the glories of Christ and of the church which he would adorn and beautify as a bride with his own grace and love, he numbers among those who should appear as guests the very symbol of commercial power and influence, saying, "the daughter of Tyre shall be there with a gift." In the age of Solomon Tyre was the seat and centre of all the traffic that was done by the sea. Its situation was such as to command the trade of the world. Its navies were built out of the forests of Lebanon. Its sails and cordage came from Egypt. Into its capacious harbor floated the wealth of all nations. Its riches came from the sea, and they were used when needed for the advancement and glory of the church and her great head. When a temple was to be built at Jerusalem the artists and architects and materials for the work were largely sent from Tyre. And looking forward to the more glorious scenes that were yet to dawn upon the church the Psalmist seemed to see what commerce would do for its advancement, and he wrote of it as "the daughter of Tyre." And in the same line of prophetic thought Moses catches a view of the coming glories of Christ's kingdom as he gives his parting blessing to the people whom he had lead out of Egypt, and says of Zebulon that he should be a haven for ships. "They shall call the people into the mountain, there shall they offer sacrifices of righteousness, for they shall suck of the abundance of the seas and of the treasures hid in the sand." So also Isaiah again and again opens to us the part which the sea shall take in the future triumphs of Messiah's kingdom, associating the conversion of its abundance with the bringing of the forces of the Gentiles, and with the growth and glory and enlargement of the church. And, again, taking up the promises of God, he re-echoes his words to his people, "Surely the isles shall wait for me, and the ships of Tarshish first, to bring my sons from far, their silver and their gold with them."

No one can mistake the import of such passages in which the Scriptures abound. And it is when we look at the ocean as associated in the sublime purposes of God, with his own glory, and the conversion of the world to him, that we may fully comprehend the meaning of the words,

"The sea is His and He made it." By it He not only separates the nations into families, leaving them to work uninteruptedly the great problem of civilization and social life, but he binds them together in a common brotherhood, bringing them year by year into closer mutual relations, breaking down the prejudices and barriers that separate them. And more than this, he will use the sea as the means of carrying to all nations the Gospel and its ordinances, and will call in the men of the sea to be his fearless, earnest and devoted laborers for the spread of the truth and the upbuilding of his kingdom. The men who go down to the sea in ships are the living links that bind the nations of the world together. They visit every shore and clime, they are intimate with all the people of the earth that live near the sea; they are brave and fearless. They are undergoing severe toil and hazard for the comfort and happiness of others, and are thus self-sacrificing, hardy and generous. And when commerce shall bestow on the church the gift of her toiling millions, all consecrated to Christ, who can estimate the results? Even now we have illustrations of what will be accomplished when the abundance of the sea shall be converted to God, and the energy, zeal and fearlessness of the sailor shall all be devoted to Christ and the spread of his Gospel. The history of the church in these later years has been fruitful in evidence of what the sailor can do when his heart is truly given to God. He carries with him into his new life and service all the qualities which mark him as a man. He never thinks of shrinking from the duties which his new captain lays upon him. He never is ashamed of his profession, or afraid to show his colors. There is no mistaking the service in which he is engaged. There is no concealment of the truth he believes.

And with the considerations we have presented there is set before us, as one of the great and important features of the work of the church in preaching the gospel to every creature, the necessity of special care and attention to the spiritual wants of the sailor. If the sea belongs to God, all that dwell upon it are his, and ought to be consecrated to his service. And yet it would seem as if the church and the world alike had been slow to recognize God's proprietorship in the ocean. Commerce has used it as her great highway, and seemingly never thought of consecrating her gifts to God and his church. Nations have used it as their bulwark and defense, or have achieved upon its waters brilliant victories over their enemies without a thought of him who rules the ways and whose ways are on the sea. Nay, it would seem as if for ages the great enemy of God and man, the ruler of the darkness of this world, had claimed as his own the sea and all that do business upon it. When we think how the pirate-ship has swept over its waters, defiantly flinging out its bloody banner to the breeze, and how the slave-ship has darkened its waters while the groans of its hapless victims have mingled with the sighing of the winds and the waves; when we recall the vice and crime, the wrong and outrage, the brutal passions, the injustice and fraud and debauchery which have marked the history of commercial and naval life, it would seem as if Satan had claimed the sea as his own, and bound its toilers in his chains and dragged them into his service. The sailor has been subjected to hardships and often to cruelties at sea, and upon the shore has been tempted and deceived and robbed. Commerce has used him for her purposes, and never cared what has become of him after he has accomplished her ends. The nations have used him for their protection in war and their services in peace, and never seemed to notice his wants or his wrongs. The church has appeared almost to have passed him by in her work of preaching the Gospel to every creature, and to have forgotten his claims to her attention. Nay, while pressing into her service almost all classes of men whom she has used in her duties, it seemed never to have entered her thoughts that the sailor might be successfully employed as her agent in spreading the Gospel over the world. But a little more than fifty years have passed since any united and organized effort was made for seamen as a class. An occasional sermon at the death of some sea captain, or an address to sailors by some pastor of a church in a sea port town, was all that was done for their conversion, was all the recognition made of *God's proprietorship in the sea.*

In a volume of pamphlets in my library is a sermon preached in 1785 on the death of Capt. Pearson, in the Presbyterian church at Newburyport, and published at the request of the Marine Society there. In the same volume is a sermon "preached at Falmouth, Feb., 1811, in the meeting erected by seamen near the water." The subject is the Seaman's Farewell, and its text is from Acts 21: 5, "And we kneeled down on the shore and prayed, and when we had taken our leave one of another we took ship." The sermon seems to have been an address to a company of seamen in Maine just before their departure for a voyage.

In the year 1813 there appeared in the *Religious Intelligencer* the "First Annual Report of the Boston Society for the Religious and Moral Improvement of Seamen." The object of this association was proposed to be accomplished:

1. By the distribution of religious tracts among seamen.
2. The establishment of regular divine service on board of merchant ships.

In 1814, a Christian gentlemen of London, while visiting the captain of the ship *Friendship*, was induced to invite the crew into the cabin and hold with them a brief religious service. This led to the establishment of similar exercises on other vessels, to which eventually the crews of neighboring ships were invited, the signal being a lantern hoisted to the main top gallant mast-head at night; by day, a blue flag with the word "*Bethel*" in the centre. This work continued with increasing interest, and resulted in great spiritual blessing to many souls. In the year 1818, a simultaneous movement was made both in England and America in behalf of seamen, which resulted in the establishment of permanent preaching places for them in Dublin, Liverpool, New York, and other prominent sea ports. Attention was called to the subject by eloquent sermons and earnest appeals through the press.

In 1826 the AMERICAN SEAMEN'S FRIEND SOCIETY was organized, and its work has been steadily increasing during the half century of its existence. And with the advance which it has made has come a fuller, deeper impression of the importance of its work, not simply in securing the personal salvation of the sailor, but in equipping him for the part he must perform in the evangelizing of the world. In the light of what has already been accomplished, the meaning of those prophecies which relate to the sea and its abundance begins to be more clearly and fully apprehended. The work of the Society, which is necessarily of a peculiar and special character, is every year becoming more hopeful. It seeks to meet the sailor at home and abroad with Christian influences. It provides for him Chaplains and Missionaries. It opens for him Bethels and Homes where he may be surrounded by friends that care for him, where his hard earned wages may be kept for his future wants, or be sent to his family for their comfort and support, where he may be lead to the house of God and the place of prayer. The Society follows him upon the sea with its well-selected libraries, by which he may be instructed and amused and cheered in his hours of leisure. It seeks to awaken a proper interest and care for him on the part of ship owners and merchants, and to secure substantial justice for him in the enactment of wise and equitable laws for his protection.

Upon its labors God's blessing has rested. Every year is giving fresh evidence of its power for good among seamen, and is bringing back to the church ripened sheaves from the seed which it has sown. It recalls the name of such a noble Christian as the youthful Earl of Aberdeen, who, leaving for a while his ancestral home and hiding his honors under the simple name of George Osborn, exerted an influence among the seamen with whom he associated that was pregnant with Christian excellence and goodness, and who but for his untimely and sudden death would have returned to give intelligent and earnest utterance to his views of the sufferings and wants of the sailor, and of the legislation which was needed in his behalf. It points to such men as Hudson and Foote and Stewart, of our own navy, as examples of the offerings which the sea has made to the church. It tells with gratitude of the work which the Missionaries and Chaplains are doing in Sweden, in Denmark, in South America, at Honolulu, in China, and elsewhere, and asks the church to aid in the continuance and enlargement of its efforts for the temporal and spiritual good of the sailor.

It claims our prayers and aid as a grand missionary agency, whose success will help on the final evangelization of the world. It seeks to make every ship a *Bethel*, and every sailor a disciple of him who "once pressed a sailor's pillow," and who chose from the hardy fishermen of Galilee his noblest and most earnest and successful apostles.

SUNDAY OBSERVANCE AND SUNDAY LABOR ON SHIPBOARD.

Any reliable contribution to our knowledge of facts in connection with this topic, must be a valuable step in the reformation of what has long been an abuse connected with the Marine service of our own and of other nations. In recent successive numbers of the London *Day of Rest*, a Sunday journal, we have noted a series of articles by Commander WILLIAM DAWSON, of the English Navy, which embody much information as to the present conditions of Sabbath observance and desecration in English harbors and upon English vessels, and we condense them for our readers in the hope of contributing something to such a reform. ED. MAG.

The facts furnished exhibit the wisdom of recognizing a distinction between the present actual observance of the Sabbath upon English Naval vessels and in the English Mercantile service. The first English "Article of War" provides that in the Queen's service, "Divine service be solemnly, orderly, and reverently performed, and the Lord's Day observed, according to law." Formerly, and in practice, the Queen's officers, on shipboard, limited the Lord's Day to the hours between 10 a. m. and 5 p. m., and took care to prepare their crews for these seven hours of bodily rest, by the useless preliminary of six hours hard and unnecessary morning labor.

It is 'the custom of the service' to give sixteen hours toil, on Saturdays, to cleansing a ship-of-war from truck to kelson, and when the crew 'turn in' at 9 p. m., the vessel is 'as clean as a new pin.' But under 'the old school,' that staunch conservator of every evil habit, the idea prevailed, that whilst the crew slept 'the new pin got rusty,' and, accordingly, at 4 o'clock on Sunday morning, 'all hands' were 'turned up' to sluice the decks and their appurtenances with streams of salt water and streamers of swab tails. To undo this gratuitous mischief, a most worrying system of polishing followed, which most sane men would think an ill-preparation of temper for the 'solemn, orderly, and reverent performance of Divine Service.' So that, after all, it was a very small mercy, the seven hours rest, which gave so much of contentment and happiness to the Queen's seamen.

It was only in 1860 that the neck of this inane 'custom of the service' was broken, and that by a most stern and able disciplinarian, who then held the chief command in the Mediterranean Fleet. His ships were, by common consent, regarded as the cleanest and best ordered fleet in the whole of the Royal Navy. Yet he ordered, and took care to enforce, a cessation of this useless Sunday morning worry, whilst putting a stop also to the customary Sunday evening exercises, &c. It required, however, all his stronghanded authority to secure a compliance, in all the vessels under his command, with the dictates of common sense. As Sir William Martin's order (all honor to the name) gave the crews, when in harbor, two hours extra sleep on Sunday morning, and a whole day of rest, instead of seven hours, the efficiency, contentment, and happiness of that fleet were greatly enhanced.

Another annoyance to the sailors of the Royal Navy, and hindrance to the observance of the Sabbath has prevailed, of late years, in the practice of opening Her Majesty's vessels, at home, to sight-seers, after noon, on Sundays. This nuisance is very considerable to all on board, interfering with all attempts at religious service and labor among the seamen, and producing among them, wide-spread discontent and ill nature, giving rise to a large increase of minor offenses on their part, and it is much to be hoped that this abuse may soon become a thing of the past. The general conclusion as to the English Navy is that in every one of its vessels, though two-thirds of them do not carry Chaplains, united daily prayers are offered, while in most of them some of the crews are to be found kneeling in individual prayer, night and morning.

Turning now, to the English Mercantile Marine, and asking for the facts concerning the subject in hand, on vessels at sea, Commander DAWSON declares that the Report of the Missions to Seamen Society (English) contains some very deplorable statistics as to the prayerless condition of a large section of the merchant shipping. It is hardly credible, he says,—we sincerely hope it is untrue, but such is the statement—that in only one ship in every 666 which leaves the port of Sunderland, is the Lord's Day kept holy at sea by assembling the crew for Divine worship. A hardly better state of things is reported of the shipping in the port of Hull. In the Downs, in one vessel in every 122 was the Fourth Commandment so observed. At Poole, one ship in 35 held Sunday service at sea. In Falmouth Roads, in one ship in 134 was public worship regularly conducted. In Swansea, the proportion is one vessel in 43; whilst in Bristol the ratio is as deplorable as Sunderland, viz., one vessel in every 647.

If these statistics be correct, one may well infer that the condition of Sabbath observance on English merchant vessels when in port, is

Vol. 48.   NOVEMBER, 1876.   No. 11.

THE ARK AND ITS LESSONS,

A SERMON

BY REV. J. E. ROCKWELL, D. D.,

Pastor of the First Presbyterian Church of Edgewater, Staten Island, N. Y.

HEB. 11: 7.—" By faith Noah being warned of God of things not seen as yet, moved with fear, prepared an ark for the saving of his house: by the which he condemned the world and became heir of the righteousness which is by Faith."

The Bible is the oldest book in the world. Its histories carry us back to the dawn of creation, and contain records which, though brief and condensed, supply us with all that we know of man for a period of more than two thousand years. While its chief aim is to teach us what we are to believe concerning God, and what duty he requires of us, yet it has notices of the progress of our race, of the dawn of science and art, of the social and political changes which have marked the progress of man, and of the manners and customs of the nations which have had the nearest relations to the Church of God, and the people through whom the blessings of redemption were introduced to the world.

In that book, we find frequent mention of the sea, and notices of ships and sailors, which show that early in the history of our race, navigation had come to be an important means of communication between the nations of the earth. It would be strange if even before the flood, men had not found some sort of vessels necessary for the purposes of commerce and of travel—and the building of so large a structure as the ark would seem to indicate, that when Noah received the command to prepare it, for the saving of himself and his house, he found mechanics sufficiently familiar with shipbuilding, to execute all the plans which he received directly from God himself. Yet, although mention is made of seas and rivers in the opening chapters of the Bible, we find no notice of any vessel until we reach the history of Noah and the flood. The ARK was not in the usual sense a ship, having neither mast nor rudder, and being designed simply to float above the waters which were to prevail over all the earth. Yet it deserves especial mention as being the first vessel of which any notice is made in history—and of which traditions are found among almost every nation and people.

I. It is a significant fact that it was constructed after a model which *God himself furnished*, and after plans which he distinctly specified. He who built all things, was the designer of this vast structure—the drawings of which he gave to Noah, with special directions as to the materials of which it should be built, and the manner in which it should be arranged. We find a statement of all these details in the same book to which we are indebted for the only reliable history of our race for a period of more than two thousand years. The Ark was built of Gopher or Cypress wood—a light and durable timber, which, in later years, was largely used by the Phœnicians in the construction of their ships, and afterwards by Alexander the Great, for the navies which he used in his conquest of the world. Bitumen, or pitch, as it is called, was employed to caulk or close up the seams, both within and without, and so to make it water-tight. Its dimensions, if we may take the cubit at 18 inches, were as follows:

Length, 450 feet, or 300 cubits.
Breadth, 75 feet, or 50 cubits.
Height, 45 feet, or 30 cubits.

This would give a ground surface of 33,750 feet and a cubical measure of 1,518,750 feet. If the cubit be taken at 21 inches, the dimensions would be one-sixth greater, and the carrying capacity of the ark proportionately increased.

In its interior arrangements there were a number of compartments, in three tiers or stories, suitable for the stowage not only of the family of Noah (eight persons in all), but of the beasts and birds both clean and unclean, who were to be housed in the ark, and for the food necessary to keep them alive. The whole was to be lighted by a window or transparency in the top, while an opening or port was to be left in the side, by which entrance was to be had to the Ark, and which the hand of God himself was to shut when all were safe within. It is a curious fact that these proportions of this vast structure have been found by actual experiment to be the most perfect for the purposes for which the Ark was built. In the year 1609, Peter Janson, a Dutch Merchant, built, at Hoorn, in Holland, a ship 120 feet long by 20 feet wide and 12 feet deep. And, though his vessel was not remarkable for her sailing qualities, it had a capacity for freightage one-third more than other ships—while requiring no more hands to work it.

II. Another fact that distinguishes the ark is, that it was built for the interest and for the salvation of the Church. It was constructed under divine guidance to keep alive the family which of all others God had found righteous, which was to be the germ of his church as well as the family by which the earth was to be re-peopled when its old population should have been swept away. For a whole year the Ark bore within its ample enclosure the Church of God. Noah had been a preacher of righteousness to his generation for an hundred and twenty years during which the Ark had been preparing. His example as well as his precept had warned men that God hated sin and loved righteousness. His works showed him to be thoroughly in earnest. No one could doubt that he believed what he preached. Men may have laughed at what they called Noah's folly. They may have called him crazy and mad. Even his workmen may have made him their jest—while receiving from him their daily wages—and as they met together at the close of the day, have been merry at his expense. Children and youth may have shouted out their ridicule as they asked amid mirth and laughter, 'when he expected his craft to set sail.' Old men shook their heads and said 'surely our neighbor has lost his senses to spend time and money on such a useless structure as that.' It is possible the ark may not have been built by any stream large enough to float it—but on some hill or plain far away from the great thoroughfares of commerce. Yet when all was finished. He who had directed its building launched it for its long and lonely voyage as never ship was launched before. When the last warning had been uttered, and the work completed, Noah heard the command 'Come, thou and all thy house into the Ark.' Crowds may have gathered to see the entrance of the beasts and birds, and then of the family of Noah into the ark. Old sailors may have wondered how he expected to float, or how to weather the storm, if his ship should ever be launched, or how to expect to reach port without sail, or mast, or rudder.

Crowds of young men returning from scenes of festivity or crime, may have looked up as they passed by the Ark and broke out into peals of laughter when they heard that Noah and his family had entered that huge craft, and were awaiting the coming flood. The great tides of business ebbed and flowed without a pause. Men bought and sold, and gave themselves up to riot and crime, and held high carnival despite the warnings of that just and good man. But the day came when God's mercy was exhausted. Seven days passed after the Ark had been closed by unseen hands.

The sun rose angry and red, and was soon darkened by thick and ominous clouds. Then came the rain, and the lightning, and the tempest. Hours and days passed with no abatement of the awful storm. The windows of heaven were opened, and the fountains of the great deep were broken up. Mothers gathered in their children as they saw the torrents sweeping by. Men talked of the great rain as something unheard of in all the annals of the world. Fathers began to move their households to higher elevations where they might find security from the dreadful inundation. The swollen rivers at length overflowed the plains. Hamlets, and villages, and cities disappeared. The hills were covered with crowds who had ascended thither for safety, and who, from their summits that rose like lonely islands in mid-ocean, looked out with terror upon the mighty and surging waters that encircled them. Higher and higher rose that vast sea that was soon to wrap the earth in a funereal shroud. The work of ruin still went on, and the last family were looking out with terror upon the scene of desolation, and saw the Ark floating by over the wreck of a drowned world—and then sank beneath the rising waters, the last of the multitude that had filled the earth with violence. There upon that lonely and shoreless sea, the family of Noah were floating in safety, protected and guided by him whom they had obeyed, and who would, in his own time, bring them forth to re-people the earth. In forty days the Ark floated, and for a hundred and fifty days more, the water prevailed, until every living thing perished, and all traces of the old earth's crimes were swept away. Days and months passed on, and still that strange craft rocked upon the billows of the ocean, until the waters subsided, and the Ark rested upon Ararat, and God remembered Noah and brought him out with his family at the end of the year, and sent him forth to replenish the earth. Looking upward the patriarch saw the bow in the clouds as the seal of God's covenant never again in like manner to destroy the earth, and offered to him sacrifices for the mercy that had saved him and his house, and the Providence that had guarded them in their long and strange voyage, over a fathomless ocean that rolled above a drowned world.

The history of this wonderful event has found a place amid the traditions of almost all nations. The Chaldeans, the Phœnicians, the Persians, Indians and Chinese, all have corrupted versions of the story which is found simply and fully narrated in the word of God. But the most remarkable attestation to the truth of the sacred record has lately been found amid the stones now placed in the British Museum, which were once part of the palace of the King of Erech, who reigned about the year 660 B. C. It claims to be the story of the flood as told by Noah himself, who is said to have obtained immortality. He relates how he was directed to build a great ship, and describes his method of building it, and how, when built, 'I caused to go up into the ship all my male and female servants, the beasts of the field, the animals of the field, and the sons of the army.' He speaks also of the coming of the tempest which destroyed all life from the face of the earth, the calming of the storm, the reappearance of the mountains, and the resting of the ship upon the top of them, the sending forth of the raven and the dove, and the final disembarkation, and building of an altar of sacrifice. Thus, in these later ages of the world, when scepticism is throwing its doubts and sneers at the simplest records of God's word, these attestations to their truth come to us from voiceless and silent witnesses which have been buried from the sight of men for more than two thousand years, and if thus, the history of this event is proved true, we may receive the lessons which it is designed to teach us, and while we learn the abhorrence with which God regards sin, flee for refuge to the hope that is set before us in the gospel, to the Savior of the world in whom alone we may have life.

III. And as this first ship of which history makes any mention was built under the direction of divine wisdom in the interests of the church, may not the church learn a lesson therefrom of the uses to which commerce shall be put, when the abundance of the sea shall be converted to God, and when every ship shall become a Bethel in which all whom it bears over the waters of the sea shall be the servants of Him who hath loved them and given himself for them. In the light of the histories and promises of the word of God, the Ark appears as a type of the part which commerce is yet to bear in the extension and triumphs of the kingdom of him who is the King of Kings, and whose is the sea, for He made it.

1st. The prophecies of the Old Testament are full of descriptions which associate commerce with the final subjugation of the world to Christ. Some of the most beautiful figures which they use are drawn from the sea, and appear to have been presented to the eyes of those who wrote, as they were moved by the Holy Ghost, in immediate and intimate associations with the growth and prosperity of the church. Amid the glories of the future which Moses saw when addressing to his people his parting words, was the part which Zebulon and Issachar were to bear in the establishment of religious institutions. Living as they were, by the most important seaport of the country, it was said of them, 'They shall call the people unto the mountains; there they shall offer sacrifices of righteousness, for they shall suck of the abundance of the seas, and of the treasures hid in the sand.'

And as we turn from this early hint of the influence which commerce was to exercise in spreading abroad the knowledge of the true religion, we find especially, amid the prophecies of Isaiah, the clearest descriptions of the uses which would be made of the sea in opening to the nations the blessings and glory of the gospel. No man can read the glowing words of this prophet without feeling that his attention was often arrested by the ships which were to be made tributary to the kingdom of Christ. He saw the abundance of the sea converted to God, and with it also the forces of the Gentiles. He beheld the ships of Tarshish engaged in bringing the sons of the church with all their treasures, back to the home from which they had been exiled. He saw the land of shadowing wings from which messengers were going, in swift ships, to carry tidings that related to the extension and triumph of the cause of Christ. And standing as it were upon the shores of some mighty ocean on which were flocking the scattered tribes of God's redeemed ones, he asked with wonder,—who are these that fly as a cloud and as doves to their windows?

2nd. And so in all the history of the church, the hint which seemed to have been first drawn from the Ark was perpetually followed in the Providence of God toward his people. In the days of Solomon, the wealth of Israel was wonderfully augmented by the navies he sent forth, which brought back from every land and clime the gold and treasures that enriched the people whom God had chosen as the depositories of his word and ordinances. It was from the sea of Galilee that Christ selected his noblest apostles, and its ships often bore him backward and forward in his missions of grace and mercy. It was by the ships of the Mediterranean that Paul was carried to and fro in his great work as the Apostle to the Gentiles, and was borne at length to Italy that he might preach the gospel as a prisoner to them who were in Rome. And so has the ship and the sailor been constantly associated with the church, in all its grandest interests and work. And the Ark has thus become a type of the part which commerce is to bear in the extension and triumphs of the kingdom of God. And as the first ship of which we have any knowledge bore within it a preacher of righteousness to that generation, so many a ship is now bearing not only messengers of the gospel to the nations that are sitting in darkness, but earnest and faithful men who from the very nature of their occupation are prompt and fearless, and who will not hesitate, whenever duty calls, to stand up for the truth, and to bear aloft the standard of their Savior and Captain.

3rd. And may not the church learn in all these lessons of God's word and providence, her duty to make use of commerce as her agent, if not for her salvation and perpetuity, for her enlargement and conquest, in subduing the world to Christ. Even now she may hear the echo of the words which Noah heard,—build thou an ark of Gopher wood, and may behold in that ancient ship which bore for a whole year the fortunes of the church—the symbol of commerce in its relations to the people of God and the kingdom of Christ.

4th. The Ark was the connecting link between the old world and the new. It bore within its ample enclosure, the fortunes of our race. Its freight was the rarest and strangest that any ship ever carried over the waters. But the most important of all that vast collection was the household of Noah, in whom all the destinies of the human race were centered.

There were God's people, for whose preservation all these arrangements had been made, there was the preacher of righteousness, who was to re-establish on the earth the institutions and ordinances of religion, and whose first act when he again walked forth upon the dry land, should be to offer a solemn sacrifice to God. And so that Ark seems to be reading to the church and to the world lessons of mighty import as to what will be the ultimate mission of commerce in advancing the interests of the church and aiding the triumphs of the Prince of Peace. We need not ask of prophecy alone what she will do for the kingdom of Christ. History opens to us, already, wondrous revelations of the uses which are to be made, of her, for the enlargement and extension of the church of God.

It is commerce that has opened up to the church new fields for her laborers, and that has helped her in her work of evangelization. It is commerce that has preceded the missionary, and prepared his way before him. She opened to the church the rich and populous countries of Southern Asia, sending her adventurous and hardy sailors thither, by the way of the Cape of Good Hope, and bringing the teeming millions of China, and India, and Japan, into contact, first with civilization, and then with the gospel. She boldly sailed westward upon the unknown waters of the stormy Atlantic, until a new world burst upon the astonished gaze of the nations, and America was opened to the church, as the theatre of some of its grandest movements for the conversion of the world to God.

5th. And besides this obvious result of commercial enterprise, we may notice what she is doing to bind the nations in a common brotherhood, and so to prepare the way for the Gospel, amid people who may yet be ignorant of its truths. We cannot pass through the busy streets of any great commercial centre without meeting the representatives of all nationalities. They come hither for the purposes of business or pleasure and they return to their homes with new impressions of what Christianity is, and what it can do for the highest interest of society. And so, too, in all the marts of Asia, Africa, Europe and the islands of the sea may be found the representatives of Christian nations, mingling with the people of China and India, Japan, Egypt, and sharing with them the influences of a common Christianity.

6th. And with this fact we notice also that commerce has given substantial aid in carrying to the nations of the earth the influences and appliances of the Gospel. Over all her vast highways she holds an undisputed sway and none can pass but with her consent. Her servants are the masters of the sea, and her swift ships bear the products of every clime and nation. They bore the first missionaries of the cross from Palestine to Italy, and ever since, they have served the church, by carrying her agents and instruments for the work of missions.

The Gospel follows in the track of commerce, and every new avenue of trade is a new opening for the church in which to enter upon the work of preaching the Gospel to every creature.

And more than this, commerce has already given to the church, fearless devoted and earnest men whose influence and labors have been of substantial service in the spread of the truth amid the nations of the earth. A hint concerning the folly of idolatry and the proper worship of the true God which dropped from the lips of one of the sailors of Capt. Cook, when he visited the islands of the Pacific, was remembered by that people for years, and prepared the way for their cordial reception of the early missionaries from America. A converted sailor has often become an earnest and faithful witness for the truth. A Christian captain, with a few sailors in sympathy with him, has often made his ship a Bethel whose influence has been felt in every port which they have entered.

But time will not permit me to enlarge upon this theme. Enough has been said to remind us of the obligations which the Christian world is under to the sailor. We form a part of that vast field which Christ opened before his disciples when he said, "Go preach my Gospel to every creature." The conversion of a sailor is the salvation of a soul for which Christ laid down his life. Were the work to stop here, that were enough to engage our noblest effort. Yet more than this is accomplished. An earnest, fearless, prompt, obedient, self-sacrificing man is given to the church to help in its work of converting the world to Christ. He will never be afraid or ashamed to show his colors, or to declare his love for his Master. He never shrinks from duty or responsibility, and so becomes a useful and important aid in accomplishing the mission of Christ's Church—as his agent for making known his Gospel to every creature. It is for such reasons that the AMERICAN SEAMEN'S FRIEND SOCIETY claims the coöperation of all Christian denominations, as being of like service to all, in this special work of caring for the spiritual interests of sailors. Its simple effort is to provide for them, Homes and Chaplains, and due attention to their general interest. It gives them libraries which they can read in their hours of leisure while at sea. It meets them when they arrive at port with an invitation to make their home amid Christian influences, where their hard earned wages are securely transmitted to their friends and families, or are kept from the miserable wretches who would rob them both of their money and their soul. It brings them to the house of God, where their own brethren of the sea are met for prayer and praise, and so seeks to lead them to Christ and to secure their highest well being and both for time and eternity. What has has thus been accomplished, while it is a subject of devout gratitude to him who has used this agency for the advancement of his kingdom, will bear a favorable comparison with all similar work for the upholding and extension of the church of God. With singular economy in the machinery it has employed, it can look over the whole field of its labors and see everywhere the happy results of its HALF CENTURY of effort in behalf of seamen.

More than 5,000 Loan Libraries are afloat, reaching with their beneficent influence over a quarter of a million of seafaring men.

Besides the establishment of Bethel churches in all important American sea-ports, it has Chaplaincies in China and Japan and Sandwich Islands, in Chili and Brazil, France, Italy, Belgium, Denmark, Norway and Sweden. Some of these Chaplains, like Dr. DAMON, of Honolulu, and the Scandinavian missionaries, are exerting a noble influence upon the outlying population as well as upon sailors, and their labors have been followed by signal spiritual blessings. Besides these agencies, Sailors' Homes and Reading-Rooms have been established in many places, and tracts and other religious reading have been gratuitously distributed on shipboard. The results of this work can never be fully known, till the issues of life are reviewed in the light of eternity. But as a means of approximating to some just idea of what has been accomplished, it may be stated that more than 800 cases of hopeful conversions at sea, are distinctly traceable to the single agency of the Loan Libraries.

And may not the Society that thus cares for seamen ask of the Church the means for continuing a work so fruitful in the past and so hopeful for the future? It has literally the world for its field, and it asks of all who love the Savior, and the souls of men, to aid it in its work of preaching the Gospel to those that go down to the sea in ships, and throwing around them influences that shall save them for Christ and his church, and that shall so help to hasten on the day when the abundance of the sea shall be converted to God, and the forces of the Gentiles come unto him,—and the knowledge of him shall fill the earth as the waters cover the sea.

A METHODIST MINISTER brought to America several young Japanese princes to be educated. One day he sat down with them and read to them the passage of Scripture which speaks about "Christ saving to the uttermost." "Well now friends," he said, "What do you think of it? Does it appear to you possible to be thus saved?" Reflecting a moment one of them said, "Why, I should think so, if Jesus Christ is to do it."

HAPPINESS IS LIKE MANNA; it is to be gathered in grains, and enjoyed every day. It will not keep; it cannot be accumulated; nor have we got to go out of ourselves or into remote places to gather it, since it has rained down from heaven, at our very doors, or rather within them.

ONE HUNDRED years the mill has stood:
One hundred years the dashing flood
Has turned the wheel with roaring sound,
Through foaming waters, round and round.

One hundred years; and overhead
The same broad roof of blue is spread;
And in the meadows, bright and green,
The miller's children still are seen.

And thus the world is still the same;
The sunset clouds are turned to flame;
And while we live, and when we die,
The lark still carols in the sky.

And others rise to fill our place;
We sleep, and others run the race:
And earth beneath and skies above
Are still the same; and GOD is love.

GIVE! as the morning that flows out of heaven;
Give! as the waves when their channel is riven;
Give! as the free air and sunshine are given—
Lavishly, thoughtfully, cheerfully give.

Not the waste drops of thy cup overflowing;
Not the faint sparks of thy hearth ever glowing;
Not a pale bud from thy full roses blowing—
But give, as He gives thee, who gave thee to live!

STAND BY THE SHIP.

"Do, grandmother, tell us about the little drummer-boy whose motto was 'Stand by the ship.'"

"Grandmother is not used to telling children stories; but, if you will be quiet, she will try." And this is the story she told us:

"During one of the fiercest battles fought in the late rebellion, the colonel of a Michigan regiment noticed a very small boy acting as drummer. The great coolness and self-possession of the boy as displayed during the engagement; his habitual reserve, so singular in one of his years; his orderly conduct and his fond devotion to his drum —his only companion (except a few well-worn books, over which he was often seen to pore)—in which he took delight: this had attracted notice, both from the officers and the men. Col. B.'s curiosity was aroused, and he desired to know more of him. So he ordered that the boy should be sent to his tent. The little fellow came, his drum on his breast and the sticks in his hands. He paused before the Colonel and made his best military salute. He was a noble-looking boy, the sunburnt tint of his face in good keeping with his dark, crisp curls; but strangely out of keeping with the rounded cheeks and dimpled chin was the look of gravity and thoughtfulness, altogether at variance with his years. He was a boy prematurely taught the self-reliance of a man. A strange thrill went through Col. B.'s heart as the boy stood before him.

"Come forward, my boy, I wish to talk to you;" the boy stepped forward, showing no surprise under the novel position he found himself. 'I was very much pleased with your conduct yesterday,' said the Colonel, 'from the fact you are so young and small for your position.'

"Thank you, Colonel; I only did my duty: I am big enough for that, if I *am* small,' replied the noble little fellow.

"Were you not very much frightened when the battle commenced?' questioned Col. B.

"'I might have been if I had let myself think about it; but I kept my mind on my drum. I went in to play for the men: it was that I volunteered for. So I said to myself, 'Don't trouble yourself about what don't concern you, Jack, but do your duty, and 'Stand by the ship.''"

"'Why, that is sailors' talk,' said the Colonel.

"'It's a very good saying if it is, sir,' said Jack.

"'I see you understand the meaning of it. Let that rule guide you through life, and you will gain the respect of all good men.'

"'Father Jack told me that, when he taught me to say, 'Stand by the ship.''"

"'He was your father?'

"'No, sir—I never had a father, but he brought me up.'

"'Strange,' said the Colonel, musing; 'how much I feel like befriending this child. Tell me your story, Jack.'

"'I will tell it, sir, as near as I can like Father Jack told it to me.

"'My mother sailed on a merchant ship from France for Baltimore, where my father was living. A great storm arose; the ship was driven on rocks, where she split, and all hands had to take to the boats. They gave themselves up for lost; but at last a ship bound for Liverpool took them up. They had lost everything but the clothes they had on; but the captain was very kind to them: he gave them clothes and some money. My mother refused to remain at Liverpool, though she was quite sick, for she wanted to get to this country so badly; so she took passage in another merchant ship just going to New York. She was the only woman on board. She grew worse soon after the ship sailed; the sailors took care of her. Father Jack was a sailor on this ship, and he pitied her very much, and he did all he could for her. But the doctor said from the first she could not live through it; he was right; for she died when I was eight days old. Nobody knew what to do with me,—they all said I would die—all but Father Jack; he asked the doctor to give me to him. The doctor said, let him try his hand, if he has a mind to,—it's no use, the little one will be sure to go overboard after it's mother. The doctor was wrong. I was brought safe to New York. He tried to find my father, but did not know how to do it, for no one knew my mother's name. He left me with a family in New York when he went to sea again; but he could never find out anything about my mother, although he inquired in Liverpool and elsewhere. The last time he went to sea I was nine years old, and he gave me a present on my birthday, the day before he sailed. It was the last: he never came back again: he died of ship fever. He did a good part by me; he had put me to a free school at seven years of age, and always paid my board in advance for a year. So you see, sir, I had a fair start to help myself, which I did right off. I went errands for gentlemen, and swept out offices and stores. No one liked to begin with me, for they all thought me too small, but they soon saw I got along well enough. I went to school just the same. I did my jobs before nine in the morning, and after school let out I had plenty of time for work and to learn my lessons. I wouldn't give up my school: for Father Jack told me to have all I could, and some day I would find my father, and *he* must not find me a poor ignorant boy. He said I must be able to look him in the face and say to him without falsehood, 'Father, I may be poor and rough, but I have always been an honest boy and 'stood by the ship,' so you needn't be ashamed of me.' Sir, I could never forget those words.'—He dropped his cap, drum and sticks: he bared his little arm and showed the figure of a ship in full sail, with this motto beneath it, pricked into the skin: 'Stand by the ship.'

"'When I was twelve, I left New York and came to Detroit with a gentleman in the book business. I was there two years when the war broke out. One day, a few months after the war broke out, I was passing by a recruiting office. I went in; I heard them say they wanted a drummer. I offered; they laughed and said I was so little; but they brought me a drum and I beat it for them. They agreed to take me. So the old stars and stripes was the ship now for me to stand by.'

"The Colonel was silent; he seemed in deep thought. 'Now, do you ever expect,' he said, 'to find your father?—you do not even know his name.'

"'I don't know, sir; but I am sure I shall find him, somehow. My father will be sure to know I am the right boy when he *does* find me, for I have something to show him that was my mother's;' and he drew forth a little canvas bag, sewed tightly all around and suspended from his neck by a string. 'In this,' he said, 'is a pretty bracelet that my mother always wore on her arm. Father Jack took it off after she died, to keep it for me. He said I must never open it until I found my father, and that I must wear it so around my neck, that it might be safe.'

"'A bracelet, did you say?' exclaimed the Colonel; 'let me have it,—I must see it at once!'

"'With both his little hands clasped around it, the little boy stood looking into Col. B.'s face; then, slipping the string from over his head, he silently placed it in his hand. To rip open the canvas was but the work of a moment.

"'I think I know this bracelet,' stammered Col. B.; if it be as I hope and believe, within the locket we will find two names—Wilhelmina and Carleton, date — May 26th, 1849.'

"There were the names, as he said. Col. B. clasped the boy to his heart, saying. 'My son, my son.'

"I must now go back in my story. In the first year of his marriage, Col. B. and his lovely young wife sailed for Europe, expecting to remain several years in southern Europe, on account of the delicate health of his wife. He was engaged in merchandise in the city of Baltimore. The sudden death of his business partner compelled his return to America, leaving his wife with her mother in Italy. Soon after he left, his mother-in-law died. Mrs. B. then made arrangements to return to Baltimore at once, and took passage on the ill-fated steamer which was lost. Vainly he made inquiries: no tidings came of her. At last he gave her up as lost; he almost lost his reason from grief and doubt. Fourteen years had passed; he did not know that God in his mercy had spared to him a precious link with the young life so lost and mourned. Restless and almost aimless, he removed to Michigan.

When the war broke out, he was among the first to join the army.

"There stood the boy, tears streaming down his cheeks. 'Father,' he said, 'you have found me at last, just as Father Jack said. You are a great gentleman, while I am only a poor drummer boy. I have been an honest boy, and tried my best to do what was right. You won't be ashamed of me, father.'

"'I am proud to call you my son, and thank God for bringing you to me just as you are.'

"My little hero is now a grown man. As the boy was, so is the man. 'Stand by the ship.'"

N. Y. Observer.

Salt Wood.

It is a curious fact that in the salt mines of Poland and Hungary the galleries are supported by wooden pillars, which are found to last unimpaired for ages, in consequence of being impregnated with the salt, while pillars of brick and stone, used for the same purpose, crumble away in a short time by the decay of their mortar. It is also found that wooden piles driven into the mud of salt flats and marshes, last for an unlimited time and are used for the foundation of brick and stone edifices; and the practice of docking timber, by immersing it for some time in sea water, after it has been seasoned, is generally admitted to be promotive of its durability. There are some experiments which appear to show that, after the dry rot has commenced, immersion in salt water effectually checks its progress and preserves the remainder of the timber. Of the oldest known timber, that in the Egyptian temples, 4,000 years old, nothing is said as to the causes of its preservation.

From the Army and Navy Journal, August 19th, 1876.

MODERN NAVIES.

NO. II.—NAVY OF THE UNITED STATES.

The war of the Revolution terminated January 20th, 1783. But although the Navy was small, the injury inflicted by our privateers upon Great Britain in her most vulnerable point, her commerce, demonstrated that there was sufficient nautical enterprise in the country to supply, if properly utilized, a good sized Navy. During the first two years of the war about eight hundred sail of the enemy's merchantmen had been captured.

On the termination of hostilities the Navy of the Revolution was disbanded, but not before it had displayed the flag in foreign waters and proved the metal of which it was made. Paul Jones had actually appeared with the *Bon Homme Richard* in the mouth of the Humber, where several vessels were taken or destroyed; and on the 23d of September, 1779, fought off Scarborough that celebrated battle, which for skill, courage, and determination has few parallels in the annals of naval warfare. The inability of the Government to maintain even a small Navy at this time, is clearly shown in the report of the agent of the marine, which stated, August 5th, 1783, "that although it is an object highly desirable to establish a respectable marine, yet the situation of the public treasury renders it not advisable to purchase ships for the present—nor until the several States shall grant funds."

"The first effort," says Kent, to relieve the people of this country from a state of national degradation and ruin, came from Virginia in a proposition from its legislature (January, 1786), in reference to our ocean commerce. This led to the calling of the convention which drew up, and, on the 17th of September, 1787, agreed to the Constitution of the United States. One month before this it had been resolved that the Commissioner of Marine accounts, in settling the accounts of the officers, seamen, and marines of the late Navy of the United States, govern himself by the principles established for the line of the Army, etc., etc." The inexperience and irresolution betrayed in the several acts quoted shows the foundation of the little Navy to have been as unsubstantial as the articles of confederation under which it was formed. On the 13th of September, 1788, the Constitution was fully ratified, and on the 4th of March, 1789, the Government as therein provided for went into operation. By that Constitution it is declared that Congress shall have power "to provide and maintain a Navy," and "make rules for the government and regulation of the land and naval forces." The second section of Article II. declares that "The President shall be Commander-in-Chief of the Army and Navy of the United States." In an act approved August 7th, the Secretary of War was directed to perform such duties as the President should entrust to him, relative to the land and naval forces.

For eleven years the United States was without a Navy. By our treaties of commerce, which have always been conceived in a liberal spirit, and have discovered an enlightened policy at times even in advance of the age, our foreign trade developed to such a degree that it soon extended to every sea. We were now to learn what every maritime nation before us had learned, that a Navy was indispensable to the safety of ocean commerce and to the integrity of the national colors. The first act of Congress looking to the establishment of a naval armament under the Constitution (Approved March 27th, 1794,) was called forth, as the preamble states, by "the depredations committed by the Algerine corsairs on the commerce of the United States." The act authorized the President to provide "four ships to carry forty-four guns each, and two ships to carry thirty-six guns each." But by the 9th section, the act was to expire should peace take place between the United States and the regency of Algiers. Peace was purchased November, 1795, by the present of the handsome frigate *Crescent*, 36. That peace cost the people of the the United States nearly one million of dollars, a sum sufficient to have put afloat a squadron large enough to have driven all the Algerine corsairs from the face of the ocean! In 1796 Congress seeing there was danger of further difficulties, this time from French cruisers, authorized the completion of two "forty-fours'" and one "thirty-six," and the perishable material of the other three to be sold. Twelve years after the sale of the last ship of the Revolution, the *Alliance*, the forty-four gun frigate *United States* was launched (Philadelphia, July 10th, 1797), and shortly afterwards the "forty-fours" *Constitution* and *Constellation*. Congress after repeated urging by the Executive, though not until the danger became imminent, authorized, little by little, an increase of the naval armament. April 30th, 1798, the act was passed for the establishment of the Department of the Navy.

The new Navy was now fairly under way. The Navy of the Revolution had died only as the sown seed, to germinate and bring forth more abundantly. All the old officers of the Revolution that were available were reappointed and brought with them the experience of their former service. Of the new frigates scarcely too much can be said as finished specimens of naval architecture, and very great credit is due to the designer, Mr. Joshua Humphreys, of Philadelphia. They were longer, proportionally, had heavier scantling, and carried heavier batteries than any ships of equal rating in the world. In fact they effected a marked change in the construction and arming of vessels of war. In support of this we may adduce here the evidence of the editor of James' "Naval History of Great Britain," Captain Chamier, R. N.: "It is but justice in regard to America," he observes, "to mention that England has benefited by her example, and that the large classes of frigates now employed in the British service are modelled after those of the United States." (James's Naval History, vol. 1, page 44, note by editor.)

The first frigate fight wherein our new ships were tried was between the *Constellation* and *L'Insurgente*. We had drifted into a species of war with the French Republic, owing to the depredations of her cruisers on our commerce, and though an act was passed (May 28th, 1798) authorizing, under certain conditions, the capture of French vessels, yet no formal declaration of war had been made. On the 9th of February, 1799, Captain Truxton, in the *Constellation*, 38, with a crew of three hundred and nine men, after a hot engagement of one hour, captured the French frigate *L'Insurgente*, Captain Barreault, of forty guns and four hundred and nine men. That is to say, an American "38" captured a French "40." But the American guns were 24 pounders, while the Frenchman had only 12s.

The *Constellation*, uninjured below her rail, was very much cut up aloft; while the Frenchman was severely damaged in the hull. But the gist of the story is told in the list of killed and wounded. *L'Insurgente* had twenty-nine men killed and forty-one wounded. The *Constellation* had but three men wounded!

Emboldened by our conciliatory policy with Algiers, Tripoli undertook to make excessive demands, which eventually brought on a war with her. This war lasted four years, and proved an admirable school of discipline for officers and men. The treaty of peace was signed June 3d, 1805. The young Republic thus leading the way in putting an end to the absurd demands for tribute by the Barbary powers, produced a great impression throughout the civilized world, and, according to Cooper, the Pope of Rome is said to have "publicly declared that America had done more for Christendom against the barbarians, than all the powers of Europe united." As this was solely the work of the infant Navy, it did much towards advancing its fortunes, character and influence, and prepared it for the higher role it was about to play.

June 18th, 1812, war was declared against Great Britain, and on the 19th of August following, the *Constitution* captured the *Guerriere*, the battle marking an important era in the history of our Navy. Cooper gives the details of the fight, and very justly remarks that he has "dwelt at length on the circumstances connected with this action, not only because it was the first serious conflict of the war, but because it was characterized by features which, though novel at the time, became identified with nearly all the subsequent engagements of the contest, showing that they were intimately connected with the discipline and system of the American Marine." (Cooper's Naval History, vol. II, page 59.)

Peace was declared February 18th, 1815, and to quote that authority once more, "the Navy came out of this struggle with a vast increase of reputation." Cooper justly ascribes the general efficiency, the high tone and the discipline of the Service "to that aptitude in the American character for the sea, which has been so constantly manifested." In 1815, just after the close of the war with Great Britain, there is trouble again with Algiers. Decatur is sent out with a squadron and soon captures the *Mashouda*, 46, and the *Estidio*, 22, brings the Dey to terms, and compels him, as far as America is concerned, to recognize the obligations of the law of nations. The year following, Lord Exmouth, with an English squadron, exacted the same for Europe.

A New Folding Boat.

The principle of these boats is not easy to describe so as to be quite comprehensible without a drawing, but we may ask our readers to imagine a canvas umbrella without a stick, and drawn out into a long shape like a boat, so that the wires which radiate from the socket, instead of all meeting in a point, touch each other two and two. Then the canvas, with its ribs, will form the bottom and sides of the boat, while the wires become the deck. When collapsed the deck doubles up in the centre, while the canvas, with its ribs, arranges itself in folds more convenient than is the case with the umbrella. Thus arranged, a boat forty feet long becomes only two and a half feet broad, and can be hung close to the side of the ship below the ordinary boats, or rather just between them and the ship.

Thus, without loss of available space, each troop-ship or transport can carry four or six large horse-boats, and they will be available for other purposes, which we shall touch upon by and by. In the act of lowering into the water the boat expands and becomes 13 feet 6 inches broad. But it is manifest that if heavy weights are placed on the sides there will be a strong tendency for the deck to rise in the middle (as an umbrella closes when the catch is freed from the socket), and the boat to collapse at the moment its expansion is most necessary. At the first experiment, some weeks ago, sufficient provision had not been made against this tendency. Horses were on board and the gun was being run over the side, when the centre of the deck rose a little, and the side went under water. The pluck and coolness of a young artillery officer, Lieutenant Buckle, and that response of the men which always comes to pluck and coolness, brought gun and horses out of the dilemma, but the accident was for the time a serious blow to the credit of the boat.

Mr. Berthon was not, however, at a loss for a remedy. He has since then stiffened the deck by cross bars, two small masts and wire ropes. Thus supported, the boat is strong enough for anything, and the experiments on the 16th ult, went off without a single hitch. The process was new to both men and horses. No systematic drill has been laid down, yet in eleven minutes from the time of the boat being arranged alongside the beach,

broadside on, the heaviest field-piece in the service was on board, with an officer, a sergeant, the gunners and drivers, and eight horses. So laden she was towed out into the harbor and again brought alongside the beach. The gun and limber were landed, and it was found that three more horses could be carried instead of the field-piece. It may be said that the boat would carry eleven big artillery draught-horses or twelve cavalry troopers. Then the three extra horses were landed, the gun and limber reembarked, and the boat, with its freight, towed across the harbor from the beach at Blockhouse Fort to Portsmouth.—*London Times.*

Leedle Yawcob Strauss.

I haf von funny leedle poy
Vot gomes schust to my knee;
Der queerest schap, der createst rogue
As efer you did see ;
He runs, and schumps, und schmabses dings
In all barts off der house—
But vot of dot ? he was mine son,
Mine leedle Yawcob Strauss.

He get der measles und der mumbs,
Und eferyding dot's out ;
He sbills mine glass of lager bier,
Pools schnuff into mine kraut ;
He fills mine pipe mit Limburg cheese—
Dot vos der roughest chouse ;
I'd take dot vrom no oder poy
But leedle Yawcob Strauss.

He dakes der milk ban for a dhrum,
Und cuts mine cane in dwo
To make der shticks to beat it mit—
Mine cracious ! dot vos druc !
I dinks mine head vos schplit abart,
He kicks up sooch a touse—
But nefer mind, der poys was few
Like dot young Yawcob Strauss.

He asks me questions sooch as dese :
Who baints my nose so red ?
Who vos it cut dot schoodt blace oudt
Vrom der hair ubpon mine hed ?
Und vhere der plaze goes vrom der lamp
Vene'er der glim I douse—
How gan I all dese dings eggsblain
To dot schmall Yawcob Strauss.

I somedimes dinks I schall go vild
Mit sooch a crazy poy,
Und vish vonce more I gould haf rest
Und beaceful dimes enshoy ;
But ven he vash ashleep in ped,
So quiet as a mouse,
I prays der Lord, " Dake anydings,
But leaf dot Yawcob Strauss."

Hartford Times.

THE GREAT BLAST.

The destruction of Hallett's Reef, in that part of the East River known as Hell Gate, was accomplished most satisfactorily on Sunday, Sept. 24th, 1876, at 2.50 P.M. The entire reef, comprising an area of three acres, was previously excavated, and the pillars supporting the reef perforated in 6,000 places, into which charges of dynamite and rendrock powder, to the extent of 52,206 1-2 lbs. had been introduced. We give below some of the details of the final preparations for this most important act in an enterprise which was commenced by General Newton seven years since.

The following is a report from Captain Mercur to General Newton, which gives the amount of explosives in the mine:

ASTORIA, September 23d, 1876.

GENERAL: The following are the numbers and weights which you desired me to give you, viz.:

	Pounds.
Dynamite in tin cartridges	24,812
Dynamite in paper cartridges	1,164
Dynamite in primers	2.925
Total number pounds dynamite.	28,901
Rendrock in cartridges	9,061½
Vulcan powder in cartridges	14,244
Total charge in mine	52,206¼
Total number of cartridges	13,596
Total number of brass primers	3,680
Total number of holes with primers	3,645
Number of iron pipes with primers	35
Number of holes charged and not primed	782
Total of holes and pipes	4,462
Number of feet of connecting wire	100,000
Number of feet of leading wire.	120,000
Number of cells in firing battery, consisting of 12 batteries of 40 cells, 4 of 43 cells, and 7 of 44 cells each	960
	Yards.
Distance of firing point from shaft	650

The following is a list of the names of the engineers in charge, and the men who have worked in the mine:

John Newton, Lieutenant-Colonel Engineers, Brevet Major-General.

James Mercur, Captain of Engineers.

Joseph H. Willard, First Lieutenant of Engineers.

Julius H. Striedinger, civil engineer, assistant.

Bernard F. Boyle, mining engineer, overseer.

James Quigley and Robert S. Burnett, assistants.

Foremen—Michael Boyle, John Furey, Bernard McLonghlan.

Miners and chargers—Jeremiah Ryan, Wm. O'Neill, John Wills, Henry Halsey, Jr., Arthur Donnelly, John Duffy, Edward Mathews, Patrick Sullivan, John Sandy, Thomas Donnelly, Peter Mathews, John Durney, Richard Kendall, Michel Ward, Edward Kennedy, Francis Sanders, Wm. Dolan, and 47 helpers.

INCIDENTS OF THE BLAST.

The mine was primed by 11 P.M. September 22d, and almost entirely "flooded," by means of a 12-inch syphon, at 7 A.M., Sunday morning. The day was very wet and disagreeable, but notwithstanding this, every point of observation on both banks of the river, and on the numerous river craft in rear of the guard boats, swarmed with a mass of people variously estimated at from 100,000 to 150,000. The firing point was about 650 feet from the mine. At 2.20 P.M., half an hour before the blast, a gun was fired from the Government scow, to give notice to all. Ten minutes before the explosion another gun

TWENTY-SEVENTH ANNUAL REPORT

OF THE

BROOKLYN CITY

BIBLE SOCIETY,

PRESENTED FEBRUARY 8, 1868.

OFFICERS.

PRESIDENT.
R. P. BUCK.

VICE-PRESIDENTS.
ABRAHAM B. BAYLIS,
HENRY IDE.

CORRESPONDING SECRETARY.
J. E. ROCKWELL, D.D.

TREASURER.
B. W. DeLAMATER.

RECORDING SECRETARY.
C. C. MUDGE.

EXECUTIVE COMMITTEE.

S. SANDERSON,   D. G. EATON,
S. B. CALDWELL,   S. B. STEWART,
W. L. PRESTON.

DIRECTORS.

H. ROWLAND,	H. BUTLER,
D. TIEBOUT,	R. BUNCE,
C. R. MARVIN,	F. BURKE,
J. BRINKERHOFF,	W. H. HAZZARD,
L. T. SMITH,	T. MUNDELL,
J. VAN CLEEK,	D. PATERSON,
E. WILLIAMS,	E. A. LAMBERT,
H. D. VAN ORDEN,	J. FRENCH,
H. G. NICHOLS,	S. GREEN,
E. W. WHITE,	H. DOLLNER,
T. C. FANNING,	W. H. MARSTON,
M. DuPUY,	I. DUBOIS.

Dr. THE BROOKLYN CITY BIBLE SOCIETY.   IN ACCOUNT WITH B. W. DeLAMATER, Treas.   Cr.

1867			1867		
	Paid American Bible Society.............................	$4,150 00	Jan. 28	By Cash on hand, per account rendered.............	$1,476 29
	Rev. B. F. Millerd, F. Millerd and A. Glenson, (Agents) salaries for 1867.........	2,307 15		Collection Anniversary Meeting	$134 40
	For rent of Depository...................................	475 00		Second Pres. Church	95 65
	Printing and Incidental Expenses...................	107 70		E. Reformed Church	14 04
Jan. 13	Balance to new account..................................	396 46		First Presbyterian, Henry st	444 50
				Christ Church	253 12
				Church of the Pilgrims	1,025 55
				Summerfield, Methodist Church	227 22
				Hanson place Methodist	180 00
				St. Peters	70 00
				Pierrepont St. Baptist	19 84
				Lafayette Av. Presbyterian Church.............	361 23
				Sands street Methodist	75 00
				First place Methodist	80 00
				First Presbyterian Ch., Remsen st	103 78
				Jane's Methodist...	18 00
				Central Presbyterian	59 61
				Church on the Heights	270 58
				Washington street Methodist	157 75
				Memorial Presbyterian	22 29
				Plymouth Church	169 05
				Donation of Mrs. E. F. Clitborn and Mrs. Nicholson..	5 00
				Cash of C. C. Mudge for sales at the Depository..	2,163 50
		$7,436 31			$7,436 41
1868			1868		
Jan. 13			Jan. 13	Balance cash on hand.....................................	396 46

ANNUAL REPORT.

The simple object of the Society which holds its anniversary to-night is the distribution of the Sacred Scriptures in this city without note or comment—and the raising of funds for this purpose and for the Bible cause generally. For more than a quarter of a century this work has been in progress—growing in magnitude and importance as the years have rolled on, and making ceaseless demands upon us for the supply of our ever-changing and rapidly increasing population with the Bread of Life. Many who were active in the formation of this Institution and who were earnest in the prosecution of its work, have ceased from their labors. And the generation then upon the stage is passing away and leaving to other hands the task which they began and which we are to carry forward until we too shall follow them. The inspired Apostle hath said, if any provide not for his own and especially for his own house he hath denied the faith and is worse than an Infidel. If this be true in regard to those things which perish in the using, how much more pertinent is it in respect to the duty of providing for the spiritual necessities of those who are members in common of the same community, and who are eminently our neighbors. And if our sympathies are aroused and our benevolent activities engaged when we hear that around us are families and individuals destitute of daily food, should we feel less practical sympathy when it is known that there are multitudes within our reach who are without the Bible, the food of the soul—the bread of eternal life. Nothing can safely be its substitute as a guide to present duty and eternal happiness, no other book can take its place in the family as the source of substantial comfort, as the support of the soul amid the trials and conflicts of life, or as the instructor of both old and young in relation to their duties and responsibilities, and in teaching them their obligations to God and the way in which to secure his favor and the salvation of the soul. It was designed to be like the air and the light free to all, and when it is permitted to diffuse its influences universally, then will intelligence, peace, virtue and order and that righteousness which exalteth a nation.

No Christian who has ever seriously inquired into the full meaning of the words of Christ, when parting from his disciples upon the Mount of Olives, could suppose that the command, "Go preach my Gospel to every creature" could be fully obeyed until the Holy Bible is placed within the reach of every living soul. The work of the church can surely never be fully accomplished, until the world is filled with the knowledge of God as revealed in his blessed Word. In this work christians of all denominations can heartily unite, as freely and heartily as in making provision for the supply of the poor and needy with the necessaries of life. Knowing as we do the value of the Bible—proving as we have in our individual experiences its preciousness and power—believing that it is the Sword of the Spirit, whose presence with it can give it efficacy in redeeming the soul from ignorance and error and sin, we should surely be recreant to our most obvious duty if with abundant means and opportunities at hand we should fail to place it within the reach of every family. Our efforts may meet with deep and bitter hostility. Infidelity on the one hand and superstition and bigotry on the other may seek to defeat our purposes; yet, wth the divine blessing, love and fidelity will at length obtain the victory, and divine grace will secure an abundant harvest where the seed has been sown. Now and then, like the dew and rain it may fall upon the desert and sink away and leave no trace of its power and influence. Yet we may often be permitted to see its results in the fertility and beauty that we find where grace was only a barren waste, and when the grand problem of life shall be summed up amid the scenes of the eternal world, many shall forever rejoice in the great salvation of which they would have remained fatally ignorant but for the Bible which this Society has placed in their hands and by which they were led to a knowledge of Him, whom to know aright is eternal life.

Here then, immediately around us do we find the field for our immediate and personal efforts for the supply of the destitute with the word of God. In the midst of a population already numbering nearly 400,000 and increasing yearly with a growth hitherto unparalleled, are multitudes who, if no efforts are personally made in their behalf must remain ignorant of the way of salvation, and who in the midst of spiritual privileges and within sight of sanctuaries, whose spires like finger-posts are pointing heavenward, must yet pass on to eternity in a darkness scarcely less deplorable than that of the Heathen world. To meet the demands thus made upon the Society two special agencies have been employed.

1st. The Visitors and Missonaries of the Brooklyn City Tract and Mission Society under the special supervision of Mr. C. C. Mudge, their efficient general agent.

2d. The services of one or more distributing agents who have given their whole time to the work of exploration and supply.

It has been their effort to meet as far as possible the wants of Mission Schools, of Hospitals and other public, humane or criminal Institutions, of the Navy Yard with its ever-changing population, and of the ships which lie at our wharves, and by faithful and constant visitation to supply destitute families or individuals with the sacred word.

At the Depository in Court St. there have been distributed as follows:

	Bibles.	Tests.
To Missionaries and Visitors of Tract Society.	159	191
At Public Institutions	174	290
Among the Shipping	140	107

To Bible Readers	35	38
" Mission Sunday Schools	826	262
" Church " "	195	
" Long Island Bible Society	59	62
At Depository to Sundry Persons	94	87
By Distributing Agents	1220	2
	2902	1139

Total Gratuitous Distribution Copies. 4041
Sold at Depository 2761

Whole Issue during the Year 6802

Eighteen months ago it was determined that there should be a thorough exploration and supply of the city, so far as this was practicable. For this purpose the distributing agent, with two assistants, was directed to make a thorough canvass of every Ward. That work has now been accomplished, and the report of Mr. Millerd to the Executive Committee presents not only the statistics of supply but some incidents of Bible distribution, which shew the difficulties sometimes encountered and the encouragements often afforded in the prosecution of the work.

The statistics found in this report reveal to us some facts, which, though they may appear discouraging, should seem as a stimulus to still more earnest efforts than we have yet put forth for the supply of our whole population with the Word of God. Of the families visited during the last year, one-fifth have been found without a Bible, and of this number nearly five-sixths have declined to receive the sacred volume even as a gift. Here is great ignorance, and an evident determination to continue therein. The reasons for this are apparent by the incidents which have been related by the agent. Indifference—deeply rooted prejudices—and the fear of priestly censures have evidently induced many to reject a gift which might have brought with it light, and hope and comfort to many a wretched heart. Yet, kindness, untiring patience, gentleness and love may at length break down all the barriers that are now reared against the truths of the Gospel. The rejection of the Bible when offered should by no means be regarded as closing up our work in that direction. We are not fully aware of the strength of that hostility to the Bible which infidelity, bigotry, and the prejudices of early education awaken in the heart. Yet, against all these obstacles, truth and Christian love have made their way to the heart. Here and there the Bible has found a place, even in the abodes of wretchedness and ignorance. And what has been done in the past may be accomplished in the future.

Our duty is plain. God will take care of the results. His word shall not return unto him void The work before us is great. Year by year these efforts to supply our city with the Bible must be continued and renewed. Thus the work of supply completed to-day must be commenced again to-morrow. For the means to carry it forward the Society earnestly and trustingly appeals to the various churches of which it is the agent. Whatever of their contributions are not needed for the supply of our own field are promptly given to aid in the great work of giving to the world the light of God's Word. Where is the church that can afford to neglect the call that comes to us with increasing power and earnestness, Send us the Gospel? Where is the Christian who knows by his own experience the preciousness of the Scriptures who can fail to give them to all nations? The field is the world. The command of Christ is imperative—" Freely ye have received, freely give." Let us give a generous aid to the work which seeks to place in the hands of every human being a copy of God's Word, and to scatter over the world the light of that blessed volume whereby we are made wise unto eternal life.

J. E. ROCKWELL,
Corresponding Secretary.

TWENTY-SEVENTH ANNIVERSARY.

The Brooklyn City Bible Society held its Twenty-seventh Anniversary at the Church of the Pilgrims, on Sabbath evening, February 2, 1868.

Mr. R. P. Buck the President of the Society occupied the chair. After the opening services he stated that the Society had never passed a more successful year than the one now closing, when the work accomplished was taken into the account. He then introduced the Rev. CHANDLER STARR, who said he had learned at the parent Society facts concerning the work, but the half had not been told him.

The speaker alluded to the influence of the Bible in forming character. No young man early trained in its teachings would be likely to become openly profligate, or if so, it would be the exception, not the rule.

Rev. Dr. STORRS said he would not make any extended remarks after the eloquent and deeply interesting speech of their venerable brother, who they were always pleased to hear, but rose only to move that the reports read be accepted and published under the direction of the Executive Committee. When we send the Bible to the families of the poor we send the words of Christ Himself—an instrument to awaken in the heart and mind of man life itself. We bring up Isaac and send him; we bring up Samuel from the dead and send him; David from his throne, nay, the Lord Himself, as when on earth.

The exercises were closed with a short but highly eloquent speech by Rev. Dr. SCHENK, of St. Ann's Church. He remarked that if the previous speaker had found it necessary to speak of lateness and of brevity, it much more became him after still farther time had passed. He would only thank the worthy President of the Society for his words of cordial greeting, and say that he regarded it as a favorable augury that it was his privilege in his first public appearance in connection with his fellow-Christians of other denominations to advocate the great cause of the Bible. This platform should be world-wide. Every man believing in God, whatever his creed, believes in the Bible.

A collection was then taken, the doxology sung, and the benediction pronounced by Rev. Dr. ROCKWELL.

EXTRACTS FROM REPORTS OF BIBLE AGENTS.

During the past year the canvass of the city, begun in the latter part of May, 1866, has been completed. The whole number of families visited is 38,311; 5,566 families were found destitute of the Bible, and 1,192 families were gratuitously supplied by the Society.

During the past twelve months, covered by this report, 15,420 families have been visited; 3,237 of these families were found without a Bible. Into 571 of these wretched homes, all that would receive the gift, the Word of God has been introduced.

The total number of Bibles distributed by the Agents (exclusive of the operations of the Depository) is 655, and the number of Testaments and Psalms 565, making the whole number of volumes through this channel 1,220.

The canvass thus completed is an important movement toward reaching the neglected masses of our city. It is a moral census which throws light upon the number and condition of these masses. The Agents have visited every house, knocking alike at the palace and the hovel, passing from the broad avenue down to the reeking alley, and thus thoroughly probing the social cancer.

But the extent of the evil has not merely been measured. A great step has been taken toward its cure—just as it is more important to excite in a patient a healthy appetite, which shall prompt him to seek food for himself, than to bring to his couch dainties which he loathes, so it is of greater consequence to awaken a *desire* for preaching than to supply the preaching itself. The Word of God is not only itself the greatest of all means of grace—it creates a demand for all the other means. Placed in the family, the Bible becomes a fountain, of which the pulpit, the press, and the school are but the streams.

The following incidents will show the reception which this movement has met from the great class it was designed to reach:

In a low street, inhabited mainly by Catholics, in the door of a comfortable and tidy dwelling, sat a young Irish mother. "Yes, I have got a Bible," said she, "it is an old one, but I would not part with it. When a child I went to the Sunday-school, and Oh, I think it leaves *such* an impression." The depth of that impression was seen in the thrift and neatness of her own dwelling, compared with the squalor and wretchedness in the tenements of her country people around her.

In an upper room of a tenement house was an intelligent-looking Irish woman who said she had no Bible, and expressed an earnest desire for one.

On receiving the copy which I handed her, and ascertaining that it was a Protestant Bible, her whole manner showed the struggle between the new desire and the old prejudice. Now she handed it back and then asked for it again, gazing wistfully upon its sacred pages, until I was compelled to tell her that she must decide whether to take it or not. She decided to take it, but just as I reached the bottom of the stairs she overtook me with a frightened look upon her face, and drawing the Bible stealthily from under her apron she said hastily, "I guess I won't take it, but I thank you."

This incident illustrates under what constraint, and oftentimes under what reluctance the Bible has been declined by so many of the destitute. Others, however, Protestants, Jews and Catholics have received it with joy, at times with tears of gratitude.

In a rear tenement was a young Irish woman with a group of children around her. In answer to my inquiry whether she had a Bible, she replied decidedly, "I don't *need* any." "I think we *all* need the Bible," said I, "especially if we have children around us." Without urging the matter further, however, I left the room, but just as I reached the bottom of the stairs she overtook me, and turning to another woman who was standing at her door in the hall, she said, "Don't you think it would be a nice thing to have a Bible in the house?" The other replied that she had taken one of me. "Well," said the other, apparently terminating a struggle, "I will take one."

In a wretched hovel was a sick woman, with her boy, and as she received with repeated thanks a Bible,—her only one—her anxiety was evidently more for her neglected child than for herself. "May I not tell him," she said earnestly "that if he'll learn to read you will come again in a year and give *him* a book.

In the upper part of a tenement house was a Catholic, with her showily-dressed daughter. "No," said the mother, "we don't want a Bible." "Let me see one," said the daughter, advancing towards me. "No," said the mother, decidedly, "You don't want to see it." "Yes, I do," said the daughter holding out her hand to me,. Please show it to me, sir. "No," said the mother, stepping between us, "don't show it to her." "I have brought you up," she said, to the daughter, in a stern tone, "in the Catholic religion." I of course, acquiesced in the mother's wishes, but the high-spirited daughter did not seem quite satisfied.

"How *small* it looks," said a woman, as she looked doubtfully at the Bible I had handed her. "What kind is it?"—Protestant. "Ah, then, we don't want it." Her daughter, a modest and pretty girl, stepped up to her mother, and in a low tone begged her to take one. "No, no," said the mother quickly. Thank you for your kindness, sir.

"You might take one," said the decent-looking Catholic woman to her slatternly neighbor, who had just angrily refused a Bible. "What, take a Protestant Bible!" "Yes, there's no harm in it." "Do you say that, and you a Catholic? You wouldn't say that if you were in the church, and Father —— heard you." The other was cowed, and when I subsequently called at her door and offered her a Bible she timidly refused to take it.

The offer of a Bible for nothing is received almost with incredulity, especially by Romanists, who often pay from thirty to thirty-five dollars for their own. "How are you able to *give* it away?" said a Catholic. I explained that the benevolent people of Brooklyn furnished the means, but he still seemed to think it a mystery.

"And am I not to return it, said an intelligent-looking woman?" "No, keep it, friend, it will last you twenty years." "Thank you, thank you," said she earnestly.

Though the city canvass has somewhat narrowed the work on ship-board, it has not suspended it. Along our docks the volume of shipping is constantly enlarging, and among the polyglot multitude which swarms on its decks the Scriptures in nearly every modern tongue has been put afloat to be borne to distant lands, where, in many cases, God has prepared the way for its reception by quickening thought and inquiry, and where it will come as a light to nations awaking out of sleep.

The following incident shows how the precious seed takes root in distant soils, there to bring forth fruit in the ages to come:

A few months since the mate of a vessel in the South American trade received in this port a package containing a Spanish Testament, with other reading matter. On entering the port of her destination the vessel was attended by a lighter whose Captain was a Spaniard, and the mate bethinking himself of the Testament gave it to him. Recently the vessel made a second voyage to the same port and was again attended by the Spanish lighter. "Have you got your Testament yet?" inquired the Mate of the Captain. "Oh, yes," said the Spaniard, "and it has showed me the way of life. I want you to get me another, for my wife has become so interested in this that she keeps it at home to read herself."

At the Navy Yard every facility for my work has been afforded by the officers, and nowhere is effort crowned with larger results. During the year I have preached every Sabbath from once to three times to seamen. However hardened these men are, they are not Gospel-hardened, and no congregation so literally *hang* upon the words of a preacher as those assembled on the open deck.

While the large screw steamer, Wampanong, soon to become the flag ship of the North Atlantic squadron, has been lying at the Navy Yard, I have held services on board on Sabbath mornings, which have been largely attended both by officers and men. At the close of my first service an officer approached me, and, taking me by the hand, thanked me warmly for the service, adding, it is the first religious service we have ever had on board, and this on a vessel with a crew of 400 men.

At the close of a recent service on the Receiving Ship, Vermont, I requested any who desired to begin a new life and wished to be remembered in prayer to arise on their feet, and scores of earnest men arose in a body.

Among the intrepid crews of our National vessels the Word of God has been welcomed with a joy which has lit up many a scarred and weather-beaten face. It comes to them as a token—of which in their toilsome and secluded life they receive too few—that they are remembered by the nation whose uniform they wear and whose flag they uphold.

As I came alongside a Norwegian ship and held up a Testament in their own tongue, the crew gathered eagerly around me, and when each had received a copy they took me one by one by the hand with a brief but earnest "Thank you," eking out their scanty English by a hearty grasp.

Near South Ferry I found a strange-looking ship, with Chinese characters on her tackle and stern. Climbing up the ladder I found but one Chinaman on board, but on my offer to bring him a Testament printed in his own tongue, being interpreted to him, he promptly accepted it.

In handing a few Spanish Testaments over the gunwale of a small Spanish vessel one dropped into the river. I passed on, and returning about fifteen minutes afterward I found a seaman patiently letting down his bucket for the lost volume, and when he at length brought it up his swarthy face lit up with pleasure.

I have *got* a Bible, said a young sailor on board the U. S. Receiving Ship Vermont, as the Agent was distributing Bibles on board, and drawing out an old pocket Bible he added tenderly, " it is the one my *mother* gave me."

"That Bible once saved my life," said another man-of-wars-man, standing in the crowd of blue jackets, who were pressing around me to get Bibles, and (pointing at the time at the imprint of a rifle ball on the cover) "no money could buy it."

The Depository of the Society is at No. 33 COURT STREET, near Joralemon where Bibles and Testaments may be had for gratuitous distribution.

A large assortment is also kept for sale, embracing every variety printed by the Parent Society, and in every kind of binding.

www.ingramcontent.com/pod-product-compliance
Lightning Source LLC
Chambersburg PA
CBHW030815230426
43667CB00008B/1232